ALLAH DOES NOT HAVE AN EXIT VISA

To FRANCES,

WITH BEST WISHES.

ALLAN M. JACK

Matador
9 Priory Business Park
Kibworth Beauchamp
Leicestershire LE8 0RX, UK
Tel: (+44) 116 279 2299
Fax: (+44) 116 279 2277
Email: books@troubador.co.uk
Web: www.troubador.co.uk/matador

ISBN 978-1783062-959

British Library Cataloguing in Publication Data.
A catalogue record for this book is available from the British Library.

Typeset in Aldine by Troubador Publishing Ltd
Printed and bound in the UK by TJ International, Padstow, Cornwall

Matador is an imprint of Troubador Publishing Ltd

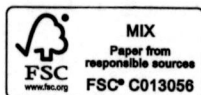

MIX
Paper from
responsible sources
FSC
www.fsc.org
FSC® C013056

To Dorothy, Alison, Kirsty, Gordon, Iona and Cara – you light up my life.

Table Of Contents

1

The Start Of It All

Why am I doing this? I wish I knew. Someone once said that the easiest part of writing a book was starting and the hardest was finishing. I'm telling myself that I'm doing this for my kids but I suppose that I am doing it for myself as well. What I don't want is for relatives and friends to have to ask, "What did he do and where did he go in his life?" after I've gone. It would be even more tragic if they had to ask those questions if I was still around but I was suffering from a condition like dementia or Alzheimer's.

Anyway, here goes!

For an explanation of the title, dear reader, you'll have to read the following dissertation. It is buried within these pages. Good hunting!

My heritage is pure Scottish. My ancestors, at least as far back as the Vikings, appear all to have been Scots, on both sides of my family. To go back a couple of generations, my mother's parents both came from the Isle of Lewis and my Dad's mother came from Argyle. My paternal grandfather was an orphan so that genealogical line has stopped dead. Although they were from Highland stock, both of my parents were born and bred in Glasgow, where I was also born (in 1951).

My Lewisian ancestors are probably where my Viking-like looks come from. Tall (6ft+), reddish hair, blue eyes and well built, I don't think I can deny my genetic code. I'll come back to Lewis later.

In 2011 I sent some of my saliva off to "ScotlandsDNA" to be analysed. It turns out my paternal ancestors were Saxons from the North German Plain who moved to Britain when Doggerland was still above water but my maternal ancestors were from the Levant (Lebanon, Syria, Jordan, Israel) even further back in antiquity. The techniques looked at the last mutations of the DNA string so giving these very interesting results. Unfortunately so far they can look only at the father-father-father—— and mother-mother-mother—— lines. The bits in between will probably have to wait for more advanced techniques.

One can't just start discussing one's own life in isolation, as none of us is an island. We are intertwined with our parents, siblings, relatives and friends. But one has to start somewhere.

I was born in a nursing home on Great Western Road in Glasgow on May 19, 1951. The family home was a tenement flat on Argyle St. but when I was 6 weeks old, we moved to the country, to a village called Gartmore, about 25 miles north of the city. There I stayed, on and off, until I was 25.

After that I went to Cape Town, got married, had a family, came back to the UK, did several stints in Saudi Arabia, the rest of the Middle East and the Caspian Sea region with a couple of years in Singapore for good measure. Hopefully you'll like the stories of these different places.

I haven't made a study of my ancestors before my grandparents but one story does stand out. My mother's mother and her family lived in a now deserted village called Calbost in the Lochs parish, south of Loch Erisort on Lewis. There was a dashing young fisherman who was either reluctant to get married to his girlfriend or just couldn't get round to it. Anyway, she got fed up and arranged to marry someone else while the young fisherman was away at sea. He got back to Calbost to find it almost empty and was told that his fiancée was getting married in Balallan, which lies at the head of the sea Loch Erisort. There were no cars, buses or taxis in these days and the roads/tracks weren't all that hot either. So our young fisherman jumped into a rowboat and headed off to Balallan. If you check the map, you'll note that it is over 20 miles. He arrived at the kirk in the middle of the ceremony but before his fiancée had been married off. The minister took it in his stride and asked the bride-to-be which one she wanted to marry. She answered, "The one in the gumboots" *i.e.* our hero. That couple is still talked about today many decades later and everybody on the island knows the story.

The other famous forebear that I can lay claim to is (Sir) Alexander Mackenzie, the first European to sail down the river named after him in western and northern Canada and which empties into the Arctic Ocean. He was looking for a quick route to the Pacific. He called it the River of Disappointment!! He eventually did manage to cross the mountains and 'Mackenzie's Rock' on the western shore commemorates his feat of July 22nd,

1793. In neither of these expeditions did he lose a man. He holds the distinction of being the first European to cross the North American continent, north of Mexico. You have no idea what kudos this gives me when talking to Canadians!

There's also a tale that Ian McLeod, a minister in Harold Macmillan's cabinet, was a relative.

My mother's father grew up on the west coast of the island in a village called Dun Carloway. 'Dun' is a Gaelic word meaning 'fort' and in this context refers to a Pictish broch on the edge of the village. This area is only a few miles from the Callanish standing stones and there are a few other such stones in the area. For those who don't know, the Callanish stones are the most important and impressive collection of standing stones in the UK outside Stonehenge itself.

Grandpa was the oldest of twelve and his father, seemingly, was a brute. Forced to work on the family croft and go to school on alternate days, he only ever attended school on Tuesdays and Thursdays. I never saw the school because they built a hotel on the site. That's the only time Grandpa ever enjoyed going there, he said. He was a John Maclean and there is a story that the Macleans originally came to Lewis from the island of Mull back in the mid to late 1700s.

Life was so harsh he ran away to sea to be a cabin boy on the fishing boats and spent some time out of the Moray Firth ports such as Portknockie, Findochty and Buckie. When we holidayed there, he came along and really enjoyed seeing all his old haunts. He eventually ended up in Glasgow, where he met my Grandma, who was in domestic service there. Gran was from the parish of Lochs, south of Loch Erisort in SE Lewis from a small village called Calbost. Calbost is deserted now but used to be a thriving crofting and fishing village in the early 20th century. It was typical of islanders to come to Glasgow round the turn of the century. In fact, Gaelic was the first language in parts of Glasgow, especially Partick, and the Highlanders' Institute and the 'Heilandman's Umbrella' – the bridge south of Central Station – were and are long standing testimony to that migration. Grandma hadn't been idle. She had already been to America "in service" and back.

Of course, World War 1 intervened and Grandpa went off to Flanders and the trenches with millions of others. He was part of the Seaforth Highlanders and I still wear his cap badge as my kilt pin. He came back but, like all who came back, he was lucky. No doubt all of them have stories but

Grandpa had a couple of beauties. On one occasion he was buried up to his neck in mud by a dud shell, which had landed a few feet away. He was wounded at another time and lost an eye to a piece of shrapnel. That got him invalided out in late 1916 and back home where he and Grandma got married. When we were young (40+ years later), Grandpa delighted in scaring the living daylights out of us by removing his glass eye. He also showed us the scars on his knees caused by the dried mud, which had caked on the hem of his kilt. That must have been day-to-day agony on top of all the other hardships.

My mother was born (in 1918), the first of three daughters and Grandpa joined the Glasgow Police. He was a marksman and trained the whole force in shooting. He also trained my mother who could shoot a rifle better than any man I have ever met. She taught me to shoot.

I mustn't forget the other side of the family, must I? Dad's mother came from Argyle, near the village of Kilmartin with cousins in Kames and Tighnabruich. She also migrated to Glasgow where she met my other Grandpa – Albert Jack. Dad was born in 1912, the first of five children, one of whom died in infancy.

This Grandpa was left a house in Gartmore (see above) as he had been evacuated there during the war, but that wasn't the house we moved to. There was some family argument and Dad's sister Ina was left the house. It had something to do with Grandpa wanting Ina to look after him after Gran died rather than my mother. That rankled for many years until Ina was on her own deathbed. I never knew either of my Dad's parents but Grandpa saw me. Both my grandfather and father were fiddlers in the Caledonian Strathspey and Reel Society band and played at concerts throughout the Glasgow area. However, my dad gave it up when we moved to Gartmore. The band held a concert in Aberfoyle sometime in the early 60's and, of course, we all attended. Dad spent the whole night chatting to his old friends in the band, about half of whom he had played with.

When my dad was young, the family lived in Shawlands in Glasgow on Kilmarnock Road. The home was right next to the bridge over the River Clyde as it snakes its way through the city. On one occasion the whole street was brought to a standstill as my father, only a small boy mind, managed to get his head stuck in the railings!

He was a fairly decent football player and even played at the old Hampden Park in schoolboy cup finals. He also was a member of the Boy's

Brigade and eventually won the King's Badge. The BB, founded by the Scot William Smith, was the model for Baden-Powell's Boy Scouts.

Although my father's father was a Jack, which is a lowland name, my other three grandparents were named Macdonald, Maclean and Mackenzie. Hence I have the 'right' to wear these three tartans. However, my middle name is Mackenzie so that is the one I usually wear. My brother has Maclean as part of his name so when he was my best man he wore a Mackenzie tartan kilt and I reciprocated by wearing a Maclean tartan one when I was his best man.

There is no doubt on where these names came from and what they mean but I've often wondered about the origin of the name 'Jack'. It is well known to be an alternative to 'John' as a Christian name but as a surname it is usually incorporated in the names like 'Jackson'. There is one intriguing explanation. In the Middle Ages, the foot soldiers wore '*jacques*', from where we get the word 'jacket', on which they bore the coat of arms of their commanders. It is where we get the term 'Jack' for a flag such as the Union Jack. The jackstaff on a ship, from where the Jack was flown, was called that because of the flag's name, not the other way round. As I'm a bit of a flag 'nut', this possible source of my surname pleases me.

The other possible alternative origin is as a maker of the medieval 'jackboots', which were waterproofed leather vessels for holding some drink or other. These vessels were known informally as 'jacks' or 'boots' and is where the phrase, "fill your boots" comes from. As Albert was an orphan, we're not sure where his origins were. Perhaps we need to do some more digging. We've always assumed that he was Glasgow born and bred.

The man after whom I am named was an uncle of my mother. He was Allan Ross Mackenzie and, after he graduated MA from Harvard, eventually he became the Director of Education in the old Southern Rhodesia. He married a girl from Richmond in the Cape. His son Calum was 'sent down' from UCT where he managed to somehow deposit a car on top of the ladies' residence. Calum married a girl from Salisbury (now Harare), a judge's daughter no less, before enrolling at Cambridge where he did a Geology (!) degree. During the war he was badly wounded in action in Burma where he won the MC. After an architectural degree (from UCT – he must have been rehabilitated!!), he designed the Leopard Rock Hotel near Umtali. In later life he invented the "Rescue" bracelet which alleviates muscle pain.

Allan's brother, John, emigrated to Argentina in 1904, to Patagonia. He seemingly married a girl from the Falkland Islands and had three daughters. He is buried in Puerto San Julian, a port almost due west from the Falklands. That must have been from where I got my wanderlust (or perhaps from Alexander (of Canada) from an earlier generation).

While I was in Saudi Arabia one summer's weekend afternoon, when it was far too hot to do anything but be indoors, I was watching some TV when a women's hockey game came on between S. Korea and Argentina. Now, I'm no great fan of women's hockey but something made me look at this game. All of the players were small and stocky with dark hair except one. One of the Argentina defenders was about six feet tall with blond, blond hair and her name was Juanita Mackenzie! I've often wondered…

As I said above, both my parents were born and brought up in Glasgow but lived on opposite sides of the city. Young people in the inter-war years met each other at the dance halls. These establishments were of varying quality but were all over the city so the whole population mingled and married. My father was a good dancer (I missed out on that gene!), told stories of how he was always ready first, and had to wait on his brothers who had to make sure their hair wasn't out of place. My father worked in a succession of offices while my mother was a telephone operator. They met in the 30's and by that time the house in Gartmore was where they spent many happy weekends. Photographs from that time show a happy couple and they even went to Lewis for dad to meet and be 'approved' by the relations up there.

However, World War II came along and disrupted everything. Dad was called up into the RAF, not as a pilot but in the ground crew. His eyesight was too poor for service in the air. Mum was promoted from operator to engineer and she used to go around all the exchanges fixing things. She came up against sexism before the term was invented but, because of the war, managed to get around it.

My parents married on a "48 Hour Pass" in 1941 (before Pearl Harbour) when the UK and the Empire stood alone, throughout the world, against the Fascist war machine. I've never seen any photos of the ceremony but have wondered whether they thought of it as some sort of statement. Maybe I'm just being over sentimental. One thing is sure; my father was then shipped off to the Middle East (Palestine) to join his RAF Squadron (261) and the newly weds didn't see each other for over five years. That puts some of the whinging of modern times into perspective.

Dad was shipped to Ceylon (Sri Lanka) in 1942 and spent some time in Trincomalee, which he always talked about with great affection. He was on his way actually to Singapore and was about a day away from there, when the fleet was told that the island had fallen to the Japanese army. The ships were diverted to Ceylon and thereafter in 1943 to Burma where he spent the next year or so. The squadron was withdrawn to India and then went back to Burma until the end of the war. He suffered recurrent malarial attacks and I remember him even having attacks back home when I was little. He always wore the lapel badge of the Burma Star Association with pride. He would be deeply distressed at the modern day occurrences and persecution in the country he so fondly remembered. Mum had a work colleague whose husband was captured at Singapore, never to see each other again.

My very existence seems to be extremely fortunate!

Eventually, Dad came home, he and Mum set up home in a flat in Argyle St., and that was where, in 1948, my sister, Pam, was born. On top of all the other problems of their early-married life, Pam was a Downs Syndrome child. It must have taken some courage, in the late 1940's, to think of having any more children after that bombshell. However, they did and I was the result. A few years later, my young brother, Torquil, was born but more of him later. Pam was my childhood companion and I never realised that anything was the matter with her until after I went to school. Eventually taking care of her became too much for my mother (as Pam would take it into her head to disappear) and my parents took the very difficult decision to put Pam in an institution. She was placed in the Scottish Institute in Larbert, between Stirling and Falkirk, and many of my youthful Saturdays were taken up accompanying Mum or Dad or both to visit her. I'll come back to Pam later on but I want now to take you to a small Scottish village unremarkable in all its aspects except that I grew up there.

2

Gartmore

Gartmore lies off all the beaten tracks. It is situated about 25 miles north of Glasgow and 20 miles west of Stirling. It is 3 miles from Aberfoyle, on the southern boundary of the enlarged Trossachs and, when I lived there, consisted of one main street and a small side road called Jellicoe Avenue, which was named after a Captain John Rushworth Jellicoe R.N. who married a daughter of the 'Big House', owned by the Cayzer family at the time. Capt Jellicoe went on to become Admiral, Lord Jellicoe, First Sea Lord, commander of the Royal Navy at the Battle of Jutland and then Governor General of New Zealand.

The village started as a stopping place on the cattle drove roads from the Highlands to the Lowland markets such as at Falkirk. The name means "Big Fold" as in an animal enclosure. Then the village was laid out as a dormitory for the workers of Gartmore House, a large manor, which looks out over the Carse of Forth to the east. The manor house was designed by William Adam and built in the early 18th century by the local landowner, Nichol Graham, who was a descendant of King Robert the Bruce, and enlarged in 1779-80 to a design by a John Baxter. The Grahams, Cunningham-Grahams, the Cayzers, the British Army and the Roman Catholic Church owned the house in turn. When I lived in the village, the De La Salle Brothers of the Roman Catholic Church ran the 'Big House' as a refuge for 'children of distressed families'. Recently (2003) some of the staff of St Ninian's School (as it was called) have been imprisoned for abuse of the pupils but, I must admit, there were no rumours of anything like that when I was young and these crimes were being committed. It has passed through a number of owners since and is, in 2003, a Christian retreat centre. In the grounds there are the ruins of Gartartan Castle, a 16th century Z-plan tower, of which I know very little other than it doesn't seem to have figured in any major historical events except for housing a Hanoverian garrison during the 1715 Jacobite uprising.

Although, the Grahams may now be "just" another family, they did hold sway at one time. They claimed descent from Robert the Bruce and the Antonine Wall was even nicknamed "Graham's Dyke". However, the Grahams of Menteith had one 'black sheep' – Sir John Menteith – and he was probably the most hated man in Scotland after he betrayed William Wallace to the English. He became known as the 'False Menteith'.

The Cunningham-Grahams had one very famous member, Robert Bontine, of that ilk, (1852-1936) who is fondly remembered in Argentina and Uruguay as "Don Roberto". So much so that there is a memorial to him on the north side of the village's football pitch dedicated to him, to the cost of which Argentina contributed and at the unveiling of which, when it was moved from near Dumbarton, the Argentine Ambassador was in attendance. "RB" was a writer of some renown, a Liberal MP, was one of the founders of the Scottish Labour party and also first President of the Scottish Nationalist Party. He is buried on the island of Inchmahome on the Lake of Menteith, which lies a few miles to the east of the estate. He was the biographer of his great-grandfather, Robert Graham (writer of the poem 'Doughty Deeds'), who became Rector of Glasgow University during which time he founded the Gartmore Gold Medal for the best essay by any student on a subject connected with 'the nature, foundation, advantages and support of political liberty'.

When the village was laid out, as a traditional 'ribbon', one street village, it housed the workers for the Gartmore Estate. For instance, the blacksmith/farrier of the estate was still alive when I was a boy and his house/workshop was known as the "Smiddy". He was known as 'Jock the Smith' although his real surname was Ferguson but I suppose only a handful of people in the village knew that. An example perhaps, even in the mid-twentieth century, of how names followed occupations.

The local church was also an historical treasure trove. The ship-owning Cayzers had their own burial ground (the Cunningham-Grahams had theirs in the grounds of the 'Big House'), while the stained glass windows showed some of the family's warrior dead. The village also showed the aftermath of the 'Disruption' when the Free Church of Scotland broke away from the Church of Scotland. The village had two churches and two manses but these had been recombined when the Free Church realised that numbers were not sufficient to justify a separate presence.

The churchyard holds a Moondial, something I have not seen anywhere else in the world. I hesitate to use the word 'unique' but it is as close anything is in Gartmore to being unique. I never saw it 'used' properly but then we hardly ever saw the Moon! I don't even know of anyone in the village who knew how to read it! It originally stood outside the front door of the 'Big House' and was moved south to the Cayzers' residence in England after the Army moved in. However, the Moondial was 'calibrated', if that's the right term, to the latitude of Gartmore and so wasn't accurate in its new surroundings. Hence it was moved back and placed in the churchyard.

The Free Church building became the church hall while the Church of Scotland manse was sold. The church hall is an impressive building just off the village square while the church is next to the local primary school, just as in so many Scottish villages. The church hall was almost the centre of the village's social life. Although the Black Bull, the hotel next door, did have a dance hall, many of the village dances were held in the church hall. There was a restriction about alcohol but as the pub was next door, that really didn't matter. Apart from dances, the church hall was used for Sales of Work, Flower Shows (Dad was the local chairman for many a year), badminton and the Wolf Cubs and Boy Scouts. I was in these movements for many a year and eventually became a Patrol Leader in the Scouts. Ironically, I was never able to pass my field-cooking badge. Funny that as I've probably cooked more meals outdoors since then, over open fires in inhospitable places, than most men have on a regular stove!

Scout camps and jamborees were great fun. We always went to the hills above Inverkip, near Largs, for our camps and we went to jamborees at Blair Drummond House and Scone Palace. Scouts were always held on a Friday night and began with the raising of the Union Jack. After this there was some activity like boys trying to gain badges/skills or learning knots, first aid, etc. During this time one or two of the boys would go over to the hotel for a can/bottle of lemonade and bring it back. One night a lad rushed back with the news that JFK had been killed. It was on the news in the pub. The first thing our Scoutmaster ordered was the flag to be flown at half-mast and the rest of the evening was rather sombre. I don't want to get all dewy eyed about JFK although it was probably a defining moment in the middle of the century. Not everybody was as devastated as some made out and my parents were among them. They had never forgiven (and would never forgive) JFK's father Joe Kennedy, when he was US Ambassador to the UK at the start of WWII, for telling FDR to "forget the British, they're finished. Don't bother helping them." after Dunkirk. Was Joe an apologist for the Nazis? Was he a friend of the Nazis? Who knows? His remarks rankled for all their lives. Thus they were not huge JFK fans although they never condoned his assassination. I suppose it was a bit of sins of the father being visited on the son. JFK was not the object of their dislike but an apple doesn't fall far from the tree, so it is said.

Bordering the village to the north and west is the Queen Elizabeth Forest Park, which is now part of the Loch Lomond and Trossachs National Park, but when I was growing up it was a working pine forest and a great playground for us kids. It also was a source of employment for local people as was the Water Board. Glasgow takes its water from Loch Katrine through a couple of tunnels, which run very close to the village. The tunnels need maintenance, which requires men to do it. The surrounding geography dictates that the village is also the centre of an agricultural community split between upland grazing and lowland dairy farms.

Gartmore has good road connections, although it lies on a semi-circular unclassified side road off the A81 Glasgow to Aberfoyle trunk road, which runs over the Flanders Moss, part of the Carse of Forth, and passes in front of Gartmore House. There is another single track unclassified road, which runs to the south west of the village and connects it to the hamlet of Dalmary and eventually to the village of Drymen. This road actually follows the old drove road mentioned above. One interesting aspect of that road is the farm of Chappelarroch, which used to be an inn. In fact, it was where Rob Roy stole the Earl of Montrose's rent money! Very close by are prehistoric 'relics'. On an outcrop, marked by a lone tree, are two bowl shaped depressions hewn out of the rock. They are known locally as 'Rob Roy's Beef Tubs', although it is more than likely he knew nothing about them. Every time I went there the 'tubs' were filled with rainwater. Next to them is a definite indentation of a foot and, with the eye of faith; it is possible to discern another foot-shaped depression at right angles to the first. What were/are they? Theories are many. The one I favour is that they mark the northeast corner of the ancient kingdom of Strathclyde and the newly elected king had to visit the site and proclaim his authority. The 'tubs' perhaps were to collect the blood of the sacrificed animals. There are also 'ball and cup' markings reminiscent of the Picts or ancient Britons nearby. People have speculated that they represent some kind of directional marks but no-one seems to really know.

On a clear day, looking east from the back of the village hall, one can easily make out the Wallace Monument on the Abbey Craig outside Stirling and, because you know that it is there, the crag where Stirling Castle stands. Main roads on the north and south side of the carse link Gartmore to Stirling. The northern road runs through Port of Menteith, Thornhill and Blair Drummond while the southern road goes through or bypasses Buchlyvie, Arnprior, Kippen and Gargunnock. On looking to the west, the very distinctive silhouette of Ben Lomond is unmistakable.

The railway once served Gartmore but because the village is on a hill, the track ran about a mile from the people and the station, appropriately called Gartmore Station, lay at the foot of the "Station Brae". The line was only ever a single track and ended at Aberfoyle. It did have a passenger service before WW2, but when I was young it was only ever used for shifting coal to, and slate from, the quarries in the hills above Aberfoyle. When the quarries closed so did the line. The line was a spur off the 'main line' from Glasgow along the Forth Valley (or Carse), which was mainly used to transport fodder for the horses in Glasgow and fertiliser back to the farms. The Aberfoyle/Gartmore spur didn't survive long enough even for Dr Beeching to cut. If you visit the area of the station today, now called Cobleland, all you will see are caravan parks and restaurants/tearooms. You may recognise where the line ran, if you have eagle eyes, but the standard railway buildings have gone. The road bridges that crossed the old line are still there but those are the only clues.

In the late 1950's, the waterworks at Loch Katrine were extended and Princess Margaret was invited to open them. Her journey from Glasgow to Loch Katrine took her by Gartmore Station. In those long gone days of more conspicuous deference to the Royal Family, we, the pupils from Gartmore School, were all marched down to the station to wave to the princess as she passed. We waved our flags as she passed and she gave us the royal wave. It lasted about ten seconds and then we trudged up the hill, back to the classrooms.

The other geographical feature of note in the vicinity is the River Forth. The river comes out of the east end of Loch Ard, passes Aberfoyle and then meanders through its floodplain (carse) on its way to Stirling and the famous Firth of Forth. To the south of Gartmore, the Claggan Burn joins the Kelty Water to become a tributary of the main river. When there are high spring tides, both of these can be backed up by the rising waters and flood. However the topography means that danger to homes etc. is minimal.

The river gave us one great amenity – a swimming pool. It was actually a loop/bend in the river but had a shingle beach and many summer afternoons saw bands of parents and children walking a mile or so down to the riverbank to "Limma Hamish", a local corruption of the Gaelic for "James' Pool". (Who James was or what he did is lost in the mists of time but my theory is that it refers to a James Graham of the 'Big Hoose'). It is where I learnt to swim and dive and I still prefer swimming in fresh water to salt water even if it is usually colder.

In the early 1950's the UK was still recovering from some of the after effects of World War II (WWII) like rationing. We didn't know anything about that, of course. We were just happy to run in the open fields and the forests and swim in the river. There were also very few cars in the village. I would think that the total number was under half a dozen. The minister had one as did the hotelier and there were one or two others and the local tradesmen e.g. the electrician, had vans. There were frequent buses but as they ran to a schedule we didn't have any problems avoiding them. Although there were a couple of shops, one of which doubled as the local sub-post office, they didn't carry a huge stock and most of the housewives relied on the delivery vans, which were a frequent and welcome sight in the village. The butcher's, the fishmonger's and the Co-op vans were the ones that I remember most.

The NHS has always been around during my life and I've seen a few changes. When I was young and Torquil a baby, we had frequent visits from the local District Nurse, Miss Macdonald. She became a very familiar figure and it was a sad day when she retired. However, she started up a kennel business in Aberfoyle and we frequently left our dogs there when we went on holiday.

Even before I went to school at the local primary, I was running around the village. These days were idyllic, as there were very few locked doors in the village and the 'grannies' were always willing to give out orange squash and biscuits to thirsty and hungry kids.

The wintertime was no barrier to play. Deep snow drifts that you could jump into with no chance of being injured plus snowball fights meant that the only problem was the short daylight span. At the back of the church hall is the most marvellous hill for sledging. Some had real sledges; others used trays or even shovels. The only drawback was in having to walk back up the hill. We couldn't afford a chair lift! In the summer the days were light until well after ten o'clock, which normally meant that some very tired kids went to bed.

Because of the light nights, football games, without floodlights, could start as late as 7.30pm and finish with easily enough light. There was a local summer league, the Forth and Endrick League, in which both Torquil and I cut our teeth in the game. It was always a social occasion for as long as I can remember on a Saturday night to cheer on the village team. Nearly all the surrounding villages had a team in the league. Aberfoyle were our big rivals as were Drymen (one of the better sides) and Thornhill. On the south of the Carse of Forth teams from Gargunnock (whose field was on the side of a hill), Kippen and Buchlyvie took part while the Endrick Valley gave us teams from Gartocharn, Balfron, Killearn and Blanefield. Gartmore was never one of the top sides as we were the smallest village but we did get to a couple of Cameron Cup finals and were second in the league during the years I played.

The day I went to school was quite memorable. Not because of the usual tears as there were none as we were shuffled into the classroom. No, the interesting incident was at playtime when I saw an older boy pull one of the girl's pigtails. My chivalrous nature demanded that I did something about that so I twisted the boy's arm up his back as punishment! Unfortunately for me the teacher only saw the second incident so I set a record as being the pupil who was given the tawse (strap) earliest in his school career – approximately 2 hours!

The school was of standard construction but did have the village air-raid shelter in the playground. It made a great place for hide-and-seek. There were outside toilets at the back of the 'play-shed', a large open faced building which was crowded during the wet play times. Sometime in my early years we had inside toilets installed which made a huge difference to our lives. The school building was divided into two large classrooms, the 'wee end' and the 'big end'. The former held primary classes 1-4 while the latter held classes 5-7. When I attended the school, the teachers were husband and wife couples with the wife teaching the junior classes and the husband teaching the seniors.

There are times and things you remember from primary schooldays which stay with you all your life. It definitely was there that I first realised that I was interested in the outside world. Maps, flags, continents, gulfs, volcanoes – were words and ideas to conjure with.

It is difficult to remember things in chronological order from so long ago. – I never did keep a diary – so bear with me as I try to give a fond impression of these days. I didn't understand until many years later how

14

lucky I was to grow up in such an environment. I've met numerous people who grew up in 'concrete jungles', high-rise flats, deprived neighbourhoods and slums but we had fresh air, green grass and a friendly word from everyone. Perhaps we didn't have a lot of money but it didn't seem to matter.

Those were the days of free school milk when every child was entitled to 1/3 of a pint of milk at the morning break. One morning, I noticed that the inside of my milk bottle had a green tinge to it. After I brought this to the teacher's attention, consternation broke out. The supplier was a local farmer (from the Freuchan Farm) and everybody in the village drank his milk. It was tracked down to a bad cleaning part and the panic was over. The only downside was that I still had to get my milk but they had run out of (or daren't give me) any 1/3 pint bottles. So my reward (punishment?) was to drink a whole pint!

This may seem a strange place to start discussing fashion trends but I've been struck by how certain materials, fabrics, etc. come in and go out of style. A couple of examples are denim jeans and cheesecloth blouses. In the 50's only manual labourers wore jeans, now everybody does while the craze for cheesecloth lasted one summer, I think. Another material is corduroy, which was dirt cheap in the 50's (I had shorts and trousers made from it), fell out of fashion and then stormed back. Every kid wore wellington boots in summer and winter. They were standard kit and allowed us to play everywhere. But our feet did stink!

When one is young, one is strictly constrained by one's age, especially to those who are in the same class in school. There were only three of us in Gartmore of my age (born 1951), myself, Jim Whitelaw who was the local electrician's son and Kay Johnston whose father owned the local garage. Kay was left-handed and in the '50s that was actively discouraged. Many were the days when she was distressed as she struggled to write with her right hand. I wonder if she's now ambidextrous. Attitudes can change, even very quickly. When my brother, Torquil, went to school, he was left-handed but there was no effort made to change him over. The Johnstons moved away to do something with cockleshells on Barra when I was about 7 or 8 so that just left two of us. Jim wasn't very keen on football so I had to play with the older boys. The outcome of that was I became a goalkeeper, as that was where the other boys stuck me! As I got older the age differences didn't seem to matter, perhaps because I got as big as, if not bigger than, the other boys.

One of the older boys was John Hutchison who was both a football fanatic and a very good player. His father was the head gardener in the 'Big House' and had been a very good player in his youth. John and I used to be always kicking a ball around after school and many's the afternoon we spent playing out fantasy games. John trained as a plumber and became a very good one. His younger brother, Alec, was more my age but only got into football in his teens. We (and Torquil) all played for Gartmore for many years.

Before Torquil went to school, he was known in the family as Iain but the school had quite a few "Ia(i)ns" so the new influx was asked if anyone had another name they could be called so "Torquil" he became. His full name is Torquil Iain Maclean Jack and, even around the Gartmore area, it was unique. You can imagine the confusion it caused when he moved to the Home Counties after he left university.

As I write (2003) Jim Whitelaw had a stroke a couple of years back, which has left him needing 24/7 care. Considering that our birthdays are only three weeks apart, it doesn't bear thinking about. Life can be cruel and not always fair.

Growing up in the country gave us plenty of time and opportunity to see Mother Nature at work; sometimes helped by the local farmers, fishers and shooters. Many of the kids collected birds' eggs as a hobby. I know that is frowned upon now, and rightly so, but there were no rules or regulations against it in the 1950s. We did enjoy watching the different migrant birds, swallows, house martins, curlews and a moorhen nested on an islet on one of the Estate ponds one summer I remember. We also had rabbits (with at least two outbreaks of miximatosis), deer would come out of the woods in the winter to feed and every now and again we would see a fox. The ponds and rivers had plenty of fish and, although I never really got into fishing as a hobby/sport, I did enjoy 'guddling' for trout from a river or pond bank. Rabbits were shot for eating and I gutted and skinned a few in my time. One incident that does stand out was watching young cattle being castrated by the local farmer. I was too young to understand fully the implications but the memory does bring tears to the eyes now!

As a community, we all pitched in when the harvest time came around. I think we all helped stack bales of hay, collect turnips and the like and, of course, take part in the 'tattie howking'. I wonder how many children today realise that the autumn mid-term school break was instituted not so that they could go to Spain for a week's sun but so that they could be employed as cheap labour, picking potatoes? It was that backbreaking work that made me decide that farming was not for me, at least as a career. I worked on farms for a couple of summers when I was a student and got to drive tractors, etc. That was much more fun.

When I traveled to other countries, the locals had a stereotype of a Brit coming from a city and knowing nothing about farming. Now, I'm no expert but I was able to carry on conversations with foreign farmers about their problems (which farmer doesn't have problems?), which helped me in my fieldwork; but more of that later.

We knew the names of all the trees (by their leaves) and the wild flowers that grew around us. The Queen Elizabeth Forest was (is) a working pine forest and the Gartmore Estate had many species of deciduous trees.

I've talked about football earlier and it will reappear throughout this tome. However, another sport close to the heart of any Scotsman is golf. When I was young, the nearby Aberfoyle Golf Club was 9 holes, with few members and, because it only leased the land from a local farmer, had flocks of sheep wandering over the course. The greens were each protected by a fence, which you had to climb over to putt! All that not withstanding, it is where I first played the game. My grandfather was a keen golfer (I still have some of his clubs) and my dad also played. Both Torquil and I have played many courses round the world but Aberfoyle remains a pleasant memory. It was cheap also. The junior membership fee for a year was half a guinea (10 shillings and sixpence in old money or 52.5p in new money) and the senior fee was one guinea. The course has changed quite dramatically in recent years. It is now 18 holes, owns the land and has a clubhouse that is well worth a visit. For those who don't know this area, Aberfoyle is on a major, although now dormant, crack in the Earth's crust known as the Highland Boundary Fault (HBF), which, as its name might suggest, separates the Highlands from the Lowlands. The first three holes are in the Lowlands, the fourth hole goes up into the Highlands and there you stay until the eighteenth brings you back to the Lowlands again. The club is a favourite venue for office golf days and many's the morning that sees a busload of workers out from Glasgow or nearby. Most, if not all, are used to playing on relatively flat city courses, which has led one or two to exclaim, after finishing their round, "That's not a golf course, it's an assault course!"

When I was in high school in Callander, I was also a member of the Callander G.C. for the princely sum of five shillings (25p) a year. So I was a member of two clubs for the equivalent of 77.5p!

Some people play golf all year round but they're nuts! So what did we do during the winter? Some played football, naturally, as did I when I was older, but my mother (and I) played badminton in the church hall for many winters. We did have some adventures playing at other village halls because of the snow! Dad was a member of the Village Club where a snooker table was the main facility. That was where I learned to play but I never did beat my dad. When he was young in Glasgow, he would play football on a Saturday afternoon and, then to pass the time until the cinema opened, he and his mates would play snooker and billiards. He had much more practice than I ever had!

Also in the 'Club', there was a peculiar table used for "Summer Ice". As far as I know it is played only in this part of Scotland. Imagine a curling rink. (For those who don't know what curling is, it's bowls on ice!) Now shrink the rink to ~3ft by ~24ft, make it of polished wood and lift it onto a table ~4-5ft off the ground. Mark it up like a curling rink and have 'stones' of ~3ins in diameter made of iron and there you have Summer Ice! There were people, usually men, who were fanatics about the game but wouldn't be seen dead on a curling rink. We did have curlers and there was a village curling pond. However 1963 saw a 'bonspiel' on the Lake of Menteith when the lake froze over sufficiently to allow open air curling. We even had reports on the TV with Fyfe Robertson (remember him?) standing gingerly on the frozen lake! It was cold enough in the nineties to allow another "Lake Bonspiel" to take place, although I didn't witness it as I was elsewhere in the world!

Holidays were always a highlight of the year. Package holidays were only just starting but I don't think my parents would have gone anyway. We used to go to the Highlands or the Islands. Lewis was one destination, Argyle another (although all I can remember about Argyle is rain and plenty of it), Ardrossan (where I remember being badly sun burnt, sitting moaning under my mother's deckchair and my back being covered in Calamine lotion to take away the pain), the Moray Firth (revisiting Grandpa's old haunts) where we made the pilgrimage all Scots should take to the Culloden battlefield, but most of all, the island of Mull. Oh, we did go to Whitby, in Yorkshire, once but that was the extent of our 'foreign' travel.

After one holiday spent on Lewis, we were coming back on the ferry, The Loch Seaforth. In those days the route was from Stornoway to the railheads at Kyle of Lochalsh and onto Mallaig. I was asleep in one cabin while Mum and Torquil shared the one next door. The ferry left Stornoway at midnight so that it would link up with the early morning trains. I awoke to the most frightful din and, before opening the cabin door, noticed that there were green fields outside the porthole. Thinking that we had arrived in Kyle, I thought that I had plenty of time to get ready. As I un-snibbed the door, in rushed my Mum in a perfect state. Seemingly, half the crew had been banging on the cabin door and walls trying to wake me up for about 30 minutes. Why? We were in Mallaig and the train was about to leave! Mum thought I had jumped out of the porthole, which is fairly ridiculous if you know the size of a porthole and the size of me!

If my memory is correct, we spent at least 4, or maybe 5, summer holidays on Mull. We always stayed in the little village of Dervaig, on the north coast. Mum, Pam (before she was institutionalised), Torquil and I sometimes went for a month and Dad would join us for the last fortnight and we would spend much of the time on the sands, especially at Calgary Bay which I still maintain has one of the loveliest beaches anywhere. As we grew up, we would spend days on the golf course or touring round the island and visiting places like Iona. Why Mull? My parents had friends from whom we would hire a house and my mum's maiden name was Maclean, whose clan castle is at Duart Point, the southeast corner of the island. Perhaps that was enough. Eventually family holidays come to an end, possibly because the children have summer jobs or they just don't want to go on holiday with their parents. That summer arrives for all families. When it happened in ours I don't recall. At the time there are few regrets, perhaps a sense that time has moved on and something innocent has gone, forever. However, little was I to know that I'd be back to Mull as an adult.

On one summer's evening back in the early sixties, I was trying to find one of my friends to spend some time with but with no luck. I must have been looking fairly down in the dumps because a retired school mistress (Miss Adams) asked why I was looking miserable. I told her that everybody seemed to be away travelling or on holiday except me. In all seriousness she looked me straight in the eye and said, "Don't you worry. When you grow up, you'll travel." My goodness was she right!

So what else was memorable about the late fifties and early sixties? I vividly remember the sound of Sputnik 1 beeping as it orbited the Earth in 1957. Suddenly the era of space exploration was upon us and would define much of the next forty to fifty years. And then in 1962, we watched the transit of Mercury across the Sun's disc. Rock and roll was starting and because it was what we heard we never thought it odd like our parents did. The Berlin wall went up amid some dark misgivings and then the Cuban Missile Crisis broke. Scenes of parents and friends looking very worried became commonplace. What did we know? Not a lot, I'm afraid. Then came the JFK assassination. And I well remember lying in bed listening on a small transistor radio to the medical bulletins of Winston Churchill's last illness.

In 1958, I watched the great Brazil team with Didi, Vava and Pele win the World Cup in Sweden. The game was shown on the Wednesday afternoon following the match because that is how long it took to get the film back from Stockholm to London. That's a far cry from the ability today to watch live events from the other side of the world wherever your living room might be. I suppose that game and the Real Madrid-Eintracht Frankfurt European Cup Final (which was the first one shown live on British TV) showed me how football should be played. I still have images in my head from these games now. 1966 had both the Aberfan disaster and England winning the World Cup. In early 1969, there was the 'Night of the Storm'. Gartmore was cut off as trees and telegraph poles were blown down. Cars were trapped under garage roofs and chimney-stacks were blown down and fell through roofs. Luckily no-one was hurt and we all got a day off school and work.

Strangely we moved twice to different houses in the village. All the time I was small, we lived on the main street in a house called Thorn Cottage. It had an outhouse, which we converted into a "Grandad Flat" after my mother's mum died and grandpa needed somewhere to stay. It consisted of a large room with a washbasin and bathroom with toilet. Grandpa always ate with us. Before conversion the bathroom held all the coal! The work on the conversion was done one summer and we all pitched in. The roof was renewed and false plasterboard walls were put over the old stone ones, which made decorating much easier.

We then moved up to the house, Woodbine Cottage, which had belonged to my other granddad. It had been left to my dad's sister and when she died Dad bought out his brothers' shares. That sat at the west end of the village football ground and beside an open field. As we grew up, it quickly became apparent that we needed more space so, eventually; my parents bought half the field and built our final home, Erisort, there.

At the time Pam was institutionalised we didn't have a car as neither of my parents could drive. Although there was more public transport than today, it was still a pain getting to Larbert from Gartmore on a Saturday and back again. An unintended advantage of this was that we got to see the football at Stirling Albion's ground, Annfield, on winter Saturday afternoons. It worked like this. After coming back from Larbert to Stirling, we would head off to the football ground whose gates would be open twenty minutes from the end of the matches. We would go in (for free) and then get a lift home on the local supporter's club bus, as my dad knew everybody. When Albion was in the first division, we would see all the top teams, even if it were only for twenty minutes.

We bought a car, second hand of course. It was a black Morris Minor, registration PUS 871. That always stuck in my memory and it was a bit spooky when a green Morris Minor appeared in the village, registration number PYS 871! A couple of years after my dad learnt to drive; my mum took her test and still drove into her 90's!

As Gartmore was off the beaten track, the local bus also doubled as a post van. Every weekday evening, the last bus to Stirling through Port of Menteith, Thornhill and Blair Drummond carried a sealed mailbag with the post from Gartmore and a small post box so that the people en route could have a late collection. Someone had to put the bag and box on the bus and I had that job for 7-8 years while I was at school. As I had become a government employee, I had to sign the Official Secrets Act and I reckon I must have been one of the youngest ever to do so.

Mum was very good at making jams and we were very good at eating it! We had strawberries, gooseberries, raspberries and blackcurrants from the garden while brambles (blackberries) grew wild all around the village. A very strong memory I have is of stewed brambles draining through a cloth overnight into a big brass pot suspended on golf clubs between two chairs. It was our job to gather the brambles and of course deal with the inevitable scratches, etc. But the reward of the bramble jelly was well worth it!

Another wild berry we collected was rose hips which went to make rose hip syrup and which many of us took to keep us healthy. The collections were organised through the schools and each pupil was given a badge depending on the weight of rose hips they collected.

I am not very musical. Although I can sing and hold a tune, I'm no good at reading music and the only way I can get a tune into my head is to hear it over and over again. All that said, my mother would have loved me to have been a piper. When you're young, you'll try anything and, I must say, I had no great dislike of pipes or piping; in fact I rather enjoy the music, the bands, the tartans and all that goes with it. So I took up the chanter, which is the mouthpiece, reed and finger holes of the pipes without the bag and drones. My father worked in the Stock Exchange in Glasgow and his boss, Matt Sloan, was a teacher of the pipes and a very good piper in his own right. When I was young, Dad worked on a Saturday morning in his office in Glasgow and sometimes he would take me with him. It became nearly every week, as Mr. Sloan would try to teach me the scales and the technique of playing. Later on I joined one of the local bands, in Balfron, but my initial interest waned and I gave the idea up. I'm not sure if Mum ever really forgave me.

Dad travelled to Glasgow every day of his working life. Today that is not really remarkable as most people in Gartmore travel to work but in the 50s, there were only about 3 men who made that journey. The others were all employed locally. The 7.10 am bus would get into Glasgow at 8.30 am and he would be home again at 6.50 pm. That was the bus that I would also get when I went with him on a Saturday morning. My Mum loved to shop in Glasgow and I have accompanied her many times. On one occasion (I was 5 or 6) we were walking east along the south side of Argyle St. when I lost sight of her and thought that she was behind me, perhaps in another shop. So I retraced my steps. I eventually got to the crossroads where Buchanan St meets Argyle St just outside St Enoch's Station. Now this was in the days before pedestrianisation, pelican crossings and the like but I crossed over and started walking up Buchanan St. Meanwhile my Mum was going crazy looking for me. I was looking in all the shops for her until a kindly shopkeeper realised that I was alone and offered me a sweet and sent someone to look for a distraught mother. It all ended happily and I still thought that I found her not the other way round!

The local church is of the (Presbyterian) Church of Scotland and Mum and Dad were members as long as I can remember. Mum came from a family of the Free Church ("Wee Frees") but consented to worship in this 'adequate' substitute. As soon as I could walk I went to Sunday School and have a number of bibles, books or certificates for attendance. Some of the things and attitudes I learnt in these days guide me still. For some reason, it became normal for the Sunday School kids to sing as a choir in the church at some of the special services such as Easter, Christmas and Harvest Thanksgiving. I had a pretty good boy soprano voice and regularly sang solos. One year it was decided that I should sing at the Watchnight Service. For those of an irreligious bent, it is the service held at 11.30 pm on Christmas Eve which takes us into Christmas Day. The rehearsals started a few weeks beforehand but I soon hit trouble. My voice started to break. It was too late to change the plans so I had hot drinks, cold drinks and throat massages. My dad even tried to get the music in a different key. In the end, we decided to go for it and my voice held out. So anytime I hear 'Mary's Boy Child', I remember that little boy in a single spotlight beside a Christmas tree.

In 1963, the then Prime Minister, Harold Macmillan, decided to retire. That would have been a big enough shock but somehow, his successor was Lord Home. As a peer and member of the House of Lords, Lord Home, if he wished to be Prime Minister, had to renounce his peerage. Sir Alec Douglas-Home, as he became, still had another problem. He didn't have a seat in the House of Commons. Our sitting MP had just died leaving a by-election in the offing but the local Conservative Part had already picked their candidate, George Younger. In a gesture that never went unrewarded, Mr. Younger stepped aside so that Sir Alex could stand. Politics in the early 60's was very different to today. The Tories had a majority of Scottish seats as recently as 1955 and our local constituency was one of the safest Tory seats in the UK.

Then the fun really started. The main opposition was the newly emerging SNP with the Liberals close behind. The Labour Party never really had a look-in. However in came a myriad of single-issue parties and those from the lunatic fringe. Screaming Lord Sutch was a candidate as was Willie Rushton. Needless to say Sir Alex romped home and those 'rogue' candidates split the other parties' votes. When Sir Alex came to Gartmore, that's the nearest I've ever been to a Prime Minister.

I'll finish this section back at the village school. The headmaster in my last few years was Jimmie Angus. Apart from teaching us the three 'R's, he also tried to educate us in classical music (afternoons listening to BBC Radio Schools programmes), art and esoteric stuff like rugby, which was basically unknown by anybody in the village, and astronomy (I bought his brass refracting telescope – the one we observed the transit of Mercury with). May I state, here and now, that I have always known the difference between astronomy –a science – and astrology – a load of bunkum! The only thing that astrology proves is that there is someone gullible born every minute. JA was from Edinburgh and loved to wind up the locals, including my dad, who were from the Glasgow area. He was also a die-hard Scottish Nationalist.

Most schools have a bell to call the children in from playtimes and lunch breaks. Gartmore did as well but JA never used it. He used to call out "Let's be having you!" and we all queued up in lines to go back into class.

It was due to JA's influence and powers of persuasion that my dad took Torquil and me to Murrayfield to see Scotland play rugby, which I've done a few times since. Another idea was to sail down the Clyde (Doon the Watter!) to hear the riveting in the shipyards (The Song of the Clyde). I think JA had foreseen that the yards were on their last legs and he thought any Scottish schoolboy should at least have some kind of idea of what the Clyde had been.

Back in the fifties and early sixties, the school system was very different from today. We had a visiting dentist; Mrs. Wallace was her name and she travelled round all the local Primary schools giving free dental care to kids who would never have received it otherwise. She also ran a mink farm. My parents were astounded but very grateful, as they didn't have anything like this when they were young. That's probably why they had false teeth in common with many of their generation. A couple of aspects of these visits are still clear in my memory. One was the foot/pedal-operated drill that she used which scared us witless the first time we heard it and the other were the pretty young girls that were her assistants. I was heterosexual from a very early age! The results of these visits are with me today. I still have all my teeth, apart from one crown, and have never had any fear of visiting any dentist.

School educates a person. That seems a simple statement of fact but school can't teach you everything. There aren't enough hours/days in your school life. What it does give everybody is the capability to learn and enquire. How people do this is usually down to the person him/herself. In my case (as many others have done) I read. Voraciously. It started with comics (Lion, Tiger, Beano, Dandy, etc.) but it culminated, in my schooldays, with the Look and Learn. I couldn't believe the amount of general knowledge in the magazine and how much I was taking in. When asked how I knew something, the response, "It was in the Look and Learn." became so routine as to be a joke. I can still remember the cover of the first edition with a picture of Prince Charles as a young boy in his kilt. It also had an article about Van Gogh. I think I took every edition until the publication ended and I still hold it in deep affection. Without it, I wonder if I would still be reading as much as I do today. Jimmy Angus gave me a book to read which I can still recall. "Twenty Years A'Growing" by Maurice O'Sullivan tells of the author's boyhood on the Great Blasket, an island off Ireland's west coast. The book is a great story, well told and started me on a long journey of book reading.

By the time I was in P7, Jim Whitelaw and I had been joined by Jim Gibson (whose father had bought the garage), by Ian Campbell (whose father was the recently arrived new minister) and by Bob Buchanan (his family was farmers and had the green Morris Minor). In those days we sat the 11 Plus (or Qualifying) Exam, which determined to which type of high school you, went after the summer. So 1963 was fairly important even though I'm not sure if we fully understood the implications.

Jim (W) was the only one who didn't make it straight to the 'local' Senior Secondary School, McLaren High in Callander, which is 13 miles away. He went to Aberfoyle Junior Secondary, which didn't go to certificate level. However, he was to join us as after a year he did so well that he transferred to McLaren. The Scottish Education system always gave you another chance.

The next part of this story concerns the six years I spent within the halls of McLaren High School.

3

McLaren High School

It was an autumn day in 1963 when I stood at the village square waiting for the wheezing, old bus from Aberfoyle Motors that would take me and all the others over the hills to Callander and who knew what. I would catch that bus nearly every morning for six years. In these enlightened times of the early 21st century, I believe that the pupils who are about to move from Primary to Secondary schools are taken to where they are destined, introduced to the teachers and shown around the buildings. No such luxuries for us. We were thrown in at the deep end and it is little wonder that we clung to those we knew for about the first week. Thinking about it, I don't think I'd been in Callander more than a half a dozen times in my life before.

On the way we picked up pupils from Port of Menteith before climbing the 'Braes of Greenock', part of the Menteith Hills and down into Callander. On the top of the hills is a small lochan, Loch Ruskie, which is a very popular fishing spot. Nowadays it is quite well hidden by some forests planted during my school years! In the middle of the lochan is an un-named island which has a legend attached to it. The Earl of Menteith, who owned the land in this area, betrayed William Wallace to the English (see above). Part of his 'reward' for betraying Wallace was to have a curse placed on him that, every time it rained, he would lose part of his lands. When it rains the level of Loch Ruskie rises and the small island, which, according to tradition, had Sir John Menteith's castle on it, disappears. Romantic story, isn't it?

The bus was crowded both with newcomers like myself and with old hands who were entering 6th Year and were very much the bosses. I didn't know it then but it wouldn't be all that long before I was a 'boss'. The journey took about forty minutes but at our ages it seemed to take forever. One of the advantages of the journey is that, through the year, it allowed those people that had forgotten to do their homework a chance to complete it. I can still remember the chattering and people catching up with the stories of what each other did during the summer. Then we were there.

Of course, the school knew that it was about to receive a bunch of new pupils who didn't know anything just as it had in years gone by and would in years to come. We were herded into the Assembly Hall and then we were allocated our classes and 'Registered Teachers'. Mrs Stark was mine along with about 20+ others. The first thing I noticed was that there were a lot more girls than boys (2:1 roughly) which was a bit of a shock as I hadn't had a female classmate since Kay Johnston had gone to Barra. I had to get used to it as this didn't change for the next six years.

Scottish education had an enviable reputation around the world and rightly so. What it did right was give the pupil a broad choice of subject with an eclectic mix. This allowed the pupil to choose, from his/her own experience, the path to follow. This didn't happen just at high school; it carried on into university. So what subjects did we have? They were English, Mathematics including Arithmetic, Science (Physics, Chemistry and Biology), Geography, History, French, German, Latin (or Technical Drawing), Woodwork (or Domestic Science), Commercial Studies, Music, Art, P.E. and R.E. We took most of these for two years before choosing those we were to take to 'O' Grade and eventually 'Higher' Grade.

It is fairly evident that things change through time and, during my life, technology has probably changed at a faster rate than at any other time even including the time of the inventions of writing and printing and of the Industrial Revolution. In our mathematics classes, we started off using logarithmic and anti-logarithmic tables (Jimmy Angus had actually given us a start on those in Gartmore Primary), progressed to slide rules – even double sided – and eventually to calculators. This was not because we should learn these techniques but because they came into general use. Even now, the name Faber-Castell means slide rules to me. Mr McNaught, one of our maths teachers, had a mechanical calculator. This contraption had a turning handle that added or subtracted a number from the total and counted how many times this had been done. This is the essence of multiplication and division. However after the first electronic calculator appeared, this machine disappeared from view. It probably will re-appear on "The Antiques Roadshow" and be worth a fortune!

The school took pupils from a huge tract of central Scotland, the whole of Southwest Perthshire, roughly 4 – 500 square miles. The, roughly triangular, area was from Tyndrum and Crianlarich in the north to Dunblane in the south with Aberfoyle and Gartmore in the southwest. It covers some of the most beautiful country on the planet and is well known as a tourist destination.

Here was I, from one of the smallest villages in the area, suddenly confronted by people who lived in towns! If the school hadn't existed, I doubt if we would ever have known each other. Yet here we were, making friendships with boys and girls from all over. We would know them for six years, some a bit longer, and then we (or, at least, I) would go our own separate ways and never see each other again.

But that was all in the future. What did this new school have in store for me?

The school had been around since 1892 and was now in its second building. The original was now the Callander Primary School. At the end of my second year the process would be repeated as MHS moved to a new building on the outskirts of the town and the Primary School occupied our old buildings. In 1963, plans were well advanced for the new school, which was just as well because we were bursting at the seams. There were portacabins all over the grounds and it was virtually impossible for all the pupils and staff to gather in the Assembly Hall. In fact, we had one boy faint because of the overcrowding. The old school was on the banks of the River Teith, which flows through Callander and this was the source of some of the problems. When the river was in spate (every year), it took away some of the underlying soil. As the school stood on the floodplain, not only did we have wet playing fields, but also some of the outer buildings were subsiding. There were huge wooden supports holding up the walls. No wonder we moved.

The school catered for a wide range of extra-curricular activities, which expanded even more when we moved. Obviously there was football and hockey alongside athletics, tennis, drama, swimming, canoeing and even skiing trips. The school now plays rugby but we never had that. All in all, it was a well-rounded education.

One facility, which allowed pupils from such a huge area to participate in these activities, was the Hostels, Ellangowan for the girls and Teithside for the boys. Some pupils from the really remote areas lived in the hostels from Monday to Friday but those who were playing in Saturday sports stayed over on a Friday night so our dads didn't have to get out of bed too early!

So first year came and went with no great dramas. I passed the exams fairly easily but English was a problem. This was to raise its ugly head as we went into second year. I failed an exam. What a shock to the system! Suddenly I remembered being told how important good English was, more than anything else. It got to such a point that I actually took extra lessons from my primary school teacher (Jimmy Angus) in Gartmore to catch up. I've never regretted it and became a convert to the cause. I deplore the incorrect use of the language and I despise bad spelling. I've been asked if it matters and could hardly answer for spluttering! If you can't communicate and make your wants and desires known to anyone, why should you be surprised when you get the wrong thing? A misplaced or omitted comma can cost you millions. A simple story told to me over 40 years ago was that the US customs service left out a comma between the two words "fruit" and "trees". Hence only "fruit trees" were subject to the rate of the customs duty applicable – NOT "fruit" and NOT "trees" as they should have been. How many millions of dollars were lost is anyone's guess!

English had set works that included novels and Shakespearean plays. Novels such as Dickens' Tale of Two Cities and, the one I never finished it was so dire, The Vicar of Wakefield. The plays were A Midsummer's Night's Dream, The Merchant of Venice, Julius Caesar, and Macbeth. Then we switched to G.B. Shaw's Arms and the Man. Every now and again, fortune smiles on you. The night before my 'Higher' English exam, I was rather nervous and couldn't get to sleep. Looking around for something to read I picked up Arms and the Man and read it from start to finish. Thank goodness it wasn't Julius Caesar, which is slightly longer. Was I happy when the first question on the exam paper started "In G. B. Shaw's Arms and the Man…"? That's probably why I passed.

We would read the plays in class and then be given assignments on certain passages and/or scenes. A pupil read each character and so we would get some idea of how the play would act out. There was one exception to this. One of our English teachers was Mr Thompson, who was a bit eccentric but no more so than others on the teaching staff. However, when The Merchant of Venice was the set work (in 2nd year), he would not let any of the pupils read the part of Shylock. Hence his nickname became 'Shylock', one he knew about and, I think, revelled in. 'Shylock' was easily recognisable in any crowd. He wasn't eight feet tall and he didn't have vivid red hair but he had the strangest facial hair I have ever seen. He didn't have a beard or a moustache but two tufts of hair growing out of his cheekbones. I've never seen that before or since.

I thoroughly enjoyed all aspects of Science and that has carried on all through my life. Experiments were great fun although one incident stands out. We were learning about the properties of light and lenses one day and the teacher had got hold of a sheep's eye, which he proceeded to dissect and show us the lens, fluid and optic nerve. We were all engrossed and never noticed that one girl had started to turn green, then white and suddenly her eyes rolled and she fell off her stool in a dead faint!

In 1964/5, a certain 'Fab Four' were in the midst of a remarkable time. They were still playing concerts in City Halls up and down the country although 'Beatlemania' was in full flow. They were due to play in the Albert Hall in Stirling but imagine the atmosphere when the rumour flew around the school that the Beatles were in town, staying at the Roman Camp Hotel. Off went the WHOLE school and stood screaming in the hotel car park. There were the four lads hanging out of an upstairs bedroom and the hotel staff besieged at the door. Girls were fainting right, left and centre but time was moving on. Would anybody get back in time for afternoon classes? Not very many made it. The sight of the Rector, Hugh Cowan, standing at the gate handing out punishment exercises to all those who didn't, must go down as one of my most memorable memories. I doubt if one pupil cared what the punishment was; they had had an experience that they could tell their grandkids about. The next day there was a rumour flying about the school that one of the Beatles (Ringo?) had written a letter to the Rector asking him to be lenient to the pupils who were back late. I doubt if the letter ever existed but can you imagine how much it would be worth now?

Second year was also the year when the school changed its badge. The old one was a monogram of MHS but the new one was, and still is, full of colour and style. There is quite a procedure for approving a new crest/badge/emblem/motto. In Scotland all has to go before the "Lord Lyon, King of Arms" which is a position none of us had ever heard of before.

Organised school trips were great fun where you could get away from the classroom. Of course they were educational and, if outdoors, held in the summer term. In first year, there was a tradition of all the pupils being taken on a trip to see the historical sites nearby. They were, in order of visiting, Doune Castle, Dunblane Cathedral, the Wallace Monument and Stirling Castle. Even in these far off (pre-Braveheart) days, we all knew the history of William Wallace, Robert the Bruce, Bannockburn and all that. So that trip was one that has stuck in my memory. It's a little advertised fact but over 70,000 people turned to watch the laying of the foundation stone of the Wallace Monument. That's more than Hampden holds for a cup final or international match these days!

Other trips included ones to the theatre in Perth to see "Arsenic and Old Lace" and to the cinema to see Zefferelli's "Romeo and Juliet". Olivia Hussey, who played Juliet, had a French boyfriend at the time called Alain Jacques that gave me a bit of "street cred" for a while.

We got quite blasé about actors, celebrities and the like. Back in the sixties, one of the most popular TV shows was "Dr. Findlay's Casebook". The opening title sequence was of Callander and most of the outdoor scenes were shot in and around the town. We got quite excited the first couple of times we saw all the crew and cast but then they became part of the scenery and we wouldn't even notice them after a while.

We all have teachers we remember, for all sorts of reasons, but we had something a bit different which makes me smile pleasantly even after all these years. There was some sort of arrangement that allowed students from France who were studying to become English teachers in France to come over to MHS and help to teach us French while perfecting their English. These students were always female and beside our normal French teachers were, to put it bluntly, stunning and chic. It's that old heterosexuality raising its head again!

Hotels abound in Callander alongside Bed and Breakfast establishments. One of the classier hotels is the Dreadnought, which, like all the others, had to find some way of being used through the winter months. There were always dances especially around Christmas and New Year but there were plenty of barren months as well. The Dreadnought solved this by running a catering school in the winter. This had students studying cooking (of all kinds), waiters, waitresses and headwaiters learning the ways of a restaurant and I'm sure there were cleaners as well. A great idea but they had one problem. All this cooking meant that there was a huge surfeit of food, far more than the students could eat. What was to be done? They hated the idea of throwing it out. Now, I don't know who came up with the bright idea of approaching the school to see if the pupils could be persuaded to come along and eat the food, which also would allow the waiters and waitresses to practice with real people. Whoever he or she was, the Nobel Prize for

Kindness to Schoolchildren would have been a walkover! The Dreadnought Lunches became legendary at McLaren.

All the pupils were divided up into groups of 25-30 and the dates (about six weeks apart) that they would go to the hotel would be put on the notice boards around the school. People highlighted these dates in their diaries with red ink and, perhaps, even blood. So for the price of a Dinner Ticket (1s/6d or 7.5p), we got a 4 – 5 course meal served to us, on bone china, with silver cutlery and menus in French. I would think that most of us had never sat down before to a meal with more than a knife, fork and two spoons in front of us and here we were confronted by a myriad of utensils. This was all part of a great education. We learnt how to behave and what to use at any high-class function. We would never be embarrassed when facing a full dinner table. That has helped me many times down the years.

The "DL's" became almost an unofficial currency. People would swap dates and, when they needed someone to do something for them, would offer their next date as payment. The lunches were so popular that one chap turned up with a newly broken leg rather than miss his turn!

The Dreadnought was also the favoured venue for the school's Burns Suppers and Christmas dances when everybody turned up in their finery. Of course this was the era of the 'Twist' and other 'modern' dances but we still had classes in the traditional ballroom dances – waltz, foxtrot and country dances – Gay Gordons, Strip the Willow, Paul Jones, etc. during our gym classes.

The first years at McLaren were also the ones where I started played organised football and ended up playing quite regularly both for the school and for Gartmore. However, those in charge were trying to make me an outfield player when all I ever wanted to be was a goalkeeper (see above). It is said that you don't have to be crazy to be a goalkeeper but it helps! It took a long time (or, at least, it seemed like it) for me to get a chance to show what I could do. It is funny how certain events stick in your mind. Gartmore was playing at home and the rain was coming down in torrents. The guy who was the regular 'keeper didn't fancy playing so I was 'promoted'. This is going to sound very bigheaded but I played a 'blinder' and the other guy never played again when I was available. That eventually led to playing for the League Select and winning the Scottish Welfare FA's Rolls Royce Trophy. I played for 7 years as the Select's goalie in every game except one when the manager wanted to give another guy a shot but kept me on the bench as a substitute. I was raging! However, I stood on the touchline and waited, seething. The game, which was part of a knockout competition, was scoreless after 90 minutes and headed into extra-time. I was the only substitute left on the sidelines when one of our defenders had to come off and I went on. I played up front for twenty minutes, got my nose broken, stayed on (no blood bins then) and five minutes from the end scored the only goal of the game! That was quite a night. I also took part in some of the earliest penalty shootouts. In one very early one, the referee got the whole thing wrong. After the first 5 shots each, there should be sudden death but he said that there were another set of 5 each. It didn't matter as we won anyway.

I get rather exasperated when pundits talk about 'tired' sport stars. My goodness, they are professionals and spend (or should) spend all their time training. When I was a schoolboy, it wasn't unusual, because of the overlapping of seasons, to play two and even three games on a Saturday. A school game in the morning would be followed by one in a local amateur league (around Stirling) in the afternoon and one at Gartmore in the evening. OK, I was a goalkeeper but my experience was not unique.

At school it took a little longer for the teachers to catch on but at last they did in my final year we won the Stirlingshire Schoolboys Football League trophy – the first time that McLaren had ever won it. That was a great side and Don Revie's Leeds Utd offered one boy, Stewart Macdonald, terms. He turned them down. He could get more money working for the Coal Board. Times have certainly changed!

The other sport that I was pretty good at was athletics – not running I hasten to add – but I could throw things, especially the shot. In fact I don't remember losing any of the shot putt competitions I entered either at school or at the County Sports. I was pretty good at the discus but the technique of the javelin eluded me and I had to rely on brute strength, which meant that I lost more often than not.

We were given the opportunity to participate in many sports even things like canoeing and skiing but the one that may seem pretty odd for a school in rural Scotland was cricket. We never played in any league but we practised during gym time and we would play on some long summer evenings in Gartmore. That brief introduction was to stand me in good stead later.

Let's get back to academia. Into third year and I was now on course to my 'O' grade exams at the end of fourth year. I was still taking Latin and French mainly because I thought I had to. I would ditch both afterwards.

French I never really got to grips with which, I now realise, was a pity and Latin I passed only because I remembered the seen translation passages and enjoyed immensely all the Roman History. Those two bits made up 40% of the total marks. I could scrounge another ten out of the unseen translation passage and general grammar. As Higher Latin had no seen translations, I ditched it. Really I was interested in Science – chemistry, physics and geography. Mathematics was a chore and I never passed another maths exam after my 'Higher' but I was beginning to appreciate English.

I was also beginning to appreciate the girls who outnumbered us boys 2:1 in every class. I don't think the appreciation was returned in any measure and living so far apart made romances pretty difficult. It was much easier to run after the females who lived around Gartmore and Aberfoyle.

I must break off here and tell you a story about how the use of terms can hurt those we least expect. The old school canteen was a couple of Nissan huts and was nicknamed 'Belsen'. When the school moved to the new building, there was a canteen facility already there. Unfortunately, the nickname didn't get left behind. It was a few weeks into the new term when Hugh Cowans, the Rector, overheard someone refer to the new canteen as 'Belsen'. No one knew this but he had been in the British Army detachment, which had relieved the concentration camp of Belsen-Buchenwald at the end of WWII. At the next assembly, he let us have it with both barrels, demanding that no one would ever use that term again and told us some home truths about the scenes he witnessed on that day. There wasn't one un-chastened pupil in that hall and 'Belsen' was never heard again.

Most people know that the education systems of Scotland and England differ in many ways. One of the fundamental ways is that there is only one examination board in Scotland. So every pupil who sits his or her 'O' grade or Higher in Swahili sits the same paper whether they are in Shetland, Callander or Dumfries. A spin off of this is that each pupil has to be identified, by name and by his or her school. This means that the name you put on the top of your answer sheet must be consistent. It is remarkable that I can still remember the afternoon when I was told that from then on I must write my name in a certain way. Henceforth, I've always been "Allan M. Jack" on any official document.

Exams were pretty much a fact of life to us back in the sixties but even we realised that these ones were something special as 'invigilators', usually retired pillars of the community, turned up rather than teachers to watch over us. The great thing was that we didn't get the results until during the summer holidays so that the last few weeks of school were spent in blissful ignorance. Of course the butterflies started as the results day drew closer but that was weeks later.

All right, I passed all eight of the 'O' grades I sat. We didn't get any A, B, or C, etc. passes for these exams in those days. If it was on the certificate, you had passed. If it wasn't, you'd failed. So what subjects was I going to take for my 'Highers'? English, Maths, Physics, Chemistry, Geography and French were on the agenda. "French!", I hear you cry. Take a piece of advice. Never listen to people telling you things they know nothing about. I was told that I had to have Higher French to study Science at University. What a load of rubbish! Once I found that out I dropped it like a hot *pomme de terre!*

I suppose that 5th year was dedicated to studying for these exams but I still played football, shot the putt and had an enjoyable year. I was also made a prefect, which meant that I was a monitor on the school bus and had to deal with the normal high jinks of pupils with too much energy on a crowded bus.

There was one incident where a female pupil was discovered having open-air sex with a male pupil at lunchtime one day. Needless to say there was a bit of an uproar. I was called to the Rector's office and given strict instructions that no one was to talk to her on the bus home. The lad was on another bus. Now, although schoolchildren like to talk, and even brag, about sex, they are all pretty prudish. Or they were in the late '60s. I didn't have any problems on that bus trip home as the lass was treated as a pariah. We never saw her (or him) again.

Of course, 1968 was the year of the Paris student riots, anti-Vietnam War rallies and really the first stirrings of 'Protest' culture. Rural high schools are not known for their political awareness but we had our moments. We wore anti-apartheid buttons (even if we couldn't spell it!) and ones saying 'Keep Gibraltar, Give England to Spain'. We had one boy who was almost a consul for the Chinese. Nice enough lad but carried copies of Mao's 'Little Red Book' and offered to get you Chinese lapel badges. Goodness only knows what the Chinese Embassy in London made of it. I wonder if they ever found McLaren on the map! Is there a file still there with all the names and addresses of those who wrote asking for badges and books? Did the lad know what horrors were being perpetrated during the Cultural Revolution? I doubt it.

After passing four 'Highers' (English, Maths, Physics and Chemistry), I decided to go back to school for a 6th year. I knew that my grades were good enough to get into university but I thought that I deserved a year where I really didn't need to do anything. I suppose it would be called a 'gap year' but back at school. I was only really interested in making the school first XI football team and enjoying myself.

Everything was going well for about a month. I mentioned above that I was a prefect. It now transpired that, instead of only the teachers deciding on whom the Head Boy and Girl were going to be for the year, the remaining prefects were also going to be asked to vote for whom they would want in the positions. There were only another four boy prefects apart from myself who were eligible so it didn't take a rocket scientist to realise that each of us had a 20% chance of being landed with the job. It didn't actually work like that because one lad was a racing certainty to get it.

The usual procedure was that the announcement of the Head Boy and Girl and the new prefects was given at the weekly assembly that was always held mid-morning on a Wednesday. The 'voting' took place on the previous Monday when we were called into rooms to be told about this new procedure and handed slips of paper to complete.

So there I was daydreaming on the bus to school on the Wednesday when I overheard a chance remark wondering who the new Head Boy and Girl were to be. I was staring out of the window at the very familiar landscape and my head was suddenly running through all the duties that the Head Boy was supposed to become instantly *au fait* with. There were speeches and bible readings (heaven help me), meeting any VIP that might turn up (sweaty palms), chairing the Burns Supper (agh!), Prefect's Council (no!) and trying to keep the whole of the male roll in order. And probably trying to keep the girls in order, too!! So there and then, I heaved a huge sigh of relief as I realised that my chances of becoming Head Boy tended towards zero!

My first class was a period of sixth year studies in physics. Approximately halfway through, the door opened and Hugh Cowans, the Rector, asked to speak to me in the corridor outside. As I passed by Ian Campbell, he whispered, 'Deputy Head Boy, then, Allan?' I replied, 'Aye'. Mr. Cowans was waiting for me, held out his hand and said, 'Allan, let me be the first to congratulate you on being elected Head Boy'. I was stunned. I had no expectation of this happening and very little time to get used to the idea before the assembly. Through my daze, I could hear him telling me to do as

I had been doing at assembly, bringing it to order before asking the minister, priest and himself to come through from his office. But I had to sit at the end of a row so as to be available for later.

I went back into the classroom, shaking my head. Ian asked what the matter was and the smiling teacher asked if I was OK. I told Ian the news. He was as stunned as I was. I told the teacher, who had known the secret all along, that I was alright. Then the bell rang to signal the end of the period. I asked Ian to keep it fairly secret but he could tell the guys in the next class he was in. I, fortunately, had a spare period in the library where I could try to get my head around this shock.

Up in the library were some of the junior pupils doing assignments but spending most of the time whispering about me, although they didn't know it. At the end of the period, during which I don't think I read a word, one asked me if I knew who the new Head Boy and Girl were. I had to mumble that I would find out at the same time they would.

The Assembly Hall was the same raucous scene it was every time and the pupils were only brought to order by the Head Boy shouting, 'Quiet!' before going out to invite the Rector and any dignitaries into the hall. (The existing prefects had been taking it in turns to do this from the beginning of term so no one suspected anything different when I did it on this occasion.) Usually the pupils split along the Protestant/Catholic divide to have separate services and then came together for general announcements. On this occasion, the short service was ecumenical and the real business got underway. Firstly the newly elected prefects were called up onto the stage to receive their new badges. Then the Head Girl and her Deputy (Alison Walker and Margaret Howie) were announced. Next the Deputy Head Boy was named (John Howie, Margaret's cousin) and 'The Head Boy will be (Hugh Cowans held it for a couple of seconds and you could see the whole school lean forward in anticipation) Allan Jack!' There was a second of incredulity broken only by a couple of cries of appreciation and then, thankfully, applause and cheering.

I can't remember much else about that day; even the trip home on the bus was a blur. Mum was out when Torquil and I got into the house but when she did come in she asked if anything interesting happened in school. I told her of the new prefects that she knew and that I had a new badge. She wanted to see it and I told her it was on my blazer which was hanging up out in the hall. She went to have a look and came back with the biggest smile ever. Of course, I then got the lecture about behaving and not disgracing my parents. As if I would!

So there was my quiet 'gap year' ruined! I can tell you that the news went round the village like wildfire. Gartmore was (is) one of the smallest of the towns and villages in the area and I don't think that anybody before me had had this type of recognition from McLaren. There had been a few prefects but never the Head Boy. Congratulations were the order of the day and my parents were as proud as anything.

However, I didn't have a clue as to what I was supposed to do! The above list from my daydreaming was only part of the story. All of a sudden I was expected to write out rosters for the prefects, read lessons at the school church services, (the Thanksgiving of Simeon springs to mind, even now) and generally to keep the whole student population in some sort of check.

The school had a tradition of putting on end of year productions, which saw alternate years have operas, usually Gilbert and Sullivan ones, and straight plays. I was involved in three such productions. I was in the chorus in the 'Gondoliers', a soldier and citizen in 'Julius Caesar' and the character 'Ferrovius' in 'Androcles and the Lion'. The latter role was at the end of my sixth year. The character is a reformed gladiator who has become a Christian convert and renounced his old life. There is one scene where he is tested to 'turn the other cheek' by a Roman citizen. This involves been slapped slightly on one cheek then the other. Then Ferrovius gets to try the same on the Roman who gently swoons as he is towered over by the ex-gladiator. Rehearsals were fine but during the first performance Alasdair Mahoney, who played the Roman, gave me an almighty slap, thinking that it would be fun as he got another go. I think he had forgotten what was to happen next so I'm not sure if the swoon was acting or for real as I glowered down at him with vivid red marks on my cheeks, the neck of his toga in one fist and my other clenched and cocked to punch his lights out! The gasps were audible even from the rest of the cast.

Being the HB gave me a lot of stature as you can imagine but the teachers liked to keep you honest. We didn't see our costumes until the afternoon of the dress rehearsal in front of the assembled school. I was handed the smallest bundle of clothes you ever saw and a pair of sandals. My costume consisted of a skimpy (!) off-the-shoulder (imitation) leopard skin leotard and matching briefs. I told 'Shylock' that if he thought I was going out in front of the whole school dressed (or not dressed) in just that, he had another think coming! He just laughed.

This had all started months before when 'Shylock' and I had met in the corridor one day and he told me that he had an ideal part for me in the school play. I didn't really think too much about it at the time but then, when I was reading the play, it all clicked. Another funny story about the production was that after we had all given in our measurements for the costumes, I again bumped into 'Shylock' in the corridor. As we passed each other by, he turned and said, "Allan, there's one thing you ought to know." "What's that, sir?" I replied. "You may be interested to know that your chest measurement is bigger than any girl's bust measurement in the school!" And with that he walked off, chuckling.

My final two weeks in school seemed to be an endless round of talks, parties, dances, church services and speeches culminating in the end of year prize giving. My task was to propose a vote of thanks to the guest speaker who, I think, was the Lord Lieutenant of the county and then give a general farewell on behalf of all the leaving pupils to the assembled school. Alison Walker (the Head Girl) had a much easier job. She just had to present a bouquet to the Lord Lieutenant's wife. I did have one moment of panic when I thought I had lost my notes. However, I had put them in a different pocket and so I had time to calm my nerves. At the time I thought that all the nerves and steeling oneself to stand up and speak publicly was a form of torture, which I didn't really need in my life. However I am now glad that I had to go through it. I have no fear of public speaking and getting up in front of any number of people to talk about or present something is second nature to me. That is just something else for which I have to be grateful to the school.

We were standing around after the ceremony, making small talk when my old PE teacher called me "Allan" for the first time ever. He had always bawled "Jack" at me no matter in what year I was or which position I held. Apart from being HB, I was also House Captain (Vennacher, the others being Achray, Katrine and Lubnaig, the names of the main lochs of the Trossachs). He was a strict disciplinarian and would not tolerate stupidity, ignorance or intransigence. I doubt if there was a boy in the school who hadn't been caned by him but I saw him use the belt only once. On that occasion, Uncle Davie (McAinsh) as he was affectionately known, had been demonstrating the correct way to jump over a horse – with your hands flat. This young lad proceeded to "bridge" his fingers, rather like a snooker player. Uncle Davie was very patient and demonstrated the correct procedure again. The lad repeated his mistake. Bend over. Thwhack! Do it again, properly! Same mistake. Bend over. Thwhack! Properly this time. Same mistake again. Just stand there, Hall. We were all engrossed. What was going to happen? Out from his office came Uncle Davie with the tawse. Hands together, please, Hall. A couple of strokes later and Hall did as he was told and jumped the horse with his hands flat!

A couple of the other teachers came past and enquired as to what I was going to do next. I was off to Glasgow University to read Science but, of course, they knew that already. They just wanted to show that they were interested. Mr. Crichton (Scratchy to every pupil) started to talk to me about the future. He was the Classics master and Deputy Rector and one of my favourite teachers. Not because I was a great classics scholar but because he had been a very good goalkeeper in his day, and, while at university, had played for East Fife. He had taught me an awful lot about playing in goal and whatever success I was to have in that field could be laid at his door.

Then it was time to leave. There are movies about the last days of your school life and everybody seems to burst into tears, hug everybody else desperately and be full of angst. I can't remember that happening. Some of us would meet up again at university or college, some we would never see again. We knew with whom we were friends and that mattered but we also somehow knew that a great big world was out there waiting for us. So off we went into the summer of '69. Isn't there a song about that?

My summer was to be spent working in the grounds of the Forest Hills Hotel near Kinlochard. One Monday I wasn't as sprightly as I should have been due to the fact that I had been up half the night watching Neil Armstrong walk on the Moon! I've always been fascinated by space, astronomy and I still think that the Apollo missions rank as one of the great achievements of mankind. I know all the political background and the belittling arguments but it still stands up as a great time to be human. I would have given anything to be part of it and, had I been an American of my generation that is what I would have set as my goal. I was privileged, some years later, to meet Harrison (Jack) Schmidt who was the second last guy to walk on the Moon. I vividly remember listening to the radio broadcasts of the Apollo 13 mission that went wrong. I admit to shedding a tear when they had to ditch the Lunar Module and, watching it burn-up in the atmosphere, said, "Aquarius, we thank you!"

Many years later (about 30 or so) I walked around the Kennedy Space Center in Florida with my kids and relived all of it.

4

Glasgow University

At the end of the summer it was time to leave for university. I had been allocated a place in the Macbrayne Hall of Residence in Park Circus Place across the Kelvingrove Park from the university. The Hall was originally founded by the same family who lent their name to the familiar Caledonian Macbrayne ferries on the west coast of Scotland. Both Roddy MacIver and Ian Campbell (from McLaren) were staying there as well. They were both studying medicine while I was in the Science Faculty. My first year subjects were Chemistry, Natural Philosophy (aka Physics) and Maths and I now realise picking them was a mistake. However I was not to know how much of a mistake that was until the end of the year.

Hindsight is a wonderful thing but I should have known that I only study subjects that interest me and I quickly lost interest in all three. I suppose Chemistry was the one in which I had most interest but even that was waning. I filled my time doing other things – chasing girls, partying and, believe it or not, boxing. Oh, and I also played a lot of football.

I did make some very good friends with whom I'm still in touch, Gordon (Sam) Murray and Mike McCulloch among them. They actually came out to Gartmore to spend New Year with my family and me.

The real kicker was at the end of the year when I failed all my exams. What a disaster! It was bad enough admitting it to myself but my parents were less than pleased, you might say. In fact, they made me even more miserable than I thought possible. Right then I decided that, if and when I had children of my own, none of them would ever be encumbered with my expectations of what they should do. I only hope I've kept that promise. Of course I'd let them (and myself) down but I would have thought that a little support would have helped. In due course, I failed the re-sits in September and the **** really hit the fan! It got so bad that I had enough and actually ran away. I packed a small case and walked out of the village. I walked over the hill to Drymen and caught a bus to Glasgow. I had my Post Office Savings Book and my school certificates and not much else. Where was I going? I hadn't got a clue. I'd got to the end of my tether and anywhere was better than my home.

After reaching Glasgow, I walked into a café and had a cup of tea and a doughnut. I then wandered down to Central Station with the plan of jumping on a train south. I didn't even know how far my money could take me. By this time the anger, frustration and red mist had all cleared and I realised that, even if I did get on a train, I didn't know what I was going to do at the other end. I certainly didn't have any friends 'down south' and purposely I had not contacted any of my university mates.

So there I was standing on the concourse of the station when I saw a family saying farewell to one of their members who was catching the train that I was looking at so thoughtfully. It was a regular family, mum, dad and two kids with the daughter leaving home, probably for the first time. That's when reality struck me. There was a family a bit like mine but they knew where the daughter was going. She would be met at the other end and she would sleep in a safe bed when she got there. So what was there to worry about? So why was her mother in tears and her dad wiping his eyes a couple of times as well? They knew that she would be looked after, something that, right at that moment, my family didn't know about me. So I walked away from the station and headed for a bus to take me home.

Right at that moment, is probably the lowest I have ever been. Was it cowardice to go back home? Some people may say it was. Was it the right thing to do? Undoubtedly. Once I did get home (before my dad who was out scouring Glasgow and the surrounding areas for me) the atmosphere changed. I was no longer somebody to be ashamed of but a difficulty which had to be resolved.

We had just moved into our new house (probably another bit of pressure for my parents) and the field, which surrounded it back and front, had to be transformed into a garden. In the back garden, a shed had to be built, with foundations, a greenhouse also with foundations and multiple vegetable plots had to be dug. The region was notorious for 'clubroot' in vegetables, which made them inedible but it could be removed by planting potatoes first. We had plenty of potatoes that autumn.

The front garden was altogether different. Mum decided to have a lawn with a rose bed and rockery around it. Where did the rocks come from? Out of where the lawn was going to be. I must have moved a ton of rocks and dug three long drains which all met at the front wall, a 'dry stane dyke' that I rebuilt myself. The lawn dropped 2 inches every six feet and was about 10 yards by 10 yards. I didn't put a square inch of turf down; it was all seeded and keeping the birds away was a full time occupation. I was really proud of that lawn but all the work put me off gardening for life. It was great to be out in the open air and seeing what I had accomplished was very gratifying but my feelings were unprintable when I went back 10 years later and the new owners had run a gravel driveway across my lovely lawn!

So what was I going to do about my education? I did hold what were known as 'class tickets' for my 3 first year subjects. These allowed me to sit the 'degree exams' at the end of the year and, always remembering that the Scottish education system gave you another chance, it didn't matter in which year you sat the exams or how many times. So I resolved to sit my chemistry and physics exams in the following June and see what happened. After that we would see. I also enrolled in the Langside College in Glasgow to 'cram'. This was a college where most of the students were either trying to pass 'A' level exams, which are equivalent to 1st year course in Scottish universities, or were on day release.

A footnote to my 'career' at Langside happened roughly a year later. One Saturday morning the phone rang asking for Mr. Jack. It wasn't my father who was wanted but ME and by the Police. The Glasgow Force on the South Side of the city was investigating a charge of embezzlement against one of the office secretaries. Seemingly, when I had paid my term fees, the full amount wasn't entered into either the books or the bank with the balance going into this lady's purse. My case was only one of many but I did have to go along and make a statement. Fortunately, the sheer volume of evidence must have been sufficient to get a conviction as I never did have to turn up at court to give evidence. My other experience with the police was one evening when I was waiting for my Dad to drive home when I was approached and asked to stand in an identity parade. I even got a fee for that and no, I wasn't picked out!

It wasn't long until I realised that I knew all the stuff and could recall it from the year I spent at university. As the months went on I got more and more confident (even when decimal currency was introduced) and I was actually looking forward to re-taking the exams.

It was strange walking into the exam hall and not knowing a single person. Maybe that helped a lot but I passed both the Chemistry and Physics papers, which meant that I could now go back to the university and start my second year. That also improved the atmosphere at home. So what was I now going to do? I had planned to re-sit my Mathematics exam in the September, which I did, but the pressure was off so I failed that one again.

I went back to see my old Advisor of Studies, Bob Murray, a lecturer in the Chemistry Dept., with whom I stayed in contact the year I was 'out'. He was delighted for me and we started to think about what subjects I was going to take in the next year. I had to take a 'Higher Ordinary' (or second year) subject, which had to be either Chemistry or Physics, so I chose Chemistry and one other 'Ordinary' (or first year) subject. The one that best fitted my projected timetable was Geology. On such small decisions are lives decided. I would need to pass my Maths eventually if I was to progress to do Honours at the end of the year but I could worry about that at the end of the year.

So off I went into my belated second year. Because of the trouble I'd got myself into in my first year, there was no thought of me staying away from home so every morning I drove into Glasgow with my Dad or caught the bus. And it stayed like that for the rest of my time in the university.

About halfway through my second lecture in Geology, I realised that I had found the subject I had been looking for. This was definitely for me. Even the fact that the first term lab time was devoted mainly to crystallography, which has to be the driest subject under the Sun, didn't deter me. The field trips were great fun, especially when some people turned up in their best clothes to go trudging through quarries and over hills!

Suddenly, studying was fun again and even exams were something to look forward to. At the time my self-confidence was so low I never dreamt that I would actually become a geologist but I didn't really care. I was enjoying myself. This even rubbed off on my Chemistry and at the end of the year; I actually passed both subjects with very little trouble.

Off I went to see Bob Murray again. As one of the committee overseeing the entrants to the Honours Chemistry class, he had put a good word in for me and there was a place in that class on the condition that I passed my Maths exam. Well, I did try but I'd been away from it for nearly two years and realistically I didn't have a prayer in passing. The fact that there was a place offered to me at all was a great boost to my self-confidence.

Now what was I going to do? Bob and I sat down and talked about it. It was apparent that I was going to have to go for a 3-year 'Ordinary' degree i.e. one without honours and we would have to try and see what subjects I would need to get the relevant credits. I started with second year Geology and added first year Geography and then, because it fitted into the timetable, first year History of Science (HoS). Geography was a breeze and HoS, because it was an Arts subject, didn't have any labs, which meant that I had some afternoons off. The really momentous part of HoS was that I got a class prize at the end of the year!

Classes in Geology followed a strange path. There were nearly 200 first year students plus a few from Engineering but in second year these figures shrank to about 30. That did allow much better student/lecturer numbers and fieldtrips were much easier to organise. The Easter fieldtrip lasted 10 days and was the one where we learned how to map rocks in the field over an extended period of time. Up till then our field maps had been drawn over the course of a day trip. It is a sobering experience to stand on a hill overlooking Girvan with the wind so cold that you can't hold a pencil and realise that you are having the time of your life and you really don't want to be doing anything else.

From the start of the year, I had been thinking about what the future held. I had resigned myself to finishing off my degree and leaving university in the summer. I could be a teacher but that never really appealed to me but one thing that did appeal was flying. As a young lad I had models and posters of aircraft hanging from my ceiling or stuck on my walls. So I wrote off to the RAF and BA to see if I had any chance of being a pilot.

This led to a kind of dichotomy. For part of the time I was looking down and scrambling around on the ground looking at rocks and for another part of the time I had my head in the clouds. I was playing a lot of football as well although all-day Saturday field trips were a bit inconvenient. However, as the teams I played for were amateur, they couldn't really complain.

At the end of the year I had enough credits to get my ordinary degree with which I would have been quite satisfied. However, one of the conventions of that time at the University was that if you did well enough in the term exams, you didn't have to sit the end of year (or degree) exams. Believe it or not, I got an 'exemption' for my second year geology. This meant that I was offered a place in the Honours class. I was now in a quandary. I had not expected this so had gone off applying for other careers and was well down the interview path for pilot training for British Airways. The teaching staff was very understanding and agreed that my place would be kept open until the beginning of the academic year (usually the beginning of October). There was one rider. The third year started early (in September) with a field trip to Arran and if I wasn't on that trip, I couldn't take up the place. So the summer was taken up with trying to make a decision. I've often found that things work themselves out but when you've been for two separate days of interviews and aptitude tests and the results aren't back 4 days before the field trip is due to kick off, panic begins to set in. However, a brown envelope arrived on the Wednesday morning saying that I'd fallen at the final hurdle and I was off to be a geologist.

Arran is often referred to as 'Scotland in miniature' and it certainly holds most of the rock types that are seen on the mainland. The ten day trip also allowed the just over a dozen of us who were in the class to get to know each other, warts and all, as we would be together for the next two years. For those who were there, the most memorable, though not the most enjoyable, part was standing on an outcrop of rock known as the Imachar Dyke. Dr Holgate had written several academic papers on this but he was not the most stimulating talker. After about 40-45 minutes listening to him droning on about textures, which can be seen only down a microscope, he asked if anyone had any questions. We were all frozen and bored so you can imagine our horror when someone (who shall remain nameless) did ask a question! It was fully another 45 minutes before we could reach the sanctuary of the bus.

So that was how my two honours years in geology started, two years that changed my life. The department was in one corner of the East Quadrangle of the university's main building. However there was a new purpose built department planned and we would be the last honours class to graduate from the 'old' building.

As the two years progressed, my love (not too strong a word) for the whole subject grew and grew. Fieldtrips are a big part of geology because the field is the start of any geological investigation. Obviously, the weather, and the light, in Scotland is not very conducive to being out in the open air for much of the year so trips had to be confined to before and after the wintertime. The 3rd year Easter fieldtrip was to Ballachulish in NW Argyllshire. We stayed in the hotel in Glen Duror, which overlooks the spot where the 'Red Fox' was shot, a true event immortalised in Robert Louis Stevenson's "Kidnapped". On the way home, we were a bit bored but the journey was enlivened by a visiting Israeli researcher (Ari Shimron – whom I was to meet again later in South Africa) singing one of the filthiest songs I have ever heard and one of the students, Reggie Nicholls, explaining the different sizes of geological hammers as sexual dimorphism!

When I was a geology student, the new 'big thing' was something called "Plate Tectonics", a theory which had evolved from another idea called "Continental Drift". Looking back from the early days of the 21st century, it may be difficult to believe that not all researchers were convinced of the validity of the theory. We were told to have an open mind as there may well be some evidence found that would shoot the whole theory down in flames. It was and is interesting to look back at some of the pre-Plate Tectonic theory papers and books. The very good and distinguished geologists made excellent field observations but when it came to a unifying theory, they were all at sea. Plate Tectonics has solved that problem.

All honours students must complete an independent, unsupervised project and the geology department insisted that the students carried out some mapping. The student sat down with the prof. (T. N. George) and decided where they would get some good experience of different rock types. I wanted to go to St. Kilda but TNG wasn't keen for a couple of reasons. One, parts of St Kilda are quite inaccessible and, two, permission to land wasn't all that easy as the Army controlled the islands. We settled on Mull (I told you I would get back there) being an easier proposition all together and the area round Lochbuie as an area that would be challenging enough. I did a recce between second and third year but I did virtually all the decent fieldwork between the two honours years.

One other major influence came into my life during these two years: I met the girl who became my wife. Dorothy started as one of the department secretaries near the beginning of my third year and we took a while to get together, what with one thing and another, mainly the facts that I lived in Gartmore, she lived in Coatbridge and I was always out in the field.

This story now gets a little complicated as Dorothy worked beside a girl also called Dorothy. My Dorothy's surname was Oliver while the other Dorothy's was Vall. You'll get the hang of it. In my class there was a mature student, Jane Macdougall, who was very friendly with Dorothy Vall. Jane was about ten years older than me and I was one to two years older than all the others in the class. Although I knew nothing about it, the two Dorothys had been discussing me and Dorothy (V) decided to sound out Jane to see if she could shed some light on me and my love life. The two Dorothys had already looked out my department card, which held all my personal details so they had a head's start. The plan was cooked up during the summer of '74 when we were out doing our independent fieldwork. While I was on Mull, Jane was in Ardnamurchan with her family where Dorothy (V) went to visit her. This might be hard to believe but I was one of the topics of conversation and all possible information on me was passed back to Dorothy (O) who was covering the departmental secretarial duties in Glasgow. Unknown to the two Dorothys, Jane had invited me to Ardnamurchan for a weekend later on in the season. There was a ferry from Tobermory on Mull to Kilchoan in Ardnamurchan, which I made by the skin of my teeth, as I had trouble hitching a lift from Lochbuie, which is at the opposite end of the island. However, made it I did and, after Jane got me to admit that I would not be averse to getting to know Dorothy (O) better, she told me of the interest from the other side. This was probably unfair as I could have cut and run but I had no intention of doing so.

After the fieldwork was over, I was back in the department cutting thin sections so I could look at the rocks under a microscope but one morning I wanted to talk to TNG. I went up to the office window and Dorothy (O) answered. TNG wasn't in so we struck up a long conversation, the outcome of which was that she would type up my 'honours thesis' and I would buy her dinner. Once I had written up the work, I met up with her (and her colleagues, including the other Dorothy and her fiancé) for dinner and drinks. I drove her home and we've been together ever since. I was never one to talk about my girls and it took many months before anyone, not in the inner circle, realised that we were an item.

The summer of '74 brought another very important person into my life. Along with me on Mull was one of my classmates (Reggie Nicholls) whose field area was just along the road from mine. Remember this was long before mobile phones so we had an arrangement that we would meet in the local pub, the Craignure Inn, every now and then. One night we were having a beer and playing darts, when another voice asked to play. That's how I first met Jo (short for John) Keenan and I was instantly aware that we would be friends for a long time. It was a strange feeling and I don't recall feeling it again anywhere. I've made lots of friends over the years but JK is still the one that I regard as being my best friend. We had a great time over the summer and we kept in touch afterwards. He came and stayed in Gartmore and I visited him in London where he was a student at Kingston Poly. He didn't believe I had a steady girlfriend by then (Dorothy) but to this day he says that he envies me my wife and kids. He has married, is divorced, but has a lovely son, Andrew.

My mother came to stay with me when I was on Mull. I had hired a small caravan so had plenty of room. While she was there the Tobermory Highland Games were on and we went along, as did Jo. The games are split into local and open events and I wanted to take part, so I turned up to register. The organisers took one look at me and saw an over 6 foot, 15 stone stranger who would have no competition in the field events from any of the locals. So they refused my registration as they said I wasn't a 'local'! Even when I told them where I was staying and why, they were adamant. I'm still convinced that they didn't want me to embarrass the 'local' athletes or win any prize money. So I tried to enter the 'open' events where the real professional athletes took part. They wouldn't allow that either, as I didn't have a kilt to compete in. That reason I understood but the other 'rule' pissed me off. I wasn't interested in the money or prizes; I just wanted to have a good time. Anyway, the weather was great, the whole day was very social and we even met up with some people from the Gartmore area.

Jo, Mum and I were in one of the local pubs one night when we fell into conversation with a local fisherman. Mum has always liked salmon and talked the guy into bringing a small one along the next evening for us. There are meals that people rave about from famous restaurants but the simple fare we had that night of shallow boiled salmon with salad is one that will live a long time in the memory.

When I was on Mull, I rode a bike, which was a great help as the caravan was not in my field area. However, it did lead to some adventures. Between the caravan and my field area was a rather high hill. At the start of my project I wasn't very fit so I walked the bike up the hill and rode down the other side. By the end of the summer I was riding up and down the hill at both ends of the day. The downside (in the morning) had a burn flowing beside it and at the foot of the hill was a bridge, at which the road turned at right angles. I was riding down the hill one morning when I noticed a small tent pitched at the side of the burn. Now I knew it hadn't been there the night before and, as I was careering down the hill, I was wondering who was in it when I realised that there was a lovely young girl washing herself in the burn, stark naked!!! I was so astonished that I very nearly ended up crashing over the bridge.

That road ran along a couple of lochs and ended at the small hamlet of Lochbuie. It wasn't very busy but, because it was only a 9-foot road with passing places, every now and then I was 'buzzed' by cars. After a while it became obvious that there was one car that was doing it more than most, being driven by the same young lady. The main social activity on the island was a ceilidh with music and dancing and these took place on the weekends at various halls. On one occasion, I noticed the female driver in question and asked her for a dance. She thought I looked familiar but when I told her I was the "boy on the bike", she flushed with embarrassment and stammered some apology. I just laughed and tried to tell her not to worry. I then learnt that she was visiting her parents with her husband and kids but the most important thing was that her dad was the local fisherman.

My area included an offshore island (Frank Lockwood's Island) and I had no idea how I was going to get onto it. After talking to her father, I was invited onto his boat one morning as he was going to pass the island en route to Oban to collect some supplies. So they dropped me on the island at about nine o'clock and disappeared off to Oban, promising that they would be back at about two in the afternoon. The island is about the same size as half a football field so it did not take me long to map it especially as it was of only one formation. So by 10am I was finished and so sat down to wait for my lift home. As usual, I had a packed lunch and a flask and I was lucky as it was a beautiful day and the sea was as calm as a millpond apart from a couple of passing squalls.

As an aside, I did wonder who Frank Lockwood had been but no-one in the local community had a clue and the question usually elicited a shrug of the shoulders. It was only many years later that I discovered that the afore-mentioned FL had been married to the sister of the 21st Maclaine of Lochbuie, who had been the Solicitor General from 1894 – 1895. I assume he was well liked.

So two o'clock came and went, as did three and four and I was getting a bit concerned. I had a good line of sight back towards Oban and would be able to see the boat a long time before it arrived. I had a couple of false alarms as boats veered off to the south and a pleasure steamer passed just half a mile away. There was one good thing, though. Scotland in the summer has light nights and darkness didn't fall until well after nine o'clock. However I was out of food and had only a little tea left, so hunger was setting in.

By seven o'clock I was cursing fishermen up and down thinking that they were all in the pub. At half past seven, I was resigned to spending the night on the island. Now I hadn't brought any tent, sleeping bag or toiletries so I wasn't too happy about the prospect. However, there was no advantage in getting upset so I just had to get used to the idea. I had stopped staring in the general direction of Oban all the time but would check every fifteen minutes or so.

At about quarter to eight, I noticed a speck on the water getting larger all the time. I resisted the temptation to get excited as I had become resigned to not seeing 'my' boat until the morning. However, as it got closer and closer, it became apparent that I hadn't been forgotten. The captain was very apologetic and explained that they had been on their way back and then realised that they hadn't taken any fuel on board and had to go back for it. Then they had to wait for a bunkering spot hence them being late. I was only too happy to see them and get back to the village. I thought I would have to ride home (forty minutes) and then cook a dinner for myself but the captain felt guilty and invited me for dinner. I still had to ride my bike back to the caravan, though.

Jo and I made friends with some of the locals and we were invited to one of the dances but it was in the village of Bunessan, near Iona. We were offered a lift there and back so didn't hesitate. The dance finished at around midnight and we went looking for our lift to be told that our 'chauffeur' had disappeared to another village. We had no option but to walk back, a mere 20 miles through the night. We had had a couple of beers so perhaps we weren't thinking too clearly. After a few miles we had gone too far to do anything else and, as we were both fit with all the hill walking, it wasn't until we reached the caravan that our legs gave way. We didn't do much fieldwork that day!

So life was going on quite well and we were heading toward the final exams. The department had a new professor (Bernard Leake) who because of his initials (BEL) became known as Ding-Dong. BEL's field areas had always been in Ireland, specifically Connemara, and so off to Ireland we went for our Easter mapping trip. Now these were the days of the 'Troubles' so it didn't bode well when BEL turned up in his trench coat and black beret, an almost exact copy of the IRA 'uniform! Off we went over on the ferry from Stranraer to Larne and across Northern Ireland to Donegal in the Republic. On the way, one of the vehicles got lost in Londonderry and crossed the Foyle into one of the dangerous areas. They pulled up at an Army post to ask directions. The officer in charge came out to direct them but kept his hand on his holstered pistol while a squaddie scanned the rooftops for snipers! They thought it could be a set-up!

Driving on we passed the bombed-out border post at Strabane and eventually arrived at the Highlands Hotel in Glenties. I learned more about mapping on that trip than any other I had been on and up till then I thought I knew how to map rocks. We all knew that this was going to be the last time that we, as a class, would be together so perhaps that is why it was so enjoyable. BEL told us a joke, which I still remember. He said that, when two bars in Ireland are out with staggering distance of each other, one would spring up in between to fill the ecological niche!

However, the local situation intruded and we had to cut the trip short as there was going to be a ferry strike and we would be marooned if we didn't leave early. The trip home was remarkable for one aspect. We were stopped and searched four times before getting out of Stranraer. The most amazing was while sitting in the car park at Larne ferry terminal where we were accosted by a tramp who turned out to be a female police officer and who demanded to see all our luggage. Student luggage is not a pretty sight at the best of times but, after about ten days out on the hills in the wind, rain and sun, it has a peculiar smell!

You would think that I would be sick of lectures but I did attend two held outside the university both of which I remember for different reasons. The first one was actually when I was in my last year in school and was a public lecture held in Strathclyde University. These were the early days of hydrocarbon exploration in the North Sea and the speaker, whose name I've forgotten (and it's just as well I have!), was giving a talk on the prospects and possibilities for the next phase. His lecture was interesting and I actually got up and asked a question about palaeomagnetism. However the big question came next when someone in the audience got up and asked if, after all the gas being discovered in the southern North Sea and in the Netherlands, was there any chance of oil being found off Aberdeen. The reply was "No chance!" The Forties field was found within the following six months and I have never really believed anything so-called "experts" have said from that day to this.

The second memorable lecture was held in Edinburgh while I was in the honours class and was given by Harrison 'Jack' Schmidt, the second last man to walk on the Moon. Not only was the lecture really interesting, mainly because Dr Schmidt was a geologist, but I actually got to shake his hand, which was a privilege. It was said that it was much less trouble to make a geologist into an astronaut then to make an astronaut into a geologist (or should that be a selenologist?).

So then we were into our final ten-week term. There were no lectures planned so every day was spent in the library revising all we had been taught. It was amazing how much started to make sense. So the day came of the first exam of the finals. We were to sit eight, three hour (9am till noon) exams in nine days starting on a Thursday and finishing the following Friday. There were five written papers followed by three practical exams and the only day off was the Sunday. There's not much studying you can do when the exams are on so the afternoons were somewhat surreal as we lazed around laced with some periods of panic as we thought we'd forgotten everything we were ever taught about mineralogy, fossils or structures. Of course, there is absolutely no studying you can do for the practical exams as you can either identify the rock or fossil or understand the structure, or not, so from the Tuesday afternoon we were at a bit of a loose end. No going to the pub, of course, because we had to have clear heads for the following morning. On the Thursday night before my final exam, my dad was playing a match in his office golf tournament at the Killermont Golf Club in north Glasgow. For something to do, I offered to caddy for him. Typically for Scotland, the weather turned wet half way round the course and I got soaked, as did everyone else. The next morning I woke up feeling dreadful. I should have gone to the pub; I would have felt 10 times better!

So in I went to my final exam feeling like death warmed up. I asked for water, aspirin, more water and didn't feel any better by the end of the exam. Funnily enough, that paper was the only one I got a first class pass for! There must be a moral there somewhere but I've never been able to work out what! We had plans to go to the bar and get hammered after the exams but I had one beer and went home for some sleep and medicine. The following Tuesday was when the results would be posted so we all met up and waited nervously, discussing what we thought we would get. Out of the dozen of us, there was one first class, one third class and the rest were split evenly between upper and lower second class. I got a 2 ii (now known as a "Bishop" (Tutu)), which I was fairly pleased with, what with my chequered university history.

5

Between Universities

There was a society in the university called the Glasgow University Exploration Society, which ran scientific visits to out-of-the-way places during the summer holidays. In the 1970s, it had been 'taken over' by the Geology Department and usually went to some region of geological interest. Since 1968, there had been a strong relationship between the departments of Glasgow and Charles University of Prague in Czechoslovakia. One of our lecturers (Don Bowes) had been caught up in the Soviet invasion of Prague in '68 and although we didn't see many Czech geologists in Glasgow, there were still some good feelings between the two institutes.

In late 1974, it was decided that the next GUES field trip was to be to Czechoslovakia and I couldn't wait to sign up. It would be the first time I had ever been abroad and so I had to get a passport – one of the old blue ones. We needed visas as well but there were no problems as the Czech government were fully supportive of the excursion.

Before setting out on the trip, I had one more important appointment. Torquil and I had tickets for the last day of the Open Championship at Carnoustie where Tom Watson and Jack Newton tied after 72 holes and had to play off on the Monday. Watson holed a long birdie putt on the 18th to force the tie and he went on to win his first Open the next day. We drove home and then I went to help my Dad in the local golf clubhouse where he was the manager since his retirement. Then I had to get up, pack and meet the others at the department before driving down to Heathrow to catch the flight to Prague. We flew on Czech Airlines who gave out free beer! I don't think they knew that they had a planeload of thirsty students.

Arriving in Prague, we were collected and driven to the student flats where we would stay for the first couple of nights before travelling up to the

Krkenose Mountains on the Polish border. We would be there for about three weeks before returning to Prague and home.

The staff of the Geology Department of Charles University could not have been nicer to us. They made us feel most welcome and showed us all around Prague. The old city, Charles Cathedral, Charles Bridge and Wenceslas Square were all on the itinerary. This was well before Prague was open to tourists from the West and we had never seen old Mid-European architecture before. We were really impressed. We were not impressed by the modern flats and housing estates built since the Communists took over.

So we were picked up by the regulation Skoda bus and set off for the Polish border. One of the Czech lecturers, Dr. Haloupski (sp?), was one of the most rabid anti-communists we had ever heard. Basically he was of the opinion that Communism couldn't find beer in a brewery and that was one of the more complimentary opinions he held. He also was not quiet about it but he was such a good geologist and held in such high regard that the authorities didn't want to (or couldn't) touch him. This was in the days when there were a fair number of politicians and opinion formers in Britain who thought that it was inevitable that the Communist system would prevail. It was interesting to hear the other side from someone living under the system. The only country this guy was allowed to travel to, apart from Eastern Europe, was Cuba. We suddenly remembered that we were not stopped by our authorities from travelling anywhere.

A few hours later we stopped at the town of Pecs where we had to get off the bus and hike the last few kilometres. That doesn't sound too bad until we realised that the few kilometres were straight up! The chalet (Lesni Bouda) where we were to stay was in the middle of a nature reserve where the only vehicle allowed was the postman's motorbike! So our introduction was a climb with full pack, which left us all gasping for beer when we eventually arrived at the bouda. I can still order a beer in Czech! Then again I had plenty of practice!

Anybody who goes to a foreign country has to contend with a language problem. For Brits the problem is less than normal as much of the world speaks English. However that was not the case in Czechoslovakia in '75. So a young female geology student accompanied us from Prague who did speak English and could act as our interpreter. One of our leaders was a guy called Con Gillen who had one both very useful and remarkable talent. He had only to listen to a language for a few days and he became fluent in it. He made more money out of translating Russian scientific papers into English than he did as a Geology lecturer. Needless to say, Czech was one of the languages in which he was fluent.

The personnel of the parties changed about so that we wouldn't get bored and the leaders would know if we were getting things wrong. I was completing a traverse with Con and another one of the leaders, John Addison, and we made our way to the restaurant on the top of the highest peak, Sneska (Snow Mountain). The other leader was Ian Vann who went onto become one of the head geologists in BP. After having some coffee, we made our way out to find that the mist was covering the summit. The Poles had fully armed border guards (the Czechs didn't bother) and one of them was standing in front of us asking for something or other. Con was paying the bill so John and I were trying to decipher the Polish which was getting louder and louder. Thankfully Con caught up with us and started to talk to the guard. He pulled out the letter (in Czech) and explained what we were doing. The only words I understood were "Glasgow University" and then something strange happened. At the word "Glasgow", the guard went silent, put his hand on his pistol butt and walked slowly backwards into the mist and disappeared! Even Con didn't know what had caused him to do that.

Because we were sometimes out on our own, the letter in Czech explained what we were doing and under whose auspices we were doing it. We also had to carry our passports around which was a little strange for us even those who had been abroad before. One day my party was stopped by some soldier and a civilian who was in charge. We were asked for our papers and it quickly became apparent that the civilian couldn't read Czech. He was a Russian who was asking Brits for papers in Czechoslovakia. That brought home to us what the locals had to put up with.

At the end of the three weeks, we decided that our last evening would be a big party so we started early and finished late. We started on beer (some on wine) and then went on to Slivovitz, which is a brandy made from peaches or plums and is quite lethal. An abiding memory was of a young local couple, who were also staying at the bouda, both dressed in Stars and Stripes t-shirts, and who insisted on multiple toasts which meant there were a lot of self-inflicted wounds the next morning.

After hiking down the mountain, we got on the bus and headed back to Prague. On our way home we stopped for a barbeque at the country house of our rabid anti-communist, complete with beer cooling in the burn at the foot of his garden. We would be in Prague for a couple of days so that we could shop for souvenirs and see some more of the city. At the top of Wenceslas Square is the National Museum. One of the highlights of the trip was when we were taken behind the scenes and shown some of the exhibits, which had yet to be out front for the public to see and some of the research material, which was never going to be on public display.

If you ever go to Prague, there is a dungeon bar just off Wenceslas Square, which sells a black beer. It's not Guinness but if you drink beer, you'll love it.

Then it was time to go home. The security at the airport was unbelievable but as most of the population wanted to leave and the authorities didn't want them to leave, I suppose it was understandable. The food had been terrible but the beer had been cold and the people warm so all in all a wonderful trip.

The trip kicked off an even stronger relationship between the two universities leading to many reciprocal visits in the following years.

All through my final year, I was conscious that the next priority after the exams would be to find a job. I had applied for a few but by graduation I had had no luck. To tide me over, I took a job working in Goldberg's in Glasgow (I had worked 3 summer vacations there), where I was Santa Claus (!) and for the Water Board digging and cleaning out ditches along the tunnel routes. That was hard work, not very well paid but in the open air and with some good people.

All through the autumn and up to Xmas, I was still applying but not even getting interviews. There were not many jobs around for geologists; it was before the North Sea had taken off and I always thought that I would have to go abroad but the lack of success was getting me down. However the Xmas and New Year season was coming up so I put a brave face on things so as not to spoil others' enjoyment.

My father had retired earlier that year from the Stock Exchange but he and my Mum would go to dinner dances with his old colleagues. I had an arrangement that I would drive them into Glasgow and I would then pick them up at the end of the evening. The only condition was that I wasn't to drink any alcohol. That seemed fair enough to me and it meant that I had a car to use for the evening.

On the Friday between Xmas and New Year, it was the yearly office function and I duly dropped my parents off at a restaurant just off Buchanan St. and went off to collect Dorothy for a pleasant night out. We had a meal

58

and some drinks with Dorothy Vall and her fiancé, Ian, in the Pond Hotel on Great Western Road. I then took my Dorothy home and drove back into Glasgow to pick up my parents. I parked just along the road (it was quiet as it was about one in the morning) and walked towards the restaurant. Before I got there I was met by my dad's great pal, Willie Stupart, who stopped me to tell me that my dad was in Glasgow Royal Infirmary after suffering a heart attack. Stunned, I walked into the restaurant to console my mother who looked as though she wasn't quite sure what was going on. Because it was so late at night, it was no use trying to get into the hospital to see if dad was OK. I had to get mum home. I had a large mug of coffee, which I really needed and phoned our local GP, both to tell him about dad and ask if I could bring mum round for some pills for her nerves. It must have been close to three in the morning when we got to the surgery and nearer four when we got home. I woke Torquil to tell him and then sat in the dark in our front room until it was time for breakfast. I would have watched night time TV but there wasn't any in these days! I can't say I had many thoughts; I just stared out the window.

We were to go into the hospital in the morning to see how dad was, so off we went back into town. Into the ward we went to find dad with wires and tubes all over him and several machines beeping away. Talking to the nurses and doctor was re-assuring, as they seemed to have got to him in time. He was lucky that the restaurant was only about ten minutes away from the hospital. If he had had the attack back home in Gartmore, he probably wouldn't have survived. So that was our schedule for the next couple of weeks, driving in to Glasgow to visit dad. It was obvious when he was ready to come home as he was driving the staff up the wall.

On the morning of Hogmanay, I got a telephone call from one of my old lecturers, Don Bowes, who asked me to come in and see him the next time I was in Glasgow. As I was just about to drive in and see my dad, I told him I would see him that afternoon. When I arrived in his office, he told me that he had a friend who needed a postgraduate student to fill a post whose funding was going to disappear if he couldn't find anyone. It turned out that the original student had been refused a work permit and the friend was getting a bit desperate. The first question I asked was where was this position? It turned out that it was at Cape Town University in South Africa and was in the Precambrian Research Unit (PRU). Needless to say, I was taken aback. There was one problem; I had to be in the field, working by the end of April.

You might think that would be quite enough time but, in the days before emails and faxes, the bureaucracy of getting a work permit/permanent residence was substantial. The rumour was that it could take up to eighteen months through the South African Embassy in London, mainly because of the numbers trying to emigrate.

Don Bowes gave me some research papers of the surrounding area and I quickly realised that the rocks were those I would like working on. So then I had to go off and write off to Piet Joubert, who would be my boss in UCT, officially applying for the position.

While I was waiting for the reply I had plenty to keep me busy. What with working for the Water Board and getting my father out of hospital, my days were full. The doctors had told my dad to stop smoking (a probable contributory factor) and give up all alcoholic drinks except whisky (in moderation). He had smoked all his life so he found that very hard and he wasn't helped by some of his friends lighting up while visiting him. He eventually started up again.

One Saturday morning in February, the mail arrived with a letter from South Africa and I received an official letter from UCT confirming my appointment as a Research Associate in the Department of Geology. Accompanying the confirmation letter was another letter, written with a note of panic, detailing whom I should contact in the SA Embassy to push my permit through. Gartmore is a long way from London but there was one advantage; it was very close to Glasgow where South Africa had a Consulate. How did I know this? It was in the same building as my father's old office! The road was officially renamed Nelson Mandela Place a few years later.

So in I walked to the consulate on the Monday morning and showed my letter of appointment to the girl at reception. She took off like a scalded cat through some large double doors and came out again a few minutes later accompanied by one of the consular officials who invited me into one of the side rooms. It took me a little while to understand his very broad South African accent and he lost me totally when he chatted about "biltong" and a "braai"! I later found out that biltong is dried meat similar to jerky and a braai is a barbeque. I was given a form to complete which I was to return with my passport and a couple of photos. I explained about the need for speed but the official didn't seem to be worried.

I was keeping UCT up-to-date but the panic letters still arrived with regularity. All I could do now was to wait.

However, there was someone else involved. Dorothy and I had decided a long time ago that we were going to be married but, all of a sudden, events were taking over. We sat down, talked it over and decided that we would get engaged before I went to Cape Town and I would come home for the wedding. I would let Dorothy know as soon as I could, when I could get home so that she could start the arrangements.

We were engaged in March, just before my permanent residence permit came through. The consular official was right to be confident. The next problem was to get a flight. South Africa was still giving assisted passages, thank goodness, so I had a flight from London to Johannesburg for 25 pounds! I would then have a train journey to Cape Town. After all the running around, I would arrive in Cape Town on 11th April 1976.

The day before I left was the wedding of the other Dorothy, which, of course, we had to attend but we left early.

The fourteen-hour flight from Heathrow to Johannesburg was uneventful if a bit longer than any journey I'd taken of any kind. SAA (the South African airline) had to fly 'round the bulge' of Africa because none of the countries of Africa, north of the then Rhodesia, would allow SAA over fly rights because of apartheid.

On arrival at Jan Smuts Airport, I was met by immigration officials and taken to a hotel in Hillbrow for a few hours. So there I was with two stamps in my passport, one South African and the other Czech. Two more different countries are hard to imagine. I was then taken to the main railway station to catch a train for Cape Town. Most people have heard of the Blue Train, which runs between Jo'burg and Cape Town and is the height of luxury. Well, that wasn't the one I got on. This trip would take two nights and a day stopping virtually everywhere along the way.

I was in a 4-berth compartment and I was lucky that one of the other young men was an English speaking South African. The other two guys were Afrikaners, only one of who spoke any English at all and both of whom were in the Army. The one chap I could talk to was on his way to Kimberley so he got off early the next morning. The whole of the next day was spent crossing the very uninteresting flat landscape of the Karoo and we lost one of the other guys, who got off at De Aar to catch a train to South West Africa (now called Namibia) with the rest of his Army unit.

So we crossed the mountains of the Du Toit's Kloof Pass during the night and I woke up to the coastal flatlands approaching Cape Town. As we got closer I could see Table Mountain and it is only when you see it for real, that you appreciate the sheer size and majesty of it.

I got off the train at the main station and went looking for a phone. I called the department and got hold of Piet Joubert who told me to wait in the café and he would come and collect me.

In the middle of the concourse of the station is an old steam locomotive. As I walked past it, I noticed that it had been made in Falkirk. I suddenly felt not so far from home. I can remember sitting in the café, drinking a cup of tea and trying not to panic over what I was getting into. You might think I would have had enough time to do that during the train journey but for most of that I was bored and not really thinking. However, just before Piet arrived, I took a deep breath and told myself I would just have to get on with it.

Piet arrived and I was off on a marvellous adventure.

6

UCT, Marriage and Namaqualand

It is impossible to discuss South Africa in the 70's without bringing up politics. Apartheid was the biggest political hot potato of the second half of the 20th century, even surpassing communism, which most people thought would rule the world anyway and life would not be too bad when that happened. I knew about apartheid, (who didn't?), but until you actually faced it, it was all a bit unreal.

The department technician was Brian, brown skinned and 'classified' as a Cape Coloured. (You have no idea how difficult this is to write.) We were downtown getting some maps and other stuff I would need and it was lunchtime. I offered to buy him lunch at a burger bar but all of a sudden where I was struck home when he told me that we couldn't sit in the same restaurant. We bought some sandwiches and sat in a park.

Of course, I was classified 'white' and so most of the iniquities of apartheid passed me by. However, it was impossible not to be affected. It would be wrong to tar all the 'whites' with the same brush, as many of them were vocal in their opposition. However the vast majority of the white population was content, mainly because the government kept them so.

UCT was one of the institutes most vocal in its opposition. In the foyer of the library was an unlit candle signifying the snuffing out of freedoms.

I was headed for an area of the north-western Cape Province known as Namaqualand. My field area lay between latitudes 30 and 31 degrees south and between 18 degrees east and the coast, a total of about seven thousand square kilometres. The region was one of sheep farming, copper and diamond mining and was deeply conservative. However before I got there I was introduced to the life in Cape Town.

Being a student, I drank beer and usually brown beer, called 'heavy' in

Scotland. Out of the UK, brown beer is rare and so I had to get used to drinking lager, which, to my palette, is alright when you are in a hot country. So I was very happy to frequent the nearby hostelries, two of which were the 'Pig and Whistle' (which was destroyed in a fire a few years later) and the 'Forester's Arms' commonly known as 'Forries'.

On my first Friday evening in the town, Piet had arranged a welcome party in his house. What he didn't tell me was that is would be a cheese and wine party. I had never really drunk wine to any extent. Some of my friends in Glasgow quite liked it but I stuck to beer mostly. So when I turned up to the party I was a bit disconcerted to find that there was no beer. The Cape is one of the world's finest wine producing areas and, right there and then; I was given a quick introduction to the produce. I have been a big fan ever since. Andy Duncan and his wife, Jean, were both enthusiastic wine drinkers and taught me a lot about the local vintages.

One of the great delights of the Cape is the sheer number of golf courses. There was an unofficial department 'school' and I was invited and became one of the regulars whenever I was in town. I hadn't brought any clubs with me but managed to beg, borrow and build up a mis-matched set, which stood me in good stead for a few years.

Rugby is huge in South Africa and the Newlands Stadium is just down the road from UCT. Football (soccer) is very much second class and at UCT, the situation was no different. I didn't have any time to look into the club but I would after my fieldwork was over.

Then it was time to go off to Namaqualand. Piet picked me up one morning in a Land Rover with a small caravan on tow and we headed up the N7 main road north towards South West Africa. Without the caravan, it would have taken us six hours but this trip was nearer eight. We were heading for a town called Springbok, which was the largest in the area. The region was famous for its copper mines and so there was a fairly robust geological community. However, historically, much of the work done in the area had been concentrated in the area near the mines. It was only in the previous few years that much research had been done in the remainder of the region. Money was now being allocated to basic geology research mainly due to the recent discovery of the huge (100's of millions of tons) polymetallic (Cu-Pb-Zn) deposits of Aggeneys and Gamsberg. In fact, Piet had been instrumental in finding these deposits. He had mapped an even larger area of Namaqualand than I had in front of me and my area was basically the bit he hadn't managed to cover. The PRU was one unit that had grasped the opportunity to put several postgraduate students in the field. The SA Chamber of Mines funded the PRU and, although the mining companies were interested in finding mines, the money allowed some very good basic research to be done. My funding was from the Anglo American Corporation and one of the reasons we were in Springbok was to visit their local exploration office.

Before getting to Springbok, we had to find a place for my caravan to stand so Piet pulled off the road just south of the village of Kamieskroon. One aspect of this area is that the people speak Afrikaans, not English, and especially not the English I spoke, coming from western Scotland. Piet was totally bilingual and had no trouble communicating. The whole area is split into farms and he found a farmer who spoke a little English and who had a couple of sons who had fairly good English. I was to be thankful for that in a little while.

I was a bit apprehensive going into the Anglo offices in Springbok, as I didn't really know what they wanted from me. I shouldn't have worried as all they wanted was for me to deliver a regular box of samples for assay either to the Springbok or Cape Town office. They didn't seem to be concerned if there were any metals in the samples or not. A couple of the geologists joined us as we went for a quick introductory tour round my area. After all, Piet was the acknowledged expert.

So, after a couple of days, I dropped Piet at Springbok airport where he caught a flight back to Cape Town. And there I was, on my own in a foreign land.

I drove back to the caravan and began to set up my camp. Coming from Scotland where water supply was never a problem, it was a shock to realise that, because Namaqualand is an arid semi-desert, I would have to rely either on rainwater (very intermittent) or water from wind pumps. Quality was iffy and drinking brackish (brak) water was to become a habit. That first night I realised I would have to buy another piece of equipment. No moon meant no light and it was probably the first time I had ever experienced total darkness. A torch was required.

The next morning I started my mapping but I quickly realised that the scale of the project meant that I had to change my techniques otherwise I would never get finished. That was one problem and relatively easily solved. However, I had another, which wasn't so easy to solve.

I suppose I was a bit of a celebrity and I'm sure that the farmers and their families talked about me, the 'Rooinek' (redneck) from Scotland. Then again I wasn't very hard to pick out. I always wore a big white, Stetson-like hat with an imitation leopard skin band and that, combined with the fact that I didn't have a heavy tan, meant that I was pretty conspicuous. The lack of a tan was due to being naturally light skinned and going through many bottles of 'Block-Out'. Namaqualand is extremely sunny as it lies at about the same latitude south of the Equator as Morocco does in the north.

The deal was that if you didn't have the permission of the farmer to walk or drive over his property then you couldn't. I suppose you could, but you risked being shot – quite legitimately. So I had to go and ask permission. My Land Rover had written on the doors 'Precambrian Research Unit' and 'University of Cape Town' in both English and Afrikaans with the UCT crest but UCT was not popular in the region. Being an English medium university and in the vanguard of trying to change apartheid from within South Africa, the local Namaqualanders did not hold UCT or its students in high regard. I thought I spoke English fairly well albeit with a Scottish accent but these guys had no clue what I was talking about. Now this was my problem, not their's. I was getting nowhere fast.

What was I to do? It didn't take a brain surgeon to work out the solution. I would have to learn Afrikaans. The next question was how. I went to my 'landlords', the Stones, and told them my problem. We sat down and decided on four phrases or sentences that I needed to be able to say to get my message across. Nothing ventured, nothing gained so the next morning I walked up to the next farmer and rattled off the four phrases. He almost fell over in surprise but from then on I didn't look back. I kept learning words and phrases and, by the end of my fieldwork, I could hold two to three hour conversations with the locals. I've always known that being a Scot is a great advantage but it now became concrete. In Afrikaans the 'g' is a guttural sound very similar to the sound 'ch' in Scots such as in the word 'loch'. So Afrikaans' pronunciation was no problem to me.

Kamieskroon sits just off the N7 blacktop, the only such road in the area and at the foot of Kamiesberg Mountains. It services the local farming community as it lies a distance from the mines. It has one great facility, a hotel and bar. The Swart family ran it and Coenie and Colla (the husband and wife team) could not have made me more welcome. Not only was I made welcome in the bar, they invited me to Sunday lunch nearly every week where I would meet people from the village that I would never meet in my normal weekly adventures.

I've already indicated that South Africans are rugby fanatics and the local Namaqualanders were no exception. Of course, this was the time of the sporting boycott but the '74 British Lions were still talked about with great reverence. One point about that tour should be made. It took place despite the boycott and had left the UK without the (Labour) government's blessing. In fact, the government did all they could to dissuade the Lions from touring and some players turned down their invitations. John Taylor of Wales was a prime example. However, the Lions didn't lose a game on the whole tour and the only game they didn't win was the final Test, which ended in a draw. Of course, the Lions returned as heroes to the UK and, wouldn't you believe it, the first person to meet them off the plane at Heathrow was the Sports Minister, Denis Howell. All that proved to me was that the hypocrisy of politicians knows no bounds.

As I frequented the Kamieskroon Hotel bar, I would be pulled into conversations about all things but eventually rugby would be the topic. We all agreed that the local Cape Town provincial team, Western Province, had a great chance of winning the inter-provincial competition, the Currie Cup. What we didn't agree on were the respective merits of the two university sides. I, of course, would not admit that the UCT side, nicknamed the Ikeys, was inferior to that from Stellenbosch, who were known as the Maties. I didn't know any of the background but the Maties were one of the strongest club sides in the country and they nearly always thumped UCT. Stellenbosch University is the Western Cape's Afrikaans medium university so most of the local students went there. It is in the heart of the South African wine country and is only about a forty minutes' drive from UCT.

There had been a yearly sports competition between the Ikeys and Maties called the 'Intervarsity', which encompassed all sports but the climax was the match between the two rugby first XVs. Because UCT had some 'non-white' students who were eligible to play in these teams and to whom the Maties objected, the formal competition had been suspended for a number of years. However, after some long, hard discussions, the Intervarsity was back on the agenda and was taking place when I had been in the country about six weeks. The upshot was that I ended up taking bets (cans of beer) on the result of the match. The game was played on a day when the heavens opened, which probably levelled matters, and UCT won a low scoring match. Needless to say I was delighted and the locals a touch peeved.

The locals did delight in 'taking the Mickey' and continually called me 'Rooinek' (a derogatory term for a Brit because of a sunburnt neck) and 'Engelsman', which needs no translation. They decided to not understand the difference between an Englishman and a Scotsman, which led me to such frustration that I ended up calling them 'Kaffir', a term so derogatory to them that I never heard the 'Engelsman' term again.

A feature of the hotel's Sunday lunches was that the Sunday newspapers were delivered there as no shops were open on the Sabbath. The papers were all in Afrikaans but one day I noticed a huge banner headline – SOWETO – and I asked what it meant to be told that it was a township outside Johannesburg. I had never heard of it (it was over a thousand miles away) but, in the next couple of weeks, I was getting letters from back in Scotland from Dorothy and my parents asking if I was OK. Letters were the only means of communication as even the phone system was rudimentary. I had an arrangement/address as Poste Restante at the local post offices. After learning what Soweto was all about and realising that I was in total ignorance, I decided that I had to buy a radio. Because Namaqualand was so undeveloped, it had to be a short wave one. As my life became more of a routine in the field, that radio became really important.

Going back to rugby, the New Zealand All Blacks were touring South Africa that year and, as I was down in Cape Town for a couple of weeks, I decided to go to the 3rd Test held at Newlands. I had seen the All Blacks at Murrayfield but this would be a chance to see two of the world's great rugby nations go head-to-head. The game was not great but it was enjoyable except for one incident. South Africa won the match but there was a loose ruck, no further than ten yards in front of where I was standing. One of the All Black lock forwards, Pole Whiting, was caught with his arms trapped in the ruck and his head sticking out on the South African side. A Springbok lock, Moaner van Heerden, was joining the ruck and I saw him look down at Whiting's head. Quite deliberately, he raked the defenceless head with his studs and almost tore Whiting's ear off. It was the most despicable, deliberate act of sheer cowardice and hate that I have ever witnessed on a playing field.

I had to go into downtown Cape Town on the Friday morning before the game and, having heard of the anti-tour demonstration on the Thursday, which had descended into violence, I didn't hang around to witness the one due at lunchtime. Many of the shops had their windows boarded up or were about when I passed on my way to the railway station to catch a train to my digs. When I got off the train at my stop I met a friend who asked me if I'd heard about the riot. I thought they were talking about the one on the Thursday but I had just missed being caught up in one that lunchtime. Some of the touring All Black's were not so lucky and they were tear-gassed, albeit by mistake.

Back in the field, I was visited by Piet taking a student field trip through Namaqualand and by a fellow PRU member, George Zelt, an American who had the deepest voice I have ever heard. Our field areas overlapped but he was a bit further on in his research. He came up to take one more look at the rocks and I tagged along. We visited some farmers that he knew but we slept under the stars for a few nights. The final day we spent way over on the west of the area along the edge of one of the dry riverbeds, which cut through the sandveld. We went to get permission from the farmer and were told, in Afrikaans, that we could drive up the river for about a few hundred yards but to stop at a certain point as the riverbed got soft after that and the Land Rover would get stuck.

Now my Afrikaans was still ropey while George spoke none at all. I was translating but George wasn't sure I had it right. Off we went, stopped the truck where we were told to and started walking along the riverbed. It was hot and dusty so, after walking a few hundred yards, George decided to go back and get the vehicle as we were making slow progress. The bed of the river seemed fairly firm so George had started to scoff about my translation of the warning we had been given. Off he went to get the Land Rover, back round a bend in the river.

A few minutes later I heard the engine start up and begin to get closer. Then I heard some loud revs and, eventually, the horn going off. I trudged back, knowing what I was going to find but hoping against hope I was wrong. I walked round the bend and there was my Landy, up to its axles in sand, salt and muck. It took the two of us over three hours to get it out but George never questioned my Afrikaans translations again!

Now, even although I was in the field all the time, I did take time off every now and again. I had to go into Springbok to get cash from the bank and supplies that I couldn't get in Kamieskroon. Seeing I was in town, I would take time to get a haircut; a restaurant cooked meal and would go and sit in the local hotel bar. I was sitting in the bar on one occasion when the owner came in a blue funk. He had a couple of Labrador dogs he was trying to get to mate but the dog wasn't performing. So there I was sitting at the bar, having a cold one when these two dogs came into the bar. The dog was obviously exhausted so that when he tried to mount the bitch, he couldn't make it and the bitch looked round and gave him such a look of contempt that the whole bar burst out laughing.

I dropped into the Kamieskroon Hotel bar one night and was asked if I had a camera. All geologists take photos of rocks and formations so I carried a reasonable SLR. It was a Russian Zenith which was Dorothy's engagement present to me. I wondered why they needed my camera but no one in the village had anything above a 'Box Brownie' and they wanted to send a photo to the newspaper of a two-headed tortoise, which had been found, on a nearby farm. It was a Siamese twin with two heads, four front feet, two rear feet and one carapace. It didn't survive long but I still have the photo!

The Kamieskroon School was organising a trip to the mineral baths at Ai-Ais in southern South West Africa and, because the local headmaster was a regular in the pub, I got the chance to tag along. Ai-Ais is the camp associated with the Fish River Canyon, which is the southern African equivalent of the Grand Canyon in the USA. It's not so extensive or as deep but it is still very impressive. The camp also had hot mineral baths, which are lovely to swim in.

South Africa was involved (far too mild a term) in the civil war in Angola and the local lads were part of the regiments who were on three-month assignments 'on the border'. The border was along the Cunene River between Angola and South West Africa. The Swarts had a son, Jan, 'on the border'. Eventually they were coming home and a whole convoy of vehicles headed for Grunau, a bleak railway stop just north of Ai-Ais where the railway turned east towards the centre of South Africa. It is the closest the railway gets to Namaqualand.

Namaqualand is an arid desert land. It gets baking hot in the summer but does get some rain in the winter and my area, being on the coast, got some strange mists rolling in off the sea. It has something to do with the cold Benguela Current and the hot air from the land intermingling.

So for most of the year, the landscape is a mixture of browns, blacks and greys. Where there are wells, there are some date palms and irrigated crops. Sheep, goats and a few head of cattle run over the hills but they share the area with some pumas and a whole host of snakes. The farmers drove around in pick-up trucks, called 'bakkies', and they usually carried a rifle in case they came across some varmint attacking their herds.

So I went to bed one night in this brown, arid landscape and woke up the next morning to a riot of colour! It was such a change that I thought I was still dreaming. This surreal image of greens, oranges, purples, whites and any other colour you can think was there in front of my eyes as the Namaqualand Daisies burst forth. For the next two months, the rainbow continued and then it was gone as quickly as it had come. Nowadays the daisies are world famous but when I was there it was only South Africans who came to see nature's palette.

Then it was time to go back down to Cape Town and get ready to head home and get married. Dorothy and I had written two to three times to each other every week (using the Poste Restante facility at the local post offices) and I was counting the days. Back at UCT, I dropped off my samples to be cut into thin sections and a box of 'economic' ones to the Anglo offices downtown.

November in Cape Town is the early part of summer and it gets warm but nowhere near what it is in Namaqualand. There is no doubt that it has a lovely climate and I had no doubt that Dorothy was going to love it. One thing I had to do before I left for Scotland was to organise a flat for Dorothy and I to live in. I managed to find a furnished 'bachelor' flat (with a double bed) very close to the Newlands Rugby stadium and within walking distance of the department. I had been in digs when I had been in Cape Town but that was no place to bring a new wife.

In the couple of weeks I had in Cape Town before going home I managed to meet some of the other members of the department who had been out in the field at the same time I was. I had been told about a couple of other Scots guys who were in the Marine Geoscience Unit, on the floor below the PRU. Steve Goodlad and Keith Martin were both from Peterhead, although Steve was originally from Shetland. Both were very good football players and we would become good friends over the years. People had trouble with my accent but Aberdonian (Doric) accents were way out of reach. It was said that when there were just one of us in a conversation, there was little trouble but when two or three of us got together, we were incomprehensible. I didn't like to tell anyone but when Steve and Keith started between themselves, they often lost me as well!

As I was about to get married, there had to be a stag night. To be honest,

I don't remember much about the evening except that I wasn't very well the next morning!

So at last I was getting on the plane for Johannesburg to catch the one to London and onto Glasgow. Dorothy met me in Glasgow and we headed for Gartmore. Back home, my mother remarked that I hadn't changed at all, which I was pleased about and we got down to planning our preparations for the wedding, two weeks hence. My mother did think, however, that I shouldn't drive as I'd have forgotten how to – on the left. She didn't know that South Africa DID drive on the left.

I had returned two weeks before the ceremony, which meant that practically all the arrangements had been made. However, that didn't mean that there was nothing to do. The two of us had to visit many, many people and we were lucky that the weather, although cold, was rather pleasant.

The 20th of November dawned as one of those crisp, blue-skied days when your breath clouds as it leaves your mouth. If I were to get sentimental I would say that those days are the ones I miss most about Scotland. We were married in Gartsherrie Parish Church where Dorothy's family worshipped and the reception was held in the Georgian Hotel in Coatbridge. Everybody seemed to enjoy themselves; I know I did and we went off on honeymoon to the usual cheers and good wishes. We spent a couple of nights in Edinburgh (funnily enough where my parents had been on their honeymoon in 1940) and then went on a tour to St Andrews, Peebles and Erskine where we were invited to dinner by my aunt Ina and Uncle George in Dumbarton. We dined on pheasant that night. Then we went back to Gartmore for a couple of days while we prepared to leave for Cape Town. We were booked on the Sunday flights so Saturday was spent packing and organising our luggage that was to be sent by freight.

Eventually we had to leave for the Glasgow airport where we also met Dorothy's family who turned up to see us off. As we kissed and shook hands with everyone we turned to go into the departure lounge where only we could go. As we were about to step out of sight, we turned to give a last goodbye wave, little realising that it would be the last time we would see my dad.

We arrived in Cape Town on the Monday morning but I had booked a room in the Newlands hotel so that we would have a day to get our flat organised.

So Dorothy was introduced to the social whirl that was the department over the Festive Season. I suppose we should have gone straight up to Namaqualand but a few weeks getting to know people was to help Dorothy settle in. The Head of Department was Prof Arch Reid originally from Fife as was his wife Mary. Arch had previously worked with NASA on Moon rocks and meteorites, both of which were part of the department's research work. Arch is the only guy I have ever been with when he got a hole-in-one. Well I was in the group behind him but there was very little conversation about anything else for a couple of weeks afterwards. Mary took Dorothy under her wing and showed her around while I was at work. It was a great help to Dorothy as she was far from home in a foreign land.

Then it was time to load up the Land Rover and head for the field. We picked up the caravan in Kamieskroon and headed for the coast and the small fishing port of Hondeklipbaai (Dog Rock Bay). Apart from a couple of short trips back to Cape Town, we spent the next nine months finishing off the fieldwork. Dorothy was my unpaid field assistant and her job included opening all the gates (and closing them) and fetching me my camera or sledgehammer if I needed them. She also drove the Land Rover over huge, white sand dunes, if required, and she is still the best female 4x4 driver I know.

The caravan was the smallest possible with the dining table being lowered at night to become the bed. We cooked both indoors and out and I became quite good at braai-ing.

The field area was half covered by a sandveld (sand desert to non-South Africans), which was cut through by four rivers (the Swartlintjies, Spoeg, Bitter and Groen) where the bedrock was exposed as it was along a small strip of the coast. At the mouth of the Spoeg River are some caves where archaeologists have discovered evidence in the form of sheep bones for a herding culture over 2000 years ago.

If you think about it, if you're alone you have to walk along a river bed and then back again to get back to your vehicle. If there are two of you, one can drive while the other walks. I would leave my camera and sledgehammer in the vehicle and signal if I needed either (I always carried a small hammer). Geologists take two things; lots of photos and lots of rock samples. Dorothy got a touch peeved when I once sent her back to get either the camera or the hammer as I had decided (late) that I needed it so the next time she brought both when I didn't need both. It was to teach me a lesson, as the deal was I always carried them back.

Hondeklipbaai has a small campground but few facilities and fresh water was scarce. We washed our clothes and dishes in water taken from a pump, which was almost seawater. Apart from the fish, this area was known for one thing – diamonds. Just to the north of the village was Koingnaas, which was being assessed as a diamond mine.

It might be appropriate to explain something about South African property rights. The whole country is split into portions of land, called farms, of different sized areas. As these were usually the only things that could be handed down from generation to generation, some became so subdivided that they were uneconomic. That was often remedied by re-consolidation of the farm by one of the children.

There was another way. The farm was divided into surface and mineral rights. The surface owner worked the farm but the mineral rights' owner owned the gold, diamonds, coal, copper or anything else that may lie below. Many farmers got out of the uneconomic dilemma by splitting the mineral rights amongst ten, twelve, twenty children while leaving the 'farm' to the eldest son. When a company wanted to prospect for minerals, it had to negotiate an 'option' to buy the mineral rights. These meant getting ALL the mineral rights' owners to sign up and tracking them all down could be a nightmare.

During the Depression of the 1930's, De Beers did something else. It was thought that the west coast could hold huge diamond deposits. After all, some old gravel beds had been mined in South West Africa and the big Consolidated Diamond Field mines there had already been proved. The farms along the coast were the targets and the farmers were desperate for cash and De Beers were solvent. They bought the mineral rights, for next to nothing, to umpteen coastal farms from the Orange River mouth southwards, right along the edge of my field area. The mines at Kleinzee and Oranjemund had already proved the theory so Koingnaas was next on the list.

We were sitting in the caravan writing letters home one Sunday when a knock came to the door. Standing there was a Scots engineer from Polmont, just outside Stirling who was working at Koingnass. We had a pleasant couple of hours talking about back home.

Like every other farm, I had to get permission to wander around but I had arranged this earlier. I had to go alone except with a guard (to see I didn't steal any diamonds), but once I'd moved out of the mining area, Dorothy came along.

The first morning that Dorothy was out with me, we were going along the coastal rocks. I was a few yards ahead when I stopped suddenly. I called Dorothy over and showed her a puff adder coiled up on the rock I was about to step on. I don't like any snake but the puff adder is the ugliest of the lot. It was a salutary lesson right at the start of Dorothy's bush life.

Being a secretary in a geology department, Dorothy was used to all the obscure terminology such as porphyroblastic gneiss. Now she was walking over some!

As I was a graduate student and on a bursary, I wasn't making much money and, of course, Dorothy wasn't getting paid as my field assistant. About one third of our monthly income was going on our flat back in Cape Town and, although I was getting expenses for petrol, I still had to pay for it first. What all this meant was that we weren't all that flush. Obviously life in the bush was less expensive than in town but we decided that we had to get back to a semblance of civilisation every now again. So we would drive down after about twelve or so weeks. Our flat was over a steakhouse and we would lie in bed and be able to smell all the lovely scents wafting up from the kitchens. To supplant our income, Dorothy registered with a Temping Agency in town, working in a number of offices and the money really helped. On occasion, we could afford to go and eat in the self same restaurant.

As we went further along the coast, we would bump into all sorts of wildlife, not forgetting the puff adder! Bat-eared foxes, ostriches, packs of seals sunning themselves on the rocks were all daily delights along with about six different species of tortoises. There were also other unforgettable times. Coming round a promontory one day we came upon Rooiwalbaai (Red Wall Bay). It was marked on the map but there was nothing to prepare us for a horseshoe shaped bay with over a hundred foot cliff made of red sand with a thin veneer of white dune sand on top.

There were no toilets in the bush and, if you needed to go, we were so isolated that it didn't matter. I would estimate that the time when a person is most defenceless is when his trousers or shorts are around his ankles. So imagine my consternation when, one day, a De Beers security helicopter flew over me at just the wrong moment! And they were only a few feet up!

Namaqualand in summer is very hot. What the exact temperature was we never knew but the high thirties (Celsius) was a pretty good guess. I wore shorts and a t-shirt with a big hat while Dorothy would be in 'hot-pants' and a skimpy top. She never did like wearing a hat but sometimes wore a bandana-like scarf when the sun was really strong. Her attire did cause some comment. Dorothy never learnt Afrikaans so when a farmer asked me if she was my girlfriend or my wife, she didn't understand the reason for my swift reassurance and my laughter when I got back in the truck. I explained that the farmer and others around weren't really prepared to see so much bare skin and we should carry a skirt so she could put it over her pants to protect her modesty and the farmers' blushes.

Our marriage was all the better for Dorothy not knowing Afrikaans. The only person she could speak to was me and, because we were so far from home, she couldn't just run home to her mother when things got rough or we weren't getting along. We were forced to talk things through and we learnt to talk without words a lot of the time.

Being my field assistant also gave Dorothy an insight into the life of a field geologist. Wives of a previous generation never went into the field with their husbands so all they ever heard were the stories of the evening braais and those spent in the hotel bars. Dorothy now learnt how the field guys deserved the little carousing they got up to when they did get back to civilisation.

Eventually we had to move our camp and found a new pitch at a hamlet called Soebatsfontein (Pleading Spring) where an early settler had begged for his life from some of the local Bushmen. In the hills above the settlement was an abandoned farm called Canariesfontein which had a running spring and where we would go on a Saturday afternoon for a swim, a hairwash and a picnic. We would also take along our short-wave radio and listen to the BBC World Service. It was there that I celebrated Scotland beating England when Kenny Dalgleish put the ball through Ray Clemence's legs!

I had been telling Dorothy all about the flower season, mainly to assure her that there would be some relief from the monotony of the landscape. Then, one morning, the miracle happened again and even a girl from a family of florists and gardeners was impressed. Every paradise has a drawback and the flower season's one was the 'blind flies'. These were small hornet-like flying insects that had an annoying bite. The bites never flared up and you knew that the flies were around only after they had bitten you!

One day we were walking back to the truck and climbing over the fence at the side of the road. When I was young, my senses were pretty acute. My sight was excellent and my hearing was just as good. Dorothy had got over the fence and I was halfway over when I heard a buzzing getting loader all the time. I jumped down off the fence and dragged Dorothy to the ground. Telling her to keep down and to stop struggling, I asked if she could hear the buzzing. Before she could answer, a swarm of wild African bees flew right over us on their way to find a new nesting place. If we had been standing up, we would have been right in their path and we would have got a severe stinging, perhaps even a fatal one.

At night, after I had drawn up my maps and written up my notes, we would listen to some of the local radio. South Africa had just become a TV nation back in 1975 but there was still a lingering affection for the good old radio. Eventually, one of the stations, Springbok Radio, would be a casualty of TV but back when we were listening it was full of light entertainment programmes and a great comfort to us out in the middle of nowhere. One of our favourite programmes was 'Check Your Mate' but more of that later.

I must admit that most of the days were repetitive in the main, but there was always something different. The area was (is) famous for Karakul sheep and, to be honest, I had my fill of lamb and mutton while I was there. However the meat was the by-product of a much more lucrative trade. Karakul pelts went to make up glamorous coats for fashion conscious westerners. What most, if not all, didn't know was that the best and softest pelts were taken from day-old lambs. One day, Dorothy and I were walking along the Swartlintjies River, and were taking slightly different tracks. I could see a pile of rotting lamb carcasses and the path that Dorothy was taking would take her slap into it. I told her to change course but she didn't and crested a small rise right on top of the pile. She started to retch and blamed me for not warning her! Although the Karakul trade was lucrative, there were farmers who wouldn't touch it because of what it entailed.

Towards the end of the fieldwork, we came up to a farm of the edge of the sandveld called Sabies. I've never professed to have any second sight but there was something about this place that wasn't quite right. As we drove up to the farmhouse, I told Dorothy to stay in the truck. She started to argue but I was a bit curt.

There was a guy standing in the yard as we pulled up cracking a whip. I walked up to him and started my usual spiel. However, he was a deaf mute! Then from inside the house and from round its sides, there appeared some urchins of different ages, cleanliness and untidiness. They all stopped and stared at me and I began to wonder what was going on. Then a middle-aged woman appeared in the doorway normal in all respects except that she had a beard! However she was coherent and I got permission to climb the one hill that I needed to. When I pulled up next to it, Dorothy didn't argue this time when I told her to stay in the vehicle, to sit in the driving seat and to keep the engine running. I went up the hill, knocked off a couple of samples and took a few readings. As I was climbing back down, I could see the guy from the yard running down the track towards the Land Rover. I started running and jumped into the cab. I told Dorothy to get going. She started to protest but I told her to look in the mirror. We got out of there, fast!

We got back to Garies, where we had moved to and were filling up with petrol. We had become friendly with the local garage owner, Mr. Malherbe, and told him our story of the 'Funny Farm'. He wasn't surprised at all as, of course, the locals knew all about the Goosens (which was their name).

We were just about finished in the field but we took one last trip to Springbok for supplies and for me to drop off some samples at the Anglo offices. We had become quite friendly with the geologists and they had arranged for me to join a field trip around the area. Apart from the Anglo geologists and the leaders from the O'kiep Copper Company, there were some from the De Beers mine at Kleinzee.

We were riding over some rough terrain when we hit a rock and I came out with some phrase or other, which was recognised by one of the De Beers geologists, Mick Hafner, as originating from Jo Keenan. So there were two friends of a guy, then in the Middle East, meeting each other in Namaqualand.

Mick invited me to visit the mine at Kleinzee, which was fascinating as the basement rocks there were similar to some in my area. The diamond guys were not really interested in these rocks as the diamonds they were after lay in the overburden. The mining method was something like this. Enormous diggers and scrapers moved the deep dune sand, sometimes offshore to create a 'new' coastline. Then the miners moved in to sift and scrape away the last few feet of unconsolidated sediment. That was where the diamonds were. At the sand/gravel and rock interface, river or seawater movements and currents had made potholes usually of about 1-2 feet across. These potholes had fist-sized pebbles in them but they also were where the diamonds were concentrated. We were walking along the mined-out area when we came across one pothole that was covered in red paint. Mick told me that it was known as the 'Treasure Trove' because when the miners were clearing it out they found the bottom inches deep in diamonds and they were picking them up in double handfuls! The miners were paid extra for 'pick-ups' as they were usually larger and better stones. We met up with one crew that was waiting for the bus at the end of their shift and Mick asked the 'Boss Boy' if they had had any pick-ups that day. The six or seven diamonds were in Mick's open palm for me to photograph when a gust of wind came through and blew them into the dirt. While we scrambled around looking for the stones, some very disgruntled miners were standing around watching the white men on their hands and knees. We found all the stones so there was no great damage.

There were very strict rules in the mine. Once a vehicle entered the mine area, it stayed there. Mick had two trucks – one inside and one outside the mine. When he was transferred a couple of years later, he offered to buy his little 4x4 from inside the mine. It had done only a few hundred kilometres. They just laughed. When any vehicle was finished with, it was driven into the sea and left to rot. There are too many hiding places on a vehicle. Miners were also not allowed out except on leave and they were all X-rayed when they left. One of the peculiar properties of diamond is that it fluoresces under X-rays. That property is now used in sorting diamonds. The conveyor belt with the gravel or crushed rock passes through an X-ray machine. When the diamond fluoresces, a jet of air at a pre-determined distance blows the diamond off the belt.

The traditional way of separating diamonds was using grease tables. Another property peculiar to diamond is that its surface tension is such that it stays dry (at the molecular level) so when it passes over grease, it sticks to it while other rocks absorb the water and don't stick to the grease.

If you ever get offered a 'diamond' and you're not sure that it's genuine, here are two tests to prove that the 'diamond' is real. One, it should scratch your watch glass. If you're still not sure take a glass beaker and fill with water. Drop the 'diamond' into the water. Then take a glass rod and put a large dollop of grease on the end. Try to pick up the 'diamond' with the greased end of the glass rod. If it picks it up, you've got a diamond. If not, walk away. You may think that it is a lot of palaver but it will save you money in the long run.

I reckoned that we had about a week left of work as we came down to a farm just outside the small village of Kotzerus. Never had a farmer denied me access in all my area, although a few needed some persuasion. I had a letter from the university explaining what I was doing but by this time I hadn't used it for months. My Afrikaans was good enough by this time that

I didn't need to revert to it. So there I was full of confidence driving up to almost my last farm when I got a very rude awakening. It was a Saturday morning and the owner was surrounded by his cronies in his front yard. I jumped out of the truck and went into my well-practised routine. I didn't get very far when I was given ten minutes to get off the property. The voice brooked no argument but I did try and then shooting was mentioned so I decided to cut and run. I suppose one bad apple out of a few hundred wasn't a bad average and I was less worried as the farm seemed to have only one rock type so the damage was minimal. However, it did leave a bad taste in the mouth.

Fieldwork being over, we headed back to Cape Town. I was to be back a couple of times but we were ready to enjoy the delights of the Cape.

7

Cape Town

We got back on a Friday evening, which meant that we would have use of the truck over the weekend. I had to hand back the vehicle and caravan on the Monday morning. We celebrated being out of the bush with a meal in our downstairs restaurant and a bottle of wine.

The rest of the weekend passed fairly peacefully as we met up with some friends and generally relaxed. So I drove up to the department on the Monday morning feeling very happy and ready to get down to some lab work. I had my samples to get ready, my map to compile and to begin writing up all the conclusions. I dropped off the Land Rover and caravan at the department garage with all the camping gear and organised for my samples to be brought down to the department.

So I rode up in the lift to the PRU on the top floor right into a storm of activity. Everybody (especially Piet) wanted to know where I'd been. No one had been able to contact me, as we'd moved camp and I hadn't picked up the last letter the unit had sent to me.

One of the specimens I had dropped off in the Anglo offices in Springbok on my last trip had got everyone buzzing. As the Springbok office did with all my specimens, they had sent this batch off to their research labs for analysis and assay. This one sample came back 'hot' with very elevated values of copper, lead and zinc. My samples were all numbered but I didn't tell Anglo where they had come from. This one result was the pay-off that both the PRU and Anglo had wanted to happen. Nobody actually expected anything to come out of my fieldwork as company prospecting teams had been all over the area for years. However, it was a way for the PRU to fill in a blank space where no detailed, published map existed and Anglo, as the paymasters of the bursary, to get first bite at any cherry.

My field notes and preliminary maps were still in a trunk in the caravan so I had no idea from where the sample came as I strolled into the unit. I very quickly had to go and find out, as Anglo wanted me down in their Cape Town offices as soon as I appeared in town. Bang went any thought of relaxing,

Piet and I jumped in his car and headed downtown to the Anglo offices. I later found out that I had been South Africa's most wanted student for about a week ever since the assay result came out. The senior geologist in head office (in Johannesburg) was the first to get the result and started everybody running around like headless chickens so relief seemed to be the biggest emotion when I walked up to the front desk. Now Piet and I didn't know which sample number was the one causing all the fuss as Anglo had kept that from the PRU. All I knew was that it was in the last batch I had handed in.

Dave Bekker was the guy in charge of the Anglo Cape Region (we'd met before) and we were ushered into his office rather quickly. His admin guy was called Dave Le Maitre, a guy whom I would get to know quite well in years to come. Then I was told the sample number and I looked it up on my rough map. I marked all sample positions in ink every night in the field so I would know exactly where they came from. I hated showing anybody my rough field map as a thing of beauty it certainly was not.

Remember the 'Funny Farm' where I had knocked off a couple of rock samples and then had hurriedly driven away? One of those samples had been of a gossan-like rock and this was the one that had got everybody jumping about. (A gossan is the oxidised cap of a mineralised sulphide deposit, appearing in an arid climate).

Dave had a map of the whole region on his wall showing all the farms that Anglo had optioned through the years. Sabies (the Funny Farm) was not one of them, a point that was probably a great relief, but there was a horseshoe of farms surrounding it, which had been optioned. We were thanked for our time and, after a cup of coffee, it was obvious that we should leave. The Anglo guys had things to do. In time, they optioned the property and spent a lot of money proving the reserves. In the end, the deposit was too small (only about 50 million tons) with the wrong combination of metals. Lead was the least common and at the time it was the most lucrative and there was no 'sweetener' of silver as in other viable deposits. However, 'The Funny Farm' did become known in the department as 'The Happy Jack Mine'!

There was one last twist. A few months later, Piet called me into his office and handed me a letter. It was from the new owner of Sabies (the bearded lady had died and the urchins and deaf mute had been taken into care) and he wanted to know the connection between one of the PRU students (me) examining the rocks on the farm and Anglo offering to option it. He wanted to see all my notes and any analyses of the rock samples I had taken. Piet was in a quandary, as he couldn't give this guy any information without compromising the relationship with Anglo and the rest of the Chamber of Mines who funded the unit. He asked me for my suggestions (which showed how shaken he was) but I had none. I never knew how he replied but I suspect he denied all knowledge.

In all the years of the department students running around mapping the rocks, only once before had one found a mine. The Rosh Pinah mine in southern Namibia was that find but that was a few years before. So I became something of a celebrity within the department, which was just as well because I was a bit of a stranger to everyone. It was a normal hazard of the department. Students would disappear for months on end into the bush and suddenly reappear in the tearoom to cries of welcome and queries about how good (or bad) were their field areas. However, everybody knew I was back. The Happy Jack Mine was a nine-day wonder. Fortunately, it all settled down but it was exciting for a while. People were even asking how much of a cut I would get. I didn't think I was due anything but I did have an idea that it might get me a job with Anglo American when I had finished at UCT.

One of the senior members of the PRU was a Czech geologist called Vaslav Vajner who had escaped communism in his old country and had ended up at UCT. He had been on secondment in a 'friendly' or 'comradely' country like Zambia or Tanzania when he and his wife walked over the border to the then Rhodesia and onto South Africa. Vaslav was quiet but extremely competent and his map of the area around Marydale and Prieska was well regarded both in and out of the department. He was always available for a chat and helped many of the post-grad students understand some aspect or other. He was also a big, well built man so I was totally shocked when I walked by his office to see a shadow of the man I knew. Vaslav had contracted cancer and the three months since I had last seen him had left him so weak that he had a camp bed moved into his office. He lasted only about a further month or so but he spent his last weeks organising all his work so that no-one would have any difficulty carrying on from where he had left off. A fine man and a great geologist and I always thought it sad that he was to die so far from home and family (except for his wife).

I had a few trips back to Namaqualand to show people over the area but one time I was going up by myself to check some of my earlier fieldwork. Another student was now using my own Land Rover so I was assigned another vehicle and as I was driving up a hill, one of the ball and socket joints on the throttle cable broke. I tied it up with some string and limped into the nearest service station which was fortunately just over that same hill. I managed to get the throttle fixed, filled up with petrol and checked my oil level. I left Vanrhynsdorp and drove north across the flat featureless plain known the Knersvlakte. The name comes from the sound made by the ox-wagon wheels on the ground as they passed over. After about 80 or 90 kilometres, the next small village appears off to the left of the highway, a place called Nuwerus. I was about 100 yards from the turnoff when the engine gave a clunk, clunk and a cloud of dark smoke obscured my vision. The vehicle lost all power and glided to a halt. I jumped out and looked under the engine. All I could see was oil everywhere and I knew that I wasn't going to go very far that night. After the local garageman had a look and confirmed that the con-rod had gone through one side of the engine block and a piston through the other, I had to look around for somewhere to sleep. I phoned the PRU and they arranged for a tow-truck to tow me back to Cape Town but it wouldn't arrive until the next day. Fortunately, the local policeman had turned up to see what all the commotion was about and he took me under his wing. The outcome was that I spent the night in a police cell, as there was no hotel! They didn't lock the door, though!

We were now in Cape Town, one of the loveliest places in the world. We were young, in love and, thanks to Dorothy's temping, we had some spare cash. The first thing we had to do was buy a car. After the fieldwork, I had lost the use of the Land Rover so if we wanted some freedom of movement, we had to buy a car. Just along the road were a few car showrooms and one Saturday morning we walked along and saw a yellow VW Beetle, which we could afford. In those days, nearly every student had a Beetle and they sold like hot cakes so in we went and bought it. We had it checked over by a friend of a friend but, apart from a bit of clutch slip, he could find little wrong. Just as we were signing the papers, a man walked in looking for a car for his student daughter. Our Beetle would have been perfect for her but we got it first.

Dorothy was beginning to get a bit tired of temping and wanted a permanent job. Many of the jobs required her to be bilingual but if she could get a job up at UCT, that requirement fell away as all business there was in English. After a couple of dry runs she managed to get two part-time jobs. One was in the Law Faculty (morning) and the other was in the Mathematics Department (afternoon). What it meant was that we went to work together and came home together. It was almost like being back in the bush! As this was all before the days of desktop PCs, Dorothy's work was all typing and the Maths typing was horrendous! She hated it and was always on the lookout for another afternoon job. She got lucky as Students' Legal Aid were looking for a new secretary. As she was already in the department, she was the ideal choice. So there we were, she in the law department and me in the geology department.

We had never had much opportunity before to explore the Cape region but with our new car, we started to run around going to all the tourist places and to the places the tourists never get to see. We started to visit the many vineyards and to build up a cellar, which was under our bed. With what went on above it, the wine tasted even better!

This may seem strange to you; it has always struck me as strange. Only two people ever came to visit us while we lived in Cape Town.

Mick Hafner, from Kleinzee, had an address in the Middle East for Jo Keenan and, as I hadn't heard from Jo in a couple of years, I dropped him a line and invited him over for a holiday. By that time, Dorothy and I had found a two bed-roomed flat with lovely views of the back of Table Mountain. It was right next door to the Kenilworth Race Course but was a lot further away from campus so it was just as well we had a car.

Jo eventually wrote back saying that he was on his way. Mick took some leave and we met up at the airport to meet Jo's plane. Jo is over six foot tall so he was quite easy to spot as he walked into the arrivals hall. He hadn't changed a bit and it seemed as though we had said goodbye only about a week before!

The first thing he said was to ask where he could find a job! He'd decided that this was a great improvement on the Middle East. Little did he know that he was going to be sent back to the desert! I had been looking around for a job myself (and had a promise of one after I had handed in my thesis) so I gave him the telephone number of a couple of guys in Personnel Departments up in Johannesburg.

We took a trip round the peninsula to show Jo the sights. He's always regarded himself as a bit of a photographer and had some great equipment so you can imagine the hoots of laughter when we got back to find that he had taken a load of photos but had forgotten to put any film in his camera!

We also decided to go up Table Mountain. Mick was a world-class rock climber so while the girls sat in the café, he persuaded Jo and I to join him in a little mountaineering. I've done a fair bit of hill walking but never was a rock climber. Even after doing one of the easiest pitches on Table Mountain, I reckoned it wasn't for me. We then decided to walk done the mountain, through Perdekloof gorge. Dorothy was very enthusiastic but not in the morning when her knees refused to work!

Jo and Mick went off on a tour of the country but I had to stay in CT as, at that time, I was too close to the finish of my work and couldn't take the time off.

The other person to visit us was one of Dorothy's sisters, Kathleen, who had decided to start up her own florist's shop but before she did she wanted a good holiday so she was heading for Cape Town.

Dorothy and Kathleen had been phoning back making plans so it was no big surprise when the phone rang one Thursday night in September. However, it wasn't Kathleen but Torquil calling me to tell me that our dad had died that morning of another heart attack. Devastation didn't come into it.

It's not really a macho thing to admit but there were a lot of tears that night and Dorothy did a lot of comforting. The next morning, I seemed back on track and went up to the department but only to say that I was taking the day off. I walked into Piet's office but broke down before I could finish. I guess I met another couple of guys on the way back to my car but I wasn't very coherent.

I knew that I couldn't afford to fly home for the funeral although Jimmy McDaid did offer to lend me the fare but I had no idea when I could pay him back so I turned the offer down. Arch and Mary Reid came round on the Sunday night on their way home from a weekend away, a gesture much appreciated.

As an aside, the funeral was held in Gartmore Church on a day when the heavens opened and stayed open. The church was full to overflowing so perhaps I couldn't have got in anyway! Dad was a very popular and well-known man in the village and roundabout. Of course, his old work colleagues came out from Glasgow and, as he was a Past Master in the local Masonic Lodge, many of his fellow masons were among the mourners. I miss him still.

So Kathleen was on her way and Dorothy was getting excited. The first thing Kathleen wanted to do was get a suntan. We tried to tell her that she should be careful but she spent the next day lying out in the sun, got burnt and spent the next few days hiding away.

She stayed for nearly a month and we went all over including Cape Agulhas, the most southern point of Africa. When she left, she was ready to start her shop. We thought that perhaps other people would follow her out to Cape Town but no one ever did.

Somewhere at the start of this, I think I mentioned that I played football and golf and had done for a long time. Golf has always been a social game for me and others in the department had like minds. We played all over the peninsula, usually on a Sunday morning plus departmental golf days. My set of clubs was a fair mixture, none of this matched set nonsense for me, but every game was enjoyable.

Football was never a social game for me. I joined the university so-called Soccer Club but too late to prevent them being relegated just after I finished my fieldwork. I had two full seasons mainly in the first team but there was another young keeper called Julian Johnson, who would eventually play pro, who kept me out of the team at times.

Eric Underhill and Stuart Leary (who had played professional football for Charlton Athletic and professional cricket for Kent) were our coaches in these two years and the second year was exceptional. The team was good enough to win the cup and the league. Well before any professional leagues or teams thought about it, we had squad numbers and players' names on the back of their shirts. One of the smallest players was called Abramowich, which meant that his name stared at his waist on one side and ran to his waist on the other! Apart from myself, we had one or two other good players, many good enough to play for the SA University Select. One was Lawrie Seeff, whose father ran one of the largest Estate Agencies in the Cape. Although Lawrie was good enough to have made it as a professional footballer, he was more interested in cricket. He went on to play for and captain Western Province and he even played for South Africa. He also had a summer in English County Cricket.

Apart from the league and cup, we also took part in one other competition; the SA University Tournament. It was to be held in Stellenbosch but only about three weeks before I was due to hand in my thesis. I took the week off as I decided I needed the break. It was the best thing I could have done as I was beginning to get a bit loopy with all the extra hours I was putting in. For the first time ever, we took two keepers and we won the title. So now I had two national medals from two different countries; Scotland and South Africa.

I was up in the department one night setting out my final master copy of my thesis when my eyes suddenly started playing tricks on me. The preferred means of typing the thesis was an IBM 'golfball' typewriter. I had split the workload between Dorothy and the unit's secretary, Judy. It was after three in the morning and I thought that the two sets of typing weren't the same. I had about a week to get the thesis copied, bound and submitted so panic set in. I drove home almost in despair. I woke Dorothy as I got into bed and told her of the problem. Her reply was that we would sort it in the morning. Of course, in the morning my eyes had settled down and there was actually no problem to solve.

A game slightly unfamiliar to a Scotsman is cricket. I had played a few knockabout games and had a bit of instruction at school but that was about all. So one Friday I was in the tearoom when I was asked if I had ever played. I said yes but didn't realise that the department was looking for players. So I ended up having to buy a set of whites and turning out in a pre-season friendly against the rest of the UCT Staff. I loved it!

It would not be too far off the mark to say that I was the most inexperienced cricket player on campus. Nearly everybody else had been brought up playing the game from schooldays onwards, whereas I had some knock-about games under my belt. I'd always liked watching the game and had a fair idea of the rules. However, nothing prepares you for that first ball from a fast bowler. I was initially in the team to make up numbers as my batting technique was nothing to write home about and my bowling needed a lot of work. Nevertheless I loved the fielding.

Dorothy was a bit non-plussed when I told her that I was in a cricket team because she had never been to a cricket match before and hadn't even watched it on the TV. She thought it boring. However I persuaded her to come along and, because all the other wives, girlfriends and families came along to watch, she began to enjoy the games. She even began to ask if I was playing and was disappointed when I wasn't.

The guys knew that I was the UCT first team goalkeeper so, when one afternoon the team didn't have a regular wicketkeeper, I was drafted into the position. All of a sudden I knew that this was for me. I must have been the tallest wicketkeeper ever, as most are relatively small and I'm over six feet but I did (and still do) have the hand-eye co-ordination required. A few years later, I met one of the professors (Martin West), to whose bowling I'd kept, at a golf club and he greeted me as "The Man with the Magic Hands"! That was probably because I was the only 'keeper on the Staff XI history who had ever stumped anybody (a total of three). While I dropping names, one of the other spin bowlers was the future Booker Prize winner, J. M. (John) Coetzee. Dave Reid (now Prof.) was one of my colleagues in the department who helped me greatly in playing the game.

I learnt the technique as I went along but the experienced players would give me tips and I had a great time. The games were social events and we had some lovely afternoons. We would go and play up in the hills against the wine farmers where the game was not the most important thing but the braai and the wine tasting afterwards were.

The UCT cricket oval is in a lovely setting on the side of the mountain surrounded by mature trees. I was batting there one Sunday when I got hit where no man likes to get hit. I dropped like a stone and just lay there. Of course, everybody was concerned except my wife, who, after she was told that I'd been hit, said that if it had been my head that had been hit I'd be OK! Luckily I had a 'box' on but I was bruised for weeks.

There was one fixture that I wanted to play in above all the others. It was on a Wednesday afternoon against the Western Province Club. Why did I want to play them? Their ground was the Newlands Test Cricket Ground and it would be the only chance I would get to play on such a ground. I didn't play very well, made a duck and dropped a couple of chances but I can always say that I did play on such a ground. I was never likely to play football in grounds like Hampden or Wembley so it meant a lot.

Dorothy's job in the Law Faculty had been a full time post originally but had been split into two part time posts of which Dorothy had one. The other part timer was a lady called Beth Gassert and she and Dorothy had hit it off right away.

Obviously the two talked as they worked and had quickly become friends. It transpired that Beth's daughter, Karen, was turning sixteen and her birthday was the same date as Dorothy's. We were invited to a select suburb of the city, as Beth's husband, Harry, was a very famous shoe designer. If you bought a Bally shoe in those days, you were buying one of his designs.

The party/braai was in full swing as we arrived and I went to get both of us a drink when I bumped into a guy who had been in the same digs as me when I had first arrived. It turned out Peter was Harry's son from a previous marriage but both of us were astounded to meet at this function.

Harry was a lot older than Beth and he was on his third marriage. Originally from Berlin, he had emigrated to South Africa in the '30's and he was fond of saying that he was the only non-Jew on the boat. As a shoe designer, he moved in a world vastly different to any that I knew and he was a friend of Adi Dassler, the brains behind the Adidas brand.

Beth and Dorothy became very firm friends and we were always welcome at her house. Harry even began to like me, so Beth told Dorothy, and Karen was to be godmother to our firstborn.

Dorothy has always liked live theatre and Cape Town had two great venues. The 'official' theatre was the Nico Malan down in the city but UCT had its own theatre at the bottom of the hill, the Baxter. We spent many a happy evening at both watching some first rate plays and musicals.

When we were in Namaqualand, we used to listen to Springbok Radio in the evenings when we were not listening to the BBC World Service. One of the shows was called 'Check your Mate' and had a format where a husband and wife team was asked questions about each other. To ensure fair play one of the couple was put in an isolation booth and then asked the same questions as their spouse and the answers checked for similarity. A simple game but it was entertaining. We found out that it was recorded at the Seapoint SABC studios and decided one night to go along and watch it being produced.

We were sitting in the audience when they asked for a couple to volunteer as one of the participants. Dorothy would never volunteer by herself but I realised that if I didn't put my hand up we would always regret it. That's how we became radio stars although a question about Olive Schreiner (the author of 'An African Farm')'s husband stumped us. We became 'famous' for a couple of days and Dorothy got her job at the Students' Legal Aid after someone heard her on the show.

I mentioned Steve and Keith earlier and how they were both very good footballers – good enough to be selected for the touring SA University squad. They were also both party animals and each of them had a string of girlfriends. Why not? They were young, fit, good looking and single. The strange thing is that I was involved in both of them meeting their wives.

The lads used to housesit for people who were away for a while but sometimes they were between houses and had to ask for a bed for a while. During one of these periods, Steve was living in our spare room. When he had been in East London earlier that year, he had met a girl and she was on her way to Cape Town. So off he went one Friday evening to meet her plane.

Although Saturday morning was not an official workday, I usually went up to the department for a few hours and, while I was away, Dorothy would clean the flat. I arrived home for lunch that Saturday and Dorothy was a bit concerned, as Steve hadn't surfaced. I told her I'd see if he was OK while she was setting the table. So I knocked on his door and poked my head round it to wake him. Steve said he'd be there in a minute and introduced me to Sue who was lying beside him trying to become invisible while red with embarrassment. They've been together ever since. I told Dorothy that she'd have to set the table for four.

The PRU secretary, Judy, was sharing the typing of my thesis with Dorothy but she was also going through a divorce. I don't know the details but the end result was that she got custody of her son, Ross, but she had to move out of the family home. By a twist of fate, I was the only student member of the PRU in the department at the time so Judy asked me to help her move. Of course I did and Judy was always grateful. In the months that followed, Judy was getting more and more withdrawn and was also being harassed by some guys in the department who thought she was an easy mark, being newly divorced.

Steve and Keith were holding a party at one of the houses they were looking after and I thought that it might be about time for Judy to have a night out. So I persuaded her to come along with Dorothy and me. As we walked in I called out, 'This is Judy and she's looking for a "lumber"!' Keith took me at my word and they've been together ever since.

One afternoon, Dorothy came to collect me before driving home. She had told me that she had a doctor's appointment that afternoon and when she turned up, she was glowing as only an expectant mother can. It wasn't really a surprise but all of a sudden I thought that I'd better find a job!

I was a few months away from finishing my thesis but I knew that with a few nights of midnight oil burning, I'd finish in time. Now I started to apply for jobs. There was never any doubt that Anglo American would offer me a position; the only question was where it would be. In the end, I was going to be posted to Kimberley to work for the New Mining Business section, which was looking for anything other than gold, diamonds or coal.

So, apart from finishing off my thesis, I had a pregnant wife and I was due to go to the SA University Soccer Tournament (which we won). A member of the organising committee was Roy Bailey who played for Ipswich Town and England and whose son Gary ended up at Manchester United and also played for England.

When I got back from the tournament, 99% of the typing was done and all that had to be done was the final layout. This was important as the thesis was to be published as the 29th bulletin of the PRU.

Finally all the research, writing and typing was complete. The PRU had a draughtswoman, Pam Eloff, who could take any of my scribbled diagrams/drawings and make a work of art out of them. Not only did she do that but she also inked all the colour separations for my map. So then we put the pictures, diagrams and drawings into the typed pages to complete the thesis. All the time, in the back of my mind were stories of people losing all their research work by some unfortunate happenstance the day before they were due to hand in the work. I made sure that my master copy was locked away every night and I was mighty glad when I went to the library to use the best photocopier on campus to make the four copies I would hand in.

So I sent off the copies to be bound before I could hand them in for examination and I thought I could relax. I had a couple of days to wait for the copies to come back but just as I thought I could spend some time arranging our move to Kimberley, I was collared as I was wandering out of the department and told that before I could go anywhere I had to 'donate' a representative sample of rocks and thin sections to the department collection. Nobody had mentioned this before so I spent a couple of days going through my samples and re-labelling my sections to give them over to the department. I only hope that they were of some use to the students in the following years.

Before we left, we had to have a going-away party to which we invited everyone we knew. Thank goodness not all of them turned up as the flat wasn't big enough! I always made a punch as a welcoming drink which had one vital ingredient. The fruit was soaked in gin for 24 hours! As the party was just after our success at the SA Varsity Football tournament, nearly all my team mates turned up as did the coach Stuart Leary and his wife. His wife was slightly snooty and she didn't usually socialise with students. She was a very successful estate agent. It so happened that we didn't have her favourite drink (?Campari and soda) but she did like the punch. However, she didn't want too much to drink so she asked for just the fruit. I didn't enlighten her so after a couple of glasses of fruit, she was several sheets to the wind and had to be helped down the stairs and home.

8

Kimberley

The arrangement was that I was to be in Kimberley on a Friday afternoon in early August so we planned to leave Cape Town late on the Thursday morning. First I had to collect my thesis copies and hand them in. Then we packed up our yellow VW Beetle and headed off to Kimberley. We knew that we wouldn't make it in one day as Kimberley is over 1000 miles away so we had booked into the hotel at Matjiesfontein, which is one of the old Karoo outposts and railway stations. The hotel is named after Alfred, Lord Milner who was an early governor of the Cape Colony and a contemporary of Cecil Rhodes. The atmosphere smacks of colonial times and the beds are all four posters.

Driving to Kimberley gave Dorothy some idea of the boring landscape that I had crossed on the train when I first arrived in South Africa. She had flown all the way to Cape Town.

Late on the Friday afternoon we arrived in Kimberley and eventually found the hotel we were booked into by the local exploration office.

I left Dorothy in the hotel on the Saturday morning and went off to find the office. When in the bush we worked a five and a half day week and sometimes more, so the office was open with some of my future colleagues. The others were out in the bush. Kimberley is not so big so I had little trouble finding the office and walked in to introduce myself. Brian King was the boss, Kim Bunting his 2IC while Malcolm Moreton was the resident geophysicist. Brian was English, Kim was from New Zealand while Malcolm was a South African. The original plan was for me to go off to the west of the area where the rocks were similar to those I had been working on in Namaqualand but another of the office geologists, Paul Caldwell, had just been given a bursary to study for a degree at the London School of Mines so I had to take over his project. He was busy looking for lead/zinc deposits in limestone sediments. Some prospects had been found which were being drilled so there had to be a geologist to oversee the work. That was to be me – someone who had never seen a drill before.

So after a couple of days of orientation I was off to the field camp near Reivilo. It was named after a Rev. Olivier (spelt backwards), which is a bit of a coincidence as Dorothy's maiden name was Oliver. There were a number of prospects, which we were trying to prove. Most of that was being done by percussion (or air) drill where the samples came up in small pieces of rock. Every now and again it was possible to see pieces of ore but we had to send of some of all samples to be assayed which allowed us to plot where the high spots were, how thick and whether they were continuous between boreholes. However there was one prospect that was so promising that we were using a diamond drill. This gave a continuous core and a much better sample of the strata. Having a core allowed a lot more tests other than assays to be done. If the prospect was going to be a mine, there were strength, analytical, metallurgical, extraction and other tests that could be done on it. It was great fun to be pitched in at the deep end at another aspect of geology and one I had had no experience in.

Reivilo is a small town lying in the middle of a plateau of almost flat lying dolomitic limestones, which are part of the Transvaal Supergroup. That's about all the stratigraphy you're going to get. I had just come from working on rocks with four recognisable folding events and at least five different faulting events to rocks that lay at about two degrees off the horizontal. If it weren't for the mineralisation, they would be the most boring rocks in the world. Lead and Zinc have always been found together in dolomites and limestones so finding them here was no great surprise.

Back at the diamond drilling, there was one fly in the ointment. The prospect was on a farm called Scheurfontein but the larger part of the deposit lay over the fence on another farm called Pering. Unfortunately, Pering had been optioned by Shell and the consequence was that, although the assays were rich enough, Scheurfontein would never be a mine by itself. A few years later, Shell bought over the option of Scheurfontein from Anglo and opened the Pering Mine. If you look at the website, you'll see that the area was a large open pit but now defunct. We still had a large part of the plateau to cover but we never did find another prospect as rich as what became the Pering mine.

I've known a lot of drillers in my time and I must say that they seem to belong to a little-known sub-species of the human race. The drilling team on Scheurfontein did little to dispel this theory. Lazy, incapable of keeping the site tidy, they had little or no idea of health and safety. I mention this because they used, to monitor the angle of the inclined drill, the most corrosive acid known, hydrofluoric acid (HF). This will burn right through a man's hand but they left it lying about with abandon and wouldn't be told to be careful. In the end, one of the driller's sons had it spilt over him and he ended up in hospital. After the drilling programme was over, we went back to check and clean up the sit and there was the bottle of HF sitting on the ground. Unbelievable!

We had to move the camp a couple of times to Vryburg and Kuruman, because apart from working on the limestones, I was also involved in prospecting for iron ore and manganese deposits. That sent me to such lovely places as Hotazel.

Many of the farms in South Africa have everyday names such as Bloemfontein (flower spring) and Soutwater (saltwater) but every now and again some lovely names come up. Names such as Hotazel (hot as hell), Rok Optel (pick up skirt), Kak in Die Nag (defecate in the night – it's rather flat there!) and my personal favourite, Twee-Buffels-Met-Een-Schoot-Deid-Geschoot-Fontein (The spring where two buffaloes were shot with one bullet!) really made some days better than others.

Kuruman is a place with a lot a history and some of it relevant to Scotland. There is a large permanent pool at Kuruman called the 'Eye' and was where the old settlement was based. About ten kilometres north of the 'Eye' is the Mission House which was built by the Reverend Moffat as that was the closest to the 'Eye' that the tribal chief would let white men stay. By the late 1970's, the tables had been turned – the white men had the 'Eye' and the Mission Station was round where the local tribal area was based. In the 1990's it all reverted. However that is not what made Kuruman relevant to a Scot. The Reverend Moffat was a contemporary of David Livingstone, the very famous explorer and missionary. Livingstone visited Kuruman but he did have an ulterior motive as he married the Reverend Moffat's daughter, Mary.

Kimberley is a very historical and interesting city. It lies between the Orange and Vaal rivers and east of the confluence of the two. The first South African diamond (the Eureka diamond) to be found was near Hopetown on the Orange River to the south and the diamondiferous gravels at Barkly West, where the rivers meet, became the first large scale digging in South Africa. These diggings brought treasure hunters from all over the world. One of these parties was known as The Red Cap Party and was travelling by ox wagon from Port Elizabeth. They camped at the foot of a hill known as Colesberg Koppie about a day's travel from Barkly West. One of the party went to relieve himself at the top of the hill and came down with a couple of diamonds in his hand. Diamonds were well known from India and now South Africa but no one had any clue where they came from. They had never been found in any host rock. There was a very good reason for this. Diamonds are part of a rock type now known as kimberlite (named after the city of Kimberley where the rock was first found). Kimberlite dissolves in wet conditions. I leave all of my other rocks out in the rain but any kimberlite remains indoors. Colesberg Koppie was the remnants of a kimberlite pipe, which had eroded somewhat, but the arid conditions had let it go only so far. The oxidised kimberlite had turned to a beige colour that became known as 'yellow ground'. The erosion meant that the 'yellow ground' was stuffed full of diamonds and the hill quickly disappeared. However the 'yellow ground' stopped at the foot of the hill and there were a few who walked away when they hit the much harder 'blue ground'. The 'yellow ground' was as easy to mine as the gravels but when the 'blue ground appeared it was much more difficult. There is a story that a Dr. Atherstone, a geologist, realised that the diamonds were likely to be in the 'blue ground' as well and revolutionised the diamond industry. Barney Barnato listened to him, buying all the discarded claims, becoming a very wealthy man overnight. Colesberg Koppie became the Big Hole, which is now where the Kimberley Mine Museum is located and four other hills became working diamond mines. At last prospectors could look for the primary source of the diamonds other than the secondary gravel deposits.

So Kimberley grew up as the 'City of Diamonds'. In its early days, it rivalled any of the Wild West towns in lawlessness and wild living but now it is much more sedate. The British Empire ruled the Cape Colony and decided that Kimberley should be part of that colony. Although the local farmers (Boers) weren't interested in mines but only in running their farms, they still wanted the boundary to be surveyed properly. However, when the surveyors came to draw the line on a map, it went right through the mining area. After some negotiation, it was decided to make an indentation eastwards to allow the diggings to remain under British control and an old grave of a tribal chief was to be the focal point. All was agreed until a pipe was found even further east. The Brits soon came up with a solution. They moved the grave!

Diamond stealing was rife and there were many horse chases of the thieves as they dashed to the safety of the Free State border only a couple of miles away. Then there were the characters. The two biggest were Barney Barnato (see above) and Cecil John Rhodes, the biggest diamond kings in town. Barnato controlled the Big Hole and when Rhodes bought it to create De Beers Consolidated Mines, he wrote the largest cheque ever seen in the western world to that time and for many decades afterwards. Rhodes went on to even greater things but Barnato is largely forgotten possibly because he died prematurely falling overboard (? murdered) and drowning on a voyage back to Britain.

Kimberley was also a strategic prize during the 2nd Boer War. It was under siege for a time and the Empire sent a column to relieve it. The Boers met the column to the south of Kimberley at a place called Magersfontein. Famous in military history as the first place trench warfare was used, Magersfontein was where Scots soldiers suffered agonies as they lay out in the veld with their kilts on and the Sun burning the backs of their legs. Eventually Kimberley was relieved but, if you go to Magersfontein now, go up the hill to the memorial where you will read, "Scotland is poorer in men but richer in heroes".

Apart from diamonds and other minerals, the area surrounding Kimberley doesn't have much to commend it. In fact it is pretty boring. We spent most of our time in the bush but we did have occasion to sample some of the delights of the town.

Hotels and bars were fairly basic but there was one four star hotel where we put important visitors, the Kimberley Sun. At the other end of the scale was our favourite bar, 'The Star of the West'. This was an old diggers' pub, alongside the 'Big Hole'. It had a couple of remarkable features. It was a men only pub because there were no toilet facilities for women. In fact, the gents consisted of plastic buckets! It also still had the original bar gantry which had come all the way from Cape Town by ox wagon back in the digging days.

There were sports clubs, the biggest was the De Beers one, but, as I was out of town mostly, I never joined. I started playing football with a social side whose members understood that I wasn't going to be around all the time. At least I was getting a game. After about a season, I was picked for the local provincial team, Griqualand West. I was the first ever player from that team selected for that side. The game I played was against Western Transvaal but imagine my surprise when the WT centre forward was Gordon Wylie who graduated with me from Glasgow University!

When we moved to Kimberley, Dorothy was five months pregnant, so by December 1979, she was ready to deliver our first child. By sheer chance our first flat was directly across the road from the local maternity hospital. I came home for lunch one day and Dorothy began to go into labour. I helped her across the road and then went back to the office to start my paternity leave. I then went back to the hospital but it seems that it was a false alarm but they kept Dorothy in overnight as a precaution.

The lads in the office (all except Brian King – he didn't drink) decided that we had to go out and celebrate the imminent birth. Well, to cut a long story short, late at night we were banging on the hospital door demanding to be let in to see Dorothy. Needless to say we were given short thrift!

The next morning I was woken by the telephone ringing to tell me that the labour had started for real, so I rushed across the road without stopping to clean up. Dorothy was not happy with my appearance and her pains had subsided again. I went home to get showered, cleaned up and to grab some lunch. When I got back to the ward, the bed was empty! Dorothy was in the delivery room so I rushed along the corridors to get there. I waited outside till I heard the first cry and the midwife came out to tell me that I had a daughter. I went in to kiss my lovely wife and our beautiful daughter, Alison. She was lying awake with large eyes looking around at the new world she was in. She's still trying to figure it out.

Alison's arrival overshadowed one other quite important event in my life. A few weeks previously I had received a call from the PRU. My thesis had been reviewed and the examiners had decided that my M.Sc. should be awarded with distinction. Unfortunately, the graduation ceremony was the day Dorothy decided to go into labour so I graduated *in absentia*.

I don't know if this is some sort of record but Alison flew when she was ten days old. On Christmas Eve we flew down to Cape Town for the holidays staying with Beth and Harry. We had Alison baptised in the Rosebank Methodist Church where we had worshipped when we were at UCT and spent a very happy time with some of our old friends.

In Kimberley we would worship at the Methodist Church in the centre of town. We found that the Methodists welcomed us wherever we were and we liked the services. One incident told us about the character of South

Africans. During a particular service the minister announced that the following week's service would be broadcast live on the radio by the SABC. We were looking forward to being part of the event but when we arrived it was pretty obvious that about 95% of the usual congregation had stayed at home to listen to the broadcast. I don't know what it sounded like over the airwaves, but I do know that ten voices don't sound like two hundred no matter how much the sound was played with. I would have loved to have heard what the minister said the following week but I had to go back to the field.

Now the two of us had to get used to having a third person in the house but we loved it. Dorothy would stay in Kimberley a bit more and would come out to the field only part of the time. Young babies mean many more trips to the doctor and some of the places I would be were not really suitable for a family. Later Alison became a feature in the camp and all the lads looked after her. She took her first steps in the caravan and loved running around in the open air. We also could go to the cinema as in Kimberley it was a drive-in, the first one we ever went to.

We lived in Kimberley for two years and, although some people thought of it as a bit of a backwater, we packed a lot in. The British Lions led by Bill Beaumont toured South Africa in 1970 the first time since the '74 Lions, who had won every match except the final Test, which they drew. The Lions were due to play in Kimberley against Griqualand West during the week before playing the second Test in Bloemfontein. Griquas had declined since the days when they had won the Currie Cup (the inter-provincial tournament) led by the old Springbok fly-half, Piet Visagie (whom I had met once in a bar in Kuruman) so the Lions were not expecting a very hard encounter. They duly won although the game was close for about a half an hour.

Ben and Margo were a couple of friends we had made since moving to Kimberley. Ben was a local doctor who, although growing up on a farm in the Free State, had trained as a doctor at UCT. Not only that but he had played provincial rugby for Free State so had managed to get a few tickets for the Test match. Ben had this wonderful idea that I should wear my kilt to the match but I had worn it to our office Xmas party and had created quite a stir. So I wasn't very sure about wearing to one of the main centres of Afrikanerdom.

Ben is very persuasive so I did wear my kilt. We had to park some distance from the ground so I walked through the centre of Bloemfontein causing traffic to come to a halt and getting some very queer looks from all around. In the end the Lions lost due to couple of bad captaining decisions but I had a great time.

By the middle of 1980, our finances were such that we could afford to go home to Scotland for Christmas and New Year. It would be the first chance for anybody from the family to meet Alison and she would be old enough to recognise and remember people. We were home for about a month and then it was time to go back to Kimberley.

We also *had* to buy (and could afford) a new car. The yellow Beetle suffered from rust as it came from the salt air of the coast but we managed to use it as a down payment on a new Opel Kadett station wagon that lasted us until we left the country.

The Kimberley Sun was part of a chain of hotels called "Southern Suns" run by a character named Sol Kerzner who was married, at that time, to the one-time Miss World, Anneline Kreil. Sol had noticed that the South African public was fairly keen on gambling, so keen that they would go off to neighbouring countries such as Swaziland and Lesotho to visit the casinos. Sol knew that casinos made money, lots of it, but how was he to get the idea past the very conservative SA government? Gambling on horse racing was allowed as it came under "Games of Skill" (?). Bookmakers had stalls on course but the government-run Tote was the only legal off-course betting.

Sol's big chance came when the government took the next step in the system of apartheid and delineated tracts of South Africa as "Independent Homelands" such as the so-named Ciskei, Transkei, Kwa-Zulu and Bophuthatswana. The last is a mouthful but is the one that concerns this story. The whole thing was a bit of a joke even to South Africans as Bophuthatswana was made up of many disparate pieces of land, usually the most unproductive bits.

We had a couple of prospects up near Mafeking run by Kim Bunting which were very similar to the ones I had been looking after. Alongside Mafeking was the 'capital' of Bophuthatswana, Mbabatho. It was here that Sol decided to test the waters and see if a casino would attract South African in sufficient numbers seeing that they wouldn't need a passport to reach it. So Kim dragged us up to look at the prospects and to visit the casino, of course.

As an aside, Kim was building an ocean-going yacht (in Kimberley – about as far from the sea as you could get in SA!). Eventually he sailed it to

Australia and home to New Zealand. He called it "The Star of the West" after the pub.

I'm not a great gambler but Dorothy and I used to go to the racecourse in Cape Town and I would still have an occasional line on the horses. This was my first visit to a proper casino and Dorothy and I spent some time just wandering around taking it all in. We stopped at a roulette wheel and I got some chips. Having spread some around the table, imagine my total surprise when, after the ball stopped, a big pile of chips were pushed towards me! I thought that was enough raw luck for that night so I cashed in and headed for the blackjack tables. I least I had a rough idea what was supposed to happen there. I had a fairly good night and came out ahead although Dorothy would have gone home straight from the roulette wheel! She even won on a slot machine.

We went back a couple of more times but the major outcome for Sol Kerzner was that the success of the Mbabatho Sun allowed him to build another larger casino on another bit of Bophuthatswana, a resort that became Sun City.

Before I go onto to other subjects, I must give you some idea of the life in the field. Unlike when we were in Namaqualand, when there were just Dorothy and me, we had a field camp of up to 30 people. At the top was the geologist (me) followed by guys called field officers who ran the teams of labourers with the help of the boss boys. The labourers were the guys who physically picked up the samples, which went for assay.

My field area covered a lot of territory and included a small settlement known as Taung. That won't mean much to anyone of you unless you are interested in the history of man. Prof Richard Dart (an Australian) of Wits University recognised "Taung Child" as a very early precursor to *homo sapiens* (i.e. you and me) and named him/her as *homo erectus africanus*. Of course, the academic establishment poured scorn on his work. After all they had found the missing link with Piltdown Man. That fraud and hoax wasn't uncovered for decades so Dart's work wasn't given its true place in science for about 50 years. And people still believe in "Scientific Consensus"!!

Our labourers were all Tswanas as they were the locals. The field officers fell into a number of categories. We had kids just out of school and hoping to go to university to study geology, we had geology students working during the holidays, there were guys who just wanted to be in the field and then we had guys who were running away from something and looked on us as something like the Foreign Legion.

One of our students was out from Glasgow University and quickly realised that fieldwork was very different to living in the west of Scotland. He didn't have a driving licence! I'm sure he didn't need one in Glasgow but as his job involved driving all over the Northern Cape, we had to get him a licence as quickly as possible. All that considered, the students were the best field officers as they were getting a lot more out of the job than just a pay cheque.

One of the misfits was so incompetent that he never seemed to do anything right. This culminated in him rolling a Land Rover, not an easy thing to do. Brian King wouldn't allow him to drive again so he left soon after. The last we heard was that he got a job in the explosives factory in Somerset West. The mind boggled.

Another had a problem with honesty and would use his vehicle for purposes he shouldn't have. We had permission to carry extra fuel but he used his to drive to Jo'burg on the weekend to see his old mates. That stopped after one month when his vehicle returns came in. He left.

The final one to tell you about was sent to us by HO. Most of our guys were fit and healthy. This guy was huge. He also drank beer instead of eating and had some outrageous stories of his previous life. Even now I'm not sure of the fact and fiction. According to him, he had a mate's ticket in the Merchant Marine but was now on shore because of some dark incident, which he never did explain. He was a great raconteur and great company but had a prodigious thirst and the night I tried to keep up with him ended in ignominy (at least for me). Like all the 'runaways', he started off well but the tedium of the job got to them after a while. Some lasted longer than others but, eventually, they left.

As an exploration office, we had to report to our head office on a regular basis. The weekly and monthly/quarterly reports were supplemented by the dreaded Regional Meetings. The reports were fairly dry and mainly contained facts and figures. Of course, you had plenty of time to write your reports but during the Regional Meetings you had to stand up and present your findings. Not only that; the men from HO would quiz you on your strategy and you could very quickly become a quaking jelly.

It meant that you had to know your prospects, what you were doing and what you would be doing in the future. One of the most difficult decisions any prospecting geologist has to make is when it is right to walk away from a prospect. A great many geologists have called it wrongly and been made to look very foolish when another company opened a mine on the old property.

By luck, (good or bad?), we hadn't had a Regional Meeting for about eight months when the first one I had to attend was due. This meant that, not only did I have a great deal of data to present; there was a lot of it that I hadn't produced, which I had to read up about. Brian King was a big help in that.

However, the Regional Meetings had a reputation of being nervous occasions and the tales of geologists being taken to task by the bosses from HO were legendary. The main ogre was the "head honcho", Dr Dave Smith who had a reputation of not suffering fools gladly. Dr Louis Coetzee (who had interviewed me originally) and some of the other Regional Managers ably backed him up. We had a young lad straight out from university in the UK, Jon Ferrier, who was so affected by the stories that he developed an ulcer!

(Jon and I had a talk one evening, where I think alcohol was involved, about taking flying lessons. The outcome was that we found that Kimberley had a gliding club. We joined and I spent a few happy hours up in the thermals. The area around Kimberley is perfect for gliding. In fact the World Championships were held up the road at Vryburg.)

The day of the first meeting dawned and there we were, all uncomfortable in our collars and ties. To be honest, we all got a fairly easy ride and, although there were a couple of probing questions, no blood was split.

In the two years I was in Kimberley, we must have had about half a dozen of these meetings and I found the bosses to be nice guys, even Dave Smith, who, I realised very quickly, liked to have animated discussions on the geology.

As well as the local guys presenting their stuff, the HO party would include geologists from other departments and they would keep us up to date on some of the advances and news from other investigations.

On one of these occasions, one of the HO photogeologists, Mike Hussey, came to give a talk on the new developments in satellite imaging and how he and Anglo American saw it being used in the future. I knew Mike from days gone by (he was married to the sister of Jimmy McDaid's wife and Jimmy had been with me in the PRU) and we had a long chat over a couple of beers when the meeting was over. He asked me to make sure I came and saw him when I visited HO.

We would go up to Johannesburg every now and again for courses so I kept my promise. I didn't really think anything of it although it was all very interesting especially the work they were doing for the Chilean office over the Andes.

A few days later, I was in the office in Kimberley when Mike called me. He asked what I thought of the set-up in HO and I had to admit to being impressed. He then dropped his bombshell. He was being transferred to Australia and had been tasked to find a replacement for himself. He thought I was the one who could fit the bill. I was astounded! He said that there would be a company wide memo coming round and I had to make sure that I responded to it.

I had to consult Dorothy as she was very happy in Kimberley and tales of living in Jo'burg didn't tempt her. As always, she was happy to go where my work would take me. So once all the hoops were jumped through we would be on our way to live in Johannesburg.

We had to have a going away party and we were persuaded to make it as Scottish as possible. Not with kilts, bagpipes and tartans but with Scottish food. I had found a butcher in Jo'burg who advertised Scotch pies, potato scones, black and white puddings and even haggis. The haggis and puddings were not as I expected, as each was 18 inches long and 3-4 inches across. When I had been up in Jo'burg visiting Mike Hussey, I had gone to the butcher and bought a double order of all the goodies. Now I was on my way to Jo'burg myself so all the food had to be either eaten or thrown out. The party was an excellent excuse. The motley mix of the different nationalities ate all the food except for a few slices of black pudding.

We packed up the townhouse we were then staying in and headed off to Jo'burg. In the morning we had heard of some bad weather up on the Highveld but didn't take any notice of it. It was only when we were passing the dumps by the mines on the West Rand that we realised that the reports were true. It was snowing! September 1981 is still remembered as the time it snowed in Johannesburg.

We had been booked into the Intercontinental Hotel by HO while we looked around for a house. Off I went to the office on the 7th floor of 40 Fox St. Anglo American owned a number of buildings around the main Head Office at 44 Main St. I had met, apart from Mike Hussey, my boss to be, Dr. Fred Cornwall who ran the Geological Services and Research Dept. and Geoff Trollope who was due to retire in about six months. I think with a trollop and a hussey in the section, some people were expecting the new recruit to be, maybe, a tart! However they got a jack.

Perhaps I hadn't been listening properly but I got a great surprise when I walked into the office. There was dust and the sound of hammering as the walls were being rearranged. Why? Oh, they must have told me that there was an all new, state of the art, image processing system going to be installed, mustn't they?

This was to be my new toy, which was a shock as I had tried to stay as far away as possible from computers. In the early 1980s, there were no PCs and each terminal was connected to a mainframe. The imaging processing mainframe was a stand-alone HP3000 with an International Imaging System bolted onto it. The disc drives (of very limited size) were as big as small desks while the tape drives held 2400ft tapes. There were no floppy discs or CDs for us. We also had an early Optronix printer, which took our digital images and made photographic films of them. Because of this and the fact that Geoff had been an aerial photographer in the RAF, we also had a darkroom where we developed both the black and white and colour negatives. As we developed the facility, the in-house drawing office built a studio where we printed 1m square images from these negatives.

Aerial photos are usually black and white but when used in stereoscopic pairs they allow you to see the ground below the aircraft in three dimensions. They have been used since the Montgolfier brothers took their balloon over Paris but they have only ever been photos. The quality of the developing process dictated the final product. Usually they got it right but there was no going back. Satellite images were/are different. Firstly, they were digital so the data could be processed on a computer and secondly, they looked at different parts of the electromagnetic spectrum (also known as all sunlight wavelengths). Some could look through clouds (something air photos could not) and at much more discriminatory regions of the spectrum. They also cover much larger areas of the Earth's surface than photos do. I'm not going to bore you with details but I will come back to some aspects of all this later.

Mike stayed around for about three weeks before he was off to Australia so I tried to get as much help out of him as I could. You must remember that all this was totally new to me and Geoff hadn't a clue about computers. However before long I was dropped into the deep end.

While I was trying to get my head around image processing, Dorothy and Alison were stuck in the hotel. Unfortunately, downtown Jo'burg had little to offer a mother and young daughter in the way of entertainment during the day so the first priority was to find somewhere to live. Alison quite liked the hotel and, for some unknown reason, would eat all the butter on the table. She never did it before and never did it after we left the hotel.

We were going to rent a house, hopefully, as we didn't fancy being in a tower block with a two year old. One of the perks to which I was entitled, was a fairly healthy rent allowance so we just had to find somewhere suitable. Dorothy would scan the newspapers and we would travel round the suburbs in the evenings, looking at potential abodes. Eventually, we came upon a house in a suburb called Blairgowrie and, this you won't believe, it was in Oban Ave! We negotiated the rent and that was where we stayed all the years we lived in Jo'burg. Once we moved in and Dorothy got to know the neighbours, life became very pleasant.

As we celebrated our first Christmas in Jo'burg, Alison was two years old and at just the right age to appreciate the whole Santa thing. As Christmas Eve went by, she became more and more excited and it became obvious that we were going to have a problem as it got later and later. She was determined to wait up and see Santa Claus. We were trying to tell her that he wouldn't appear if she wasn't in bed but she didn't believe us. Luckily, a plane flew over with all its lights flashing and we managed to convince her that that had been the sleigh and she was being missed out. That got her to bed at about 11.30p.m. and gave us a chance to get all the presents out and arranged in front of the fire and to pour ourselves a drink. We were about to go to bed just before 1.00 a.m. when Alison came through shouting, "Oh, he's been!" and started to rip open the presents. We left her to it as we were bushed.

9

Johannesburg

For those of you who know Jo'burg, Blairgowrie is near Randburg and that was the nearest shopping centre to our house so we spent a lot of time there. I took a bus into work at first (about 40 minutes) so that Dorothy could have our car during the day.

Mike Hussey had been working on images over the Chilean Andes where Anglo had a gold prospecting team. As he left, Chile became my first priority along with all the other jobs from the exploration teams. As the Andes don't have much vegetation, the images reflect the rock characteristics so prospective areas are easier to delineate.

I mentioned that Geoff was about to retire and, as I was pretty new, the section needed someone with experience to run it. Dr Fred Cornwall was in overall charge and he advertised worldwide for someone.

As this was still in the days of apartheid, we were all surprised when Dr. Aurelio. A. de Gasparis arrived from the USA. Known as Lillo, his name caused great trouble for the great majority of the staff and some hilarity as people struggled with it. However he had worked with NASA on the Landsat programme, so he brought great experience into the division and, looking back, stimulation to the ideas within the company. Lillo was of Italian extraction but had been born in Abyssinia (Eritrea) and had studied at Wits University some years before.

After Lillo had found a house, he applied for a telephone line. Imagine his surprise when he was told he already had one! Seemingly, when he had been at Wits some 15 years before, the telephone in the flat he shared was in his name. No one had ever bothered to change the name in which it was held, so Lillo had the line and number transferred to his house. I'm sure there were some very surprised and shocked students that day!

So work progressed. We were still interpreting images and photographs from all over the world and slowly but surely we were being accepted. We shared a floor with the Geophysics and Geochemistry departments both of whom shared our computing facility. Geochemistry was only two people, John Coles and Clinton Smythe. Clinton I had known in UCT where he had been an undergraduate. He was active in his opposition to the apartheid regime; a fact we all knew but we were still surprised when he let slip that he had a 'black' student lodging with him. This was in the days of 'dompas' and the pass laws when the different races were supposed to 'go home' to the townships at night. There was no way that this student could attend classes and live 'at home', so Clinton put him up. There was always a chance that Clinton could be reported to the authorities but he seemed confident that that wouldn't happen. However, he did admit that the student would head for the cupboard under the stairs if there were an unexpected knock at the door! He never was caught.

Clinton came to me one morning with a question. Did I know a place in SWA (Namibia) called Solitaire? I admitted that I did. He then asked if I could advise him where he should arrange to meet some people there when he was passing through during a holiday he was taking. I was a little confused and asked him to elaborate. He replied that he wanted to know at which hotel or street junction he should tell his friends to wait for him. I almost burst out laughing as it was obvious that Clinton knew nothing about Solitaire. I told him that if he and his friends arrived in Solitaire on the same day they would meet each other. He started to argue but I told him to trust me. A few weeks later he got back to work and I asked him if he and his friends had met up. Rather sheepishly, he admitted that they had. To explain, Solitaire is well named as there is no other 'town' within a radius of several hundred kilometres. It is important and hence marked on the map as it has a petrol station and store, which is the only place you can buy beer for many miles, and a church. Nothing else.

Clinton was a very clever lad and was sent by Anglo to Imperial College in London for a year. When he came back he admitted that it was the hardest work he had ever done and the only time off he had had was between the Christmas and New Year. He decided to go to Skye in the Inner Hebrides and he showed me some photos that he had taken. One was of the Cuillins from the Sleat peninsula at the southern end of the island. I must admit that it was probably the clearest and best photo of the Cuillins that I had ever seen outside a professional calendar shoot. He told me that it was taken on the 28th of December and I was stunned. He didn't realise how lucky he had been to get that shot even after I told him I knew of people that visited Skye every year and had never seen that view.

Clinton loved travelling and always seemed to end up in some exotic locale. He went off to India on one trip but it was only after he returned that we found out that he was on a train which passed through Bhopal a couple of hours before the Union Carbide tragedy.

Ken Beisheuval, who had been with Anglo all his working life, ran the Geophysics section. He was a very keen runner and would run to and from his house at least twice a week. I have learned that he dropped dead on a visit to the Himalayas while on a walking tour a couple of years ago. His deputy was Eddie Kostlin who had been born in Germany during the war and had escaped from East Germany by crawling under a wire fence. Phil Klinkert ran a project where Anglo were outfitting an aircraft for geophysical exploration while Peter Leggatt did most of the data processing which meant that he was the main user of the computer along with myself.

Above I mentioned that I was thrown in at the deep end and I was picking up the techniques as I went along. We had a short training course from IIS, the company who had supplied the image processing system but it was really a case of monkey see, monkey do. What I needed was an in-depth course that went to first principles and took me up to the then present and beyond to the future developments.

Like every other office in the world, we were inundated with fliers and one day a small inconspicuous notice passed across our desks. A course was being held in a few places in the USA and was perfect for what I thought I needed. Never thinking that there was a chance I could go, I passed it onto Lillo. Imagine my shock and joy when he said that he was going to send me so I had better get started organising the whole thing.

Anglo had its own travel agency so they could handle the tickets. I had to organise my visa and then apply for some foreign exchange. South Africa had draconian exchange laws so I had to jump through the usual hoops. The course was to be held in the Americana Hotel in Fort Worth, Texas and the most popular show in SA at the time was "Dallas", so I kept being asked if I was going to visit 'Southfork'.

SAA had a flight from Jo'burg to New York's JFK airport on a Friday night. It was an eighteen-hour flight with a re-fuelling stop on Sal Island in the Cape Verde Islands. Off I went to Jan Smuts to catch the flight and be seen off by the family where I bumped into Eric Underhill, one of my old football coaches from UCT, who was on the same flight. It was good to have a friendly face to talk to and to go through arrivals at JFK together. When we touched down it was raining so hard that I doubt if the pilots on the flight deck could see the runway.

I was supposed to be in Fort Worth for first thing Monday morning so I had booked a flight from New York on Sunday afternoon which meant that I had a day or so to look around the city. I was in a Manhattan hotel but the weather was so foul that I only got to stroll outside for a short time on Sunday morning. Even then I was offered some dodgy diamonds in the street. I turned the offer down; I didn't have the heart to tell the guy that I worked for Anglo American/De Beers!

So then I was off to the Pan Am terminal to catch flight PA 081 to Dallas-Fort Worth (DFW). When I got to the check-in desk, I was told I wasn't booked on the flight and it was the wrong flight number anyway. Stunned, I suddenly realised that my bag had already gone down the chute and I had been put on the stand-by list.

As I was sitting in the departure lounge, I could see that this flight was going to be full so I went over to the ground staff and asked if I had a chance. Not likely was the reply and they checked my ticket. Oh, it was a full economy ticket and I could catch any flight. Were there any other flights to DFW? American had one that left in about ten minutes so I couldn't catch that one but United had one, which left in about an hour. I could use the little train, which connected all the different terminals. So off I went to the relatively deserted United terminal. Again I was told I on the stand-by list but the flight wasn't full so I had a good chance of getting on the flight.

Waiting around gave me a chance to think things over and try and work out why this had happened. Needless to say I was a bit stumped. Then I was called for the flight and realised that I was going via Chicago! One aspect I haven't mentioned is that this was in March and the weather was a bit severe. We taxied out to the runway but then we sat there for about an hour as the weather in Chicago meant that our landing couldn't be guaranteed. Eventually we took off for our approximately two-hour flight to O'Hare airport.

This part of the journey was uneventful until we got to Chicago. The pilot came on the intercom to tell us we were in a 'stack' waiting to land but we were running out of fuel so we would have to go to Cedar Rapids, Iowa, to fill up! This was getting beyond a joke! Cedar Rapids is probably a very nice place but it is flat and I had the impression that the guy who worked the tower was the same guy driving the fuel truck. In later life I met a guy who came from Cedar Rapids who couldn't believe that a Scotsman had ever heard of it. Terry Farrell, who played Jadzia Dax in 'Star Trek – Deep Space 9' and had a part in the Ted Danson comedy series 'Becker', also grew up there.

We flew back into O'Hare airport and we were lucky that the 727 we were on was the largest type of plane allowed to land that night because of the snow. All the people for Chicago de-planed and left about five of us heading for DFW. A new cabin arrived but the flight crew had to be changed as well. Because of the weather, our new flight crew was in Minnesota and we had to wait for them to arrive, which would mean another delay of at least a couple of hours. The time was after 11 at night so we weren't going to get away until at least 2 in the morning. I needed a drink!

Believe it or not, the cabin crew couldn't serve us alcohol while on the ground so I drank a lot of coffee. It turned out that a previous flight to DFW had been cancelled so our flight was going to be absolutely full. Eventually, the pilots arrived and we started to load the other passengers. I was in an aisle seat and the middle seat beside me was the last to be filled. I'm a big lad but the guy who squeezed into that seat made me look tiny. No chance of any sleep because of the squeeze and the fact that my fingertips were tingling from all the coffee!

The big chap (on his way to Temple, Texas) and I chatted and I told him of my troubles. He remarked that he would be in tears and I agreed that if I hadn't been forcing myself to smile, so would I.

We landed at DFW at just after four in the morning, before the dawn and then I remembered that my case had been on the PanAm flight the previous night. Oh, dear. How was I going to get it? I walked over to the only baggage handler around and spelt out my problem. He said that he had been handling the baggage off the PanAm flight from JFK but didn't recognise my description of my bag. He promised to take me to the other terminal when all the passengers off the United flight had gone.

I telephoned the Anericana hotel to tell them that I was going to arrive very late and they advised me to use their courtesy bus, which would make its first run from the airport at about 0630 hours.

There I was alone in DFW with the baggage handler and off hopefully to find my case. As we drove along he told me that they had put all the unclaimed bags in a locked cupboard. As I walked into the terminal, I could see my bag through a glass door. I've never been so relieved in all my life. I caught the bus, checked into the hotel and was shown to my room.

I realised that if I lay down, I would not get up again for hours and I was due in a classroom in less than an hour. Off I went to breakfast (more coffee!) and down to the course. Apart from me, the other people on the course were all from USA or Canada, but my story quickly broke the ice and we all got on very well.

I must admit that by four in the afternoon I was struggling to keep my eyes open so I never did make the 'ice-breaker' in the evening.

Being a fairly intelligent chap, I was determined that I wouldn't be caught out on the next leg of my trip. I was booked to fly to London on the Friday night (to see Jon Ferrier (studying at Imperial College) and to spend the weekend with Torquil who had moved to just outside London) and then onto Jo'burg. The airline was American and they had an office just down the street from the hotel. Imagine my anger when I was told that I was a 'no show' on their flight AA081 from JFK to DFW on the Sunday night and my onward reservations were cancelled. As you may remember my ticket had PA 081 on it. However it was handwritten and the right hand tail on the A was not complete hence the confusion. I was composing a tirade to give the lady back in our travel office when I was told that I could get a seat on the Saturday afternoon flight.

This meant that I would have to stay another night – not a great hardship.

On the last evening we were in the bar of the hotel having a farewell drink when I asked how many of the lads had been in Vietnam. Perhaps not the most diplomatic question I could have asked. It turned out that ALL the American lads were Vietnam Vets although none had served together. One was an ex-marine, another had been a medic and another had been flying a helicopter. They all had stories and, for me, it was remarkable that none actually regretted their time there. They regretted having to go in the first place but they all looked back with some nostalgia.

After getting back to Jo'burg, I found that the girl who had booked my flights and issued the ticket had left so I never did get to give her a piece of my mind.

As we carried on with our image processing, we found that we began to get more and more work from all over the organisation. A part of that was that I was acting the part of that Mike Hussey did when I listened to him in Kimberley. It was rather a pleasant experience being on the other side of the table and realising what the office geologists were going through.

We continued to get work from all over including from covert operations in Angola and China. De Beers were active in both these countries but the links with South Africa were kept as secret as possible.

I was asked to interpret images over the diamond digging on the Angola/Zaire border, one of the most dangerous mining areas in the world. Fortunately I was not required to do any fieldwork as the head geologist was coming down to HO. His route was Luanda-London-Johannesburg as there was no direct flight between Angola and South Africa. There were still SA troops in northern South West Africa (Namibia) and probably in Angola as well so the attitudes were understandable. I was used to meeting and discussing images with geologists from all over but this guy was the most nervous I have ever come across. Not surprising really as one of his last duties, as the head guy at the mines, was to identify the body of one of his junior geologists who had been murdered by panga/machete wielding bandits.

De Beers always worked in different parts of the world, in many places not under the De Beers name. For example, in Australia the work was in Stockdale Prospecting's name. There was a monopoly suit against De Beers in the USA and the directors were under danger of arrest if they went there.

However, one of the last places you would expect them to be working was China. Although the De Beers name was suppressed, the consulting work was at the invitation of the Chinese government. I'd liked to have been a fly on the wall at those negotiations! They had a problem understanding the distribution of the indicator minerals and the known kimberlite pipes and asked me to look at the images. With the definition of the Landsat Thematic Mapper, I was able to decipher the intricate structures and explain the distributions. When the guys from HO took my report to China, the Chinese disappeared with the images and report, which were never to be seen again!

Our offices and lab were along on side of a large open plan office with the rest of the floor being given over to engineering draughting tables. Needless to say, I became quite friendly with some of the draughters and the banter helped to lift spirits when required. One of the lads came to me one morning as he knew I was a Scot. He had bought some books at a jumble sale and was trying to read one but he couldn't make any sense of it. He was Irish but the book was in Doric! It was an autobiography written by a ploughman in NE Scotland but this guy couldn't understand a work. He passed the book to me and I read it and loved it! When I told him, he just shook his head.

I tried to get in first in the morning but the draughtsmen and ladies always beat me in. One morning I was called over to the far windows. Our offices were on the seventh floor of 40 Fox Street and we looked onto the seventh floor of the block across Fox Street, a block also occupied by Anglo American. I was told to look at a certain window and wait. I could see a chap sitting in his office with his back to the window and it all seemed perfectly normal. Told to be patient, a few minutes later, the door to his office opened and closed behind a young lady with whom the guy in the office proceeded to "make out". As they disappeared onto the floor, we all burst out laughing and I was told that this was regular morning entertainment.

The original Landsat (Multispectral Scanner – MSS) tapes had only four bands of data and computer-generated images were generally of three of the four bands to give a colour picture. This led to 'false colour composites' being the norm but further processing was generally fairly simple and could lead to washing out the images or enhancing details of one feature while depressing others. Techniques such as Principal Components or Edge Enhancing were useful to a certain extent but their full potential required a data set of more complexity. Fortunately such a development was on the way. Known as the Thematic Mapper or TM, it was to have seven bands of data, one in the thermal region of the EM spectrum, but the really good news for geologists was that one band was in the region of the spectrum where clay minerals absorb energy. You may be asking why that should be important. Let me enlighten you.

Some precious metal deposits are formed when hot, metal carrying fluids move through country rocks. These fluids deposit the metals, in a certain sequence, as the fluids cool and become less pressurised. If that were all that happened, prospecting would be quite difficult. However, many country rocks contain minerals called feldspars, which are altered by the hot fluids and the products of that alteration are various clay minerals. So, if you can identify the alteration zone, you can target the possibility of precious metal deposit. One important fact is that the alteration zone is always much larger than any deposit. On MSS images, alteration zones were very difficult to distinguish from many other rock types. However, on TM images, the alteration zones are easily distinguished so the prospecting was much more effective.

The MSS satellites were originally designed so that the USA could map the potential grain harvest of the USSR and know how much they would be selling to the Soviets. The TM satellites were going to help so many more disciplines including geology. So you can imagine the anticipation as the first TM satellite was about to be launched. However, it was NASA'a bad luck (and ours) that the shuttle chosen to take the satellite in space was the Challenger. Not only did we lose a TM satellite, Lillo lost a friend on board.

Chile was one of the regions where satellite imagery really worked. Even the MSS images were useful and we were looking forward expectantly to being able to help the effort there. However, it was obvious that we had two problems. One was that the computer system was too small and too slow and we were going to need some in-house programming to produce images, which were different from the run-of-the-mill ones.

To get another computer system, Lillo was going to have to convince the powers above that it was worthwhile. Into our laps fell a data set, which gave us a good excuse. Somehow, we acquired a tape with ground gravity data over most of southern Africa. The processing of this was slow on our old machine and we found that when we were working on that data set, we couldn't work on anything else.

The data allowed us to look at the distribution of diamond pipes and to see that there was a correlation between the pipes and triple point junctions in the gravity data. That combined with the potential of TM in finding gold/silver deposits meant that the budget was approved and we were going to get a new machine.

Lillo met a mathematics post-graduate student called Neil Pendock and offered him use of our machine to write programs on the understanding that any 'useful' ones we would get to use first. Neil is one of the cleverest people I have ever met and we became a pretty good team as he would run a program over an area and I would see if it showed anything of interest or potential.

However all the big works would have to wait until the Landsat 5 satellite was operational. Neil was working on some sample data and I was kept busy doing interpretations of MSS images and aerial photos.

I was being sent on trips to field offices for their regional meetings but also Lillo was keen that I kept up my skills with going on training/seminars. Tim Wilson was a world-renowned photogeologist from Australia who ran a yearly course at Rhodes University in Grahamstown in the Eastern Cape. Lillo decided that I should go on this as an external student and try to hone my skills and learn any new tricks that Tim could pass on. It was a course that I thoroughly enjoyed and Tim eventually was very successful. He discovered a hitherto unknown fossil beach deposit of ilmenite (titanium dioxide) and he became a rich retired photogeologist.

The ERIM conferences were international affairs where other image processing people could meet and exchange ideas. Lillo decided that I should go to the one held in San Francisco and combine it with a radar interpretation course in Houston, Texas. I wasn't going to be caught out like the last time so I made sure that I was going straight through to 'Frisco. Another 18 hours with a stop at Sal Island followed by a 6 hour flight from New York to San Francisco meant that I hadn't a clue what time it was when I arrived. I just fell into bed and slept. I woke up in the early hours wondering where I was but a few more hours and a good breakfast got me back on track.

The conference was being held in the Westin St Francis Hotel on Union Square slap bang in the middle of town. A fascinating hotel and it was where the Queen had stayed when she visited California during Ronald Reagan's term. How do I know this? When you switched on the hotel TV, it defaulted to the information channel, which showed the Queen arriving in the pouring rain at the hotel. This threw me for a while, as the weather was warm and sunny outside. Perhaps the jetlag was worse than I thought. Another fascinating fact about the hotel was that down in the basement was a guy who washed all the coins that were used in the hotel. This meant that all the coins given back to you in change were bright and new. Not only that but you also got brand new banknotes back as well. All the 'old' dirty money was taken out of circulation.

Part of the conference was a fieldtrip around San Francisco and the San Andreas Fault. We were shown images and their relevance to the earthquake dangers. I got the impression that the locals seemed to ignore the danger. We walked along the beach where the fault trace disappears into the Pacific Ocean, south of the Golden Gate. At the top of the cliff, where the fault trace was shown by a depression in the countryside, the authorities had built a school!

I loved walking around San Francisco and sitting on Fisherman's Wharf looking over to the island of Alcatraz was a highlight. One of the bars there had a speciality of serving Irish Coffees and I had a few.

Everybody knows that American beer is pretty poor so imagine my delight when I found out that the hotel bar was selling bottles of McEwan's Export. Not only that but one evening they were on special at $2 a go! I seem to remember drinking them all. As I was walking along the corridor to my room, a young lady was coming out of another. Even in my befuddled state, I could recognise a good-time girl. As I passed she asked if I was interested. "Only if you want to practise", I replied. She went off giggling.

The conference was due to finish on the Friday afternoon at about 4.30pm. As the final talk was being delivered, we noticed that the hotel staff was massing at the sides of the hall. As soon as the conference was wrapped up, the staff rushed in to set up tables, etc. for a formal dinner. Casper Weinberger, the Secretary of State, was due to speak at a fund raising dinner that evening and we were holding things up.

We dropped our bags in our rooms and met up in the bar. Across the street was the almost obligatory rent-a-demo against 'Cap the Gun'. As we watched, a section of the National Guard proceeded to march down the street and face the demonstration, which seemed very well behaved behind the barriers, which had been put up.

One of the delegates I had met was from New Orleans but it took me about three days to understand what she had been saying as her accent was so strong. While we were in the bar, she came in looking quite worried. She explained that she had to go up to the top of the hill to get a taxi so that she could catch her flight home but she didn't fancy walking out alone into the poisonous atmosphere. Needless to say, my gallantry took over and, in the company of Pete Wilson from CSIRO in Australia, I accompanied her and her luggage to the taxi rank.

The following morning, I caught a flight to Houston, Texas and the radar interpretation course. We were in the Marriot Hotel in the Galleria but there was only one other guy on the course and he was from Kentucky.

I thoroughly enjoyed the course but the highlight was going to a baseball game at the Astrodome. The Houston Astros were playing the LA Dodgers and I was really lucky as I was with a baseball enthusiast. He talked me through the game and now I love baseball. I suppose you only really enjoy a game when you know what the players are trying to do.

As there were only three of us on the course, we used to drink and eat together. The hotel bar served free fajitas in happy hour. We used to load up with the free food and then drink the night away. A word of warning. Don't drink Wild Turkey bourbon for any length of time on a few small fajitas. I did and had the worst hangover of my life. I've not touched that particular bourbon since.

We all know that Americans have a peculiar parochial outlook on life and the Texans are probably the worst exponents. So imagine my surprise when the morning TV show had a list of towns and cities weather forecasts with all the usual suspects Houston, Dallas, New York, Chicago, LA, etc., with the only non-American city listed being Aberdeen!. Yes, even the Texans had to admit to the importance of Aberdeen in the oil industry.

My alarm clock was set for 0800 hours so imagine my shock when the phone by my bed stared ringing at about 7.30am. In my half sleep, I realised that Lillo was on the other end. I had to go to Ottawa and meet with a company that was offering us a new image processing system. That meant rearranging my flights and that I wouldn't be home at the weekend as planned with Dorothy.

So I stayed another night in Houston, and then flew to Dallas, Montreal and Ottawa on the Saturday. One thing I hadn't planned for was the temperature change. Frisco and Houston were relatively warm so I hadn't packed any cold weather clothes. I had only one thin pullover with me. Ottawa Airport was undergoing renovations and the wind whistled through it, exaggerating the already cold −1C temperature.

The Sunday morning was bright and clear so I decided to go for a walk after breakfast. I only got a couple of steps out side the hotel. It was too cold, even for me! I stayed in my room and watched Curtis Strange throw the Masters away by hitting into the water on both the 13th and 15th holes to let Bernhard Langer win it for the first time.

After the meeting on the Monday morning, I flew back to JFK airport to wait for the SAA flight back home. I hate layovers but when it is over 8 hours and the terminal is also undergoing reconstruction, my feelings were well and truly ugly when it was time to clamber on board the Jumbo to Jo'burg.

As before there was a re-fuelling stop at Sal Island in the Cape Verde Islands. Looking out the aircraft window (I'd once spent a very uncomfortable couple of hours in the Sal Island's poor excuse for a lounge – a tin shed was a fairer description) I could see the very distinctive tailplane of an Ilyushin aeroplane.

Sal Island was not just a re-fuelling stop for SAA. It was also a layover for the Cuban soldiers which were propping up the communist regime in Angola; that same regime that the South African forces were fighting on the ground. This must have lead to a few awkward moments when these two 'communities' were juxtaposed on this small island.

I had two more memorable events on planes while flying to the USA. On one flight was the star of "*Knight Rider*", David Hasselhoff, long before "*Baywatch*", who had been on a promotional tour of South Africa. Another bunch of Americans who had been visiting South Africa were the Mormons, all well-scrubbed and polite youngsters. By coincidence, they were sitting all around me on my flight to JFK en route to San Francisco. As we approached JFK, one of the missionaries, asked a flight attendant if it was possible to play something over the in-flight entertainment system. As that is a closed system, all that could be offered was the tannoy system. I was cringing as I was imagining some sort of Mormon religious music being imposed upon us all. Imagine my surprise and joy when the Bruce Springsteen's "*Born in the USA*" blasted out of the speakers.

I was glad to be home and I do promise that I will bring you up to date on our home life. So that you're not too confused, I'll try to stick to my work life.

We were processing TM images by this time and some of the images, which we were producing, were creating waves. Neil had some programs using Hue, Saturation and Intensity, which allowed us to isolate alteration zones and the exploration crews in Chile were getting very excited. The chief geologist in Chile was Bob Lyall (another Scot) and he came across to our lab. He even sent a couple of his young geologists over to see how we did it. There was to be a IMM conference in Santiago and it was decided that I should go over and then join a fieldtrip round some of the prospects – some of which I had been instrumental in discovering.

There were no direct flights from South Africa to South America so I had to go on a long detour; firstly by TAP to Lisbon, stopping at Abidjan en route. A day's layover in Lisbon was followed by an eight-hour flight on SAS to Rio de Janeiro and then onto a Varig flight to Santiago via Montevideo.

Unfortunately the transfer at Rio was really short so I didn't have a chance to see the sights. There was something uncomfortable about the flight to Montevideo but it was only when we landed I realised what it was. There, at the bottom of the aircraft steps, was the incongruous sight of several late middle-aged men in Lederhosen. They could only be Nazi refugees. We've all heard the stories of Nazis escaping to South America after WWII and here was the evidence in front of my eyes.

As we flew across the flat expanse of Argentina, we crossed one of the largest saltpans I had seen, called *Salinas del Bebedero* near San Luis, and I realised that 'Don Roberto' (of Gartmore) may well have ridden across these very same pampas. My granduncle, John Mackenzie, had lived much further south, in Patagonia.

I was dreamily looking out of the window and thinking that the clouds I could see better not mean rain, when I realised that they weren't clouds. They were the snow-capped peaks of the Andes! As we got closer, they got higher.

It became fairly evident that we were not going to fly over the mountains; we were going through them! The approach to Santiago airport is one of the most hair-raising in the world. As the plane flies through the mountains with seemingly little or no margin for error, you're sitting there hoping that the pilot knows what he is doing. Then you heave a sigh of relief as the mountains disappear only to find that the plane is flung over to the left in one of the most violent manoeuvres that you'll ever experience on a commercial flight to land at Santiago. You need a drink after that one!

I was staying in the Sheraton Hotel in Santiago and it was there that I learnt that Chile produces wine – very good wine. In fact, we still drink Chilean and South African wines at home in preference to other national vintages.

Bob Lyall invited me round to his house for a barbecue on the Sunday to discuss the arrangements for the fieldtrip and to show his new horse. I hadn't been on a horse for years but I was persuaded to give it ago. The horse was the easiest I've known to ride. If you wanted to go forward, you leant forward and the more you leant forward, the faster the horse went. It was the same with leaning back (go backward), lean right (go right), lean left (go left) and, if you wanted to stop, you sat up straight. It was exhilarating!

One other aspect of Bob's garden was that the snow-covered Andes loomed over it. In fact he could be skiing within a couple of hours from smog-polluted Santiago.

The IMM conference was being held in a downtown hotel, which was within easy walking distance from my hotel. Santiago has a unique way of trying to overcome downtown congestion. A six-lane highway, which is a one-way street in the morning, is still one-way in the evening but the direction of the traffic is reversed. That can be tricky when crossing the road if you don't know about it.

Chile has been a mining country from time immemorial. Some of the largest copper mines in the world are to be found there but the latest impetus to all the activity was the potential for gold. Above I gave a short explanation on the formation of alteration zones. These are not just in two dimensions i.e. on the surface, but also go deep into the earth. There is also a sequence of metals dropping out of solution. That starts with base metals at the bottom (is that why they're called base metals?), metals like copper, lead and zinc, followed by silver and gold with finally mercury right at the top. Chile has a north-south line of copper deposits all at about the same height above sea level (+/- 2000m). However the Andes go to over 5000m high, so there is plenty of "room" for the gold deposits to be left un-eroded.

Exploration programmes always start with an idea. They then run into problems as the potential doesn't seem to be realised. Sometimes the rocks tell you that your ideas are wrong but sometimes they show that the ideas were spectacularly correct. A discovery of a "Bonanza" – type gold deposit at El Indio showed that the potential for gold in Chile was very real. The rock had so much gold in it that it was shipped straight to Sweden for smelting. In fact it was known as the DSO (Direct Shipping Ore) and started a new gold rush of which we were a part.

After the conference was over, I was on a small plane to Copiapo in the north of the country where I was collected and taken on a tour of some of the prospects. I had a chance to wander around Copiapo and saw that it had a number of Jacaranda trees. Pretoria is known in South Africa as the "Jacaranda City" as it is stuffed with these trees. I was told that the tree is native to South America so all the ones in Pretoria have been introduced.

If you look on a map of South America, you will notice that Chile is a long thin country running north to south and bounded by the Andes on one side and the Pacific Ocean on the other. Because of the orientation of the country, there is a great variation in the climatic regions. The northern end of Chile can be split into the coastal region of the Atacama Desert, which spills into southern Peru, and the Alto Plano (High Plains), which consist of the upper stretches of the Andean foothills. The Atacama Desert is one of the driest places on Earth and can go decades without seeing any rain. The Alto Plano is also dry but does get snowfall in the winter. However, much of the snow ablates (goes straight to vapour from solid) rather than melts because the air is so dry.

As we drove around the prospects we passed the large copper mine of Chiquicamata where peasants dug in the discharge streams for the little bit of copper still left by the refining process. My notebook has a note "hell on earth" for this place (Pueblo Hundido). Thinking about it still makes me shudder.

We were going to meet some of the others at one of the field camps so this little trip was to show me how accurately my image interpretations were. As it became obvious that all my targets were of interest, I could relax. We drove up to 4,400m, where native sulphur was present, the highest I've ever been without the aid of an aeroplane and then we dropped down to 3,750m to the field camp. The rest of the party had arrived and we settled down for the night. There were some guests along and Bob warned me not to talk about the images I had produced. They were a company secret. Two of the guests were the independent consultants Bernstein and Thompson who had first recognised the precious metal potential in the Andes and they were definitely not to know anything about these images.

I remembered that I had left something behind in the truck and decided to run back and get it. I was reasonably fit but the 30 odd yards running left me gasping for breath. There's not a lot of oxygen at that altitude! But they say you can get used to anything. The camp workers regularly had a game of football just before sundown!

One evening I complained about a headache and everybody started muttering about altitude sickness. It was nothing so exotic. Part of the cap I had been wearing was a latticework and, when I touched the top of my head, I realised I was sunburnt; hence the headache. A few beers got rid of the dehydration.

The prospects we were working on included Marte, Lobo and Escondido, prospects with high gold values. Other good areas included Aldebaran and Refugio. The fieldtrip included both rock bashing and photo opportunities. We passed herds of alpaca, vicuna and guanaco and flocks of flamingos. After a couple of nights at Escondido, we moved to another camp near a mountain lake called Laguna Del Negro Francisco. The lake was split into two by a sandspit. One half was red and the other blue. All the flamingos stood in the blue water. Another feature was a small boat tethered about half a mile from shore, which surely indicated that the region had been getting drier over the previous years.

One of the other guests on the trip was Dr Dick Sillitoe, who had based his career on understanding the geology of the Andes. Dick was fluent in Spanish as was everyone else on the trip except me. He had honed his language skill by spending some time as a doorkeeper in a brothel in Punta Arenas. He was also an extremely good geologist and was giving some valuable advice to the exploration team.

The last night of the trip was a celebration and there was a quite a lot of drinking. I told a joke and Dick Sillitoe translated it into Spanish so that some of the others could understand. Jokes are usually dependent on word plays or idioms which may translate but don't convey the same hilarity in the other language. Dick was so fluent that, no matter how convoluted or obscure the joke was in English, he managed to translate it and get the locals laughing outrageously. One of the most impressive linguistic feats I have ever witnessed.

So the trip was over, we drove back down to Copiapo and flew back to Santiago. I then had to get on another plane and retrace my steps through Rio, Lisbon and onto Jo'burg. Before I leave Chile, I have to say something about the politics of the place. General Pinochet was in power and, in Santiago, every street corner had a couple of armed soldiers. Coming from South Africa, that was a bit unusual but I had learned that talking about politics usually ended in acrimony. So it was with a bit of trepidation I broached the subject with one of the local geologists. He said that, although Allende had been elected, his administration was never going to last very long. He never had the confidence of the powerful farmers, for instance, and Santiago was about to run out of food within a day or so before Pinochet launched his coup. That didn't keep me from being nervous all the time I was in Santiago, though.

While I was working on finding gold mines and diamond prospects, Dorothy was working on making our house in Jo'burg a happy home. I would catch the bus into town in the morning, which meant that she had the car during the day. Alison was growing up and we were getting ready for the arrival of our second child.

As she found her way round the Randburg area, Dorothy gradually lost her nervousness in driving in the suburbs. She got to know the shopping centres and became very friendly with our next-door neighbours. Rob was a metallurgist with the Chamber of Mines and Deirdre looked after their two children, Kevin and Tracey. Not only that but she and Dorothy found that they were both due to give birth at about the same time. They were also our landlords as we were renting our house from Rob's mother who lived in a flat in Hillbrow.

Dorothy also picked up some part-time work when Alison was at her nursery school. One memorable job was promoting "Rooibos" (redbush) tea in local supermarkets. The leaves come from a bush, which grows in southern Namaqualand and is unique to the area. It has a distinctive taste and was once only found on SA shelves. Now you can find it all over the world.

Our local church was Linden Methodist, which was a five-minute drive away. Dorothy joined the Young Mothers' Club where she took Alison. It was a great place to meet other women in the same situation. One of the older helpers at the church was a lady called Erica Lundie. Her own grandchildren lived far away from Jo'burg and she instantly took a great like for Alison. She quickly became "Granny" Lundie to us.

It was quite a while later that we discovered that Erica was an expert on Beatrix Potter and had handmade a full set of soft toys based on the Peter Rabbit characters. Each of these was over two feet tall and authentic. Erica used to show her models and even had newspaper articles and radio shows devoted to her work.

The church was an important 'anchor' for us in the crazy city of Johannesburg. Dorothy spent a lot of time there and made a lot of friends through the church. She used to go to talks and most were interesting but sometimes they seemed a bit weird to me. One lady talker told them to get rid of all the images, models, pictures, etc. of owls (!), which made me laugh. Another lady talker told them that she fell pregnant even though she didn't have all of the requisite "bits" in her lower abdomen. She ascribed it to a miracle due to her long and heartfelt prayers. Laughingly, I asked Dorothy to inquire if praying could stop babies if you DID have all of the requisite "bits"!

I was a member of the "Breadwinners' at the church which was made up of the fathers in the congregation and we would have evening meetings every few weeks. The church ran a fete to raise money for an extension and we were assigned the White Elephant Stall. I ended up collecting stuff and making sure it all ran smoothly. In the end we raised the largest amount of money and the extension was built. I also sang in the church choir.

Just after we arrived in Jo'burg, we had discovered that Dorothy was pregnant again and in July 1982, our lovely second daughter, Kirsty, was born in the Sandton Clinic. The theatre sister started to clothe me for going into the delivery room but that wasn't for me. I believed that I would be more in the way than a help so I stayed in the corridor. I was first in, as soon as I heard the cries. However, Kirsty was instantly different from Alison. Rather than staring with wide eyes at the world around her, she fell soundly asleep.

The garden of our house had a couple of fruit trees (peach and plum) although they never did give us a great harvest. Over our back wall, our neighbours had an avocado tree, which produced a lot of fruit, and one of its branches hung over our back lawn. Our kids grew up eating avos and still love them.

When we moved in, it was obvious that the previous owners had been in the throes of building a swimming pool – there was a big hole on the back garden! We filled it in and watched the birds feasting on larvae, which hatched from the infill. Some seeds had obviously got mixed up in the fill and we had quite a crop of large squash fruit. There was also a brick built braai (barbeque), which we would use either just for ourselves or to entertain (just like real South Africans!). As an aside, those boxed wines that you can buy in the supermarket had the name of "boom-wyn", literally "tree-wine", because people would hang the boxes in trees to make them easier to pour from.

Another tree in the back garden had a tree-house in it but after both Alison and Kirsty broke their arms in accidents, playing in it was stopped.

I told you earlier that I have little love for gardening and, although I would cut the grass, it was obvious that the rest of the garden was getting out of hand. I knew that suburbia had got me when I bought my first lawnmower. Something had to be done so I hired our one and only 'servant', a casual gardener by the name of Daniel. I'm not going into all the in and outs of the Apartheid laws but I would pick Sam up on a Saturday morning and he would work in the garden all day. We would give him coffee and food as required plus a fee, which he was happy with. The house did have maid's quarters where he would leave his day clothes while he worked and where he could wash and change at the end of the day. I would then drive him back to where I had collected him.

Daniel was a bricklayer by trade and the gardening was to raise some extra cash. One day I asked him to pull down the ivy, which was on the back wall of the garden. As it came down, it became obvious that the wall had not been built level and there was a significant step effect on the top of the wall. In fact it looked so weird that, when Dorothy came back from the morning's shopping trip, she burst into tears. No problem, as we had a friend in the building trade who got us some bricks and the next Saturday, Daniel smiled and whistled his way to rebuilding the wall. Once Daniel had 'broken the back' of the gardening work, he kept it running very smoothly.

Jon Ferrier (ex-Kimberley colleague) and his wife, Catherine, came to stay with us one weekend on his way back to Kimberley from a holiday in the Kruger Park. As we sat around after the barbeque, we discussed the "Million Dollar Golf Tournament" which was taking place at Sun City and which, unusually for South Africa in the days, was holding its final round on the Sunday. We watched the highlights of the third round on the TV and started to wonder if we should go to Sun City to watch the final round. In the end after much persuasion of the wives, we decided that we should all go.

This decision had its inherent problems. One was that in those days due to sanctions and an oil boycott, the petrol stations were closed on the weekends. So if you planned to drive anywhere on the weekend, you had to fill up by 6.00pm on the Friday. Jon drove a two-seater Carmen Ghia so our sturdy Opel Kadett station wagon would be pressed into service for the trip and, though not full, it did have enough fuel to get us there and back. The next problem was cash. ATMs were unknown at that time and we pooled what loose cash we had. We reckoned that we had enough to get in – just – but we would be struggling for any food or drink so we would have to take some along.

Off we went on the Sunday morning and it wasn't long before we realised that half of Jo'burg had made the same decision as we had the night before. A long stream of traffic wound its way to Sun City but the hotel complex was prepared with organised parking and shuttle buses up to the course. When we got to the gate, we realised that we were right that we had only just enough cash to get in with only a few Rand left over.

We were wandering around and I bought a programme. Big mistake! Dorothy gave me a verbal going over for wasting precious change. Then we walked round to the practice green and she grabbed the programme so that she could get autographs from all the celebrities and golfers!

In that first tournament, there were only five pro golfers; Gary Player, Jack Nicklaus, Johnny Miller, Lee Trevino and Seve Ballesteros. There were also some female pro golfers and some international film and entertainment stars to bring in the crowds.

The crowd wasn't huge but there were grandstands, one at the eighteenth greenside. As we wandered round, Dorothy was getting tired. She was several months pregnant with Kirsty at the time so she wandered over to the eighteenth green with Alison as both were feeling the heat, which was intense.

The grandstand was deserted with an area roped off. Dorothy managed to get right against the rope and kept spaces for us three (Jon, Catherine and me) for when we decided to head for the last hole. When we got there, the place was packed but Dorothy waved us over and there we sat. Dorothy was like the cat with the cream as she was sitting right beside Sean Connery!

Johnny Miller eventually beat Seve after a 9-hole play-off, but Sol Kerzner couldn't present the trophy and cheques. He'd been drinking for too long!

It was late when we arrived back home, very tired but very happy. I wasn't that keen to get up the next morning, though.

Here's one more story about golf. I was at a loose end one Saturday and decided to go off to Royal Johannesburg to watch the final round of the SA Open. There was a great field with stars like Gary Player and Nick Price taking part. In fact I walked around with Price and was standing on the side of the eighteenth fairway when someone asked me if the ball lying close to us was Price's.

I told him, without looking at him, that the ball belonged to Price's playing partner, Warren Humphreys and Price's ball was behind the bunker. Hearing my accent, he asked where I was from. I turned to look at him and the man talking to me was the golfing legend, Bobby Locke. He waxed lyrical about golf in Scotland and especially about Royal Troon where he won the Open in 1950. He related the fact that he didn't three putt once in four rounds and he said that the greens were the best he ever played on. This from one of the greatest ever putters. I was wide mouthed but did have the presence of mind to ask him to sign my programme. Bobby Locke was always criticised by the American press for having a weak left-hand grip. He said it didn't matter as he always took the cheques with his right!

That SA open ended in a tie among Gary Player, Warren Humphreys and John Bland and needed an 18-hole play-off on the Sunday. Due to South African Sunday observance laws, entrance fees were nil and a huge crowd watched Bland and Player tie after 18 holes. Player then won in sudden death. I don't think Warren Humphreys ever got that close to a big title, before or since.

I never did join a golf club in Jo'burg. It was too expensive for a guy with a young family. However I had to do something. There was a Chamber of Mines Social Club but that would have meant socialising, playing and working with the same people, something that I didn't really fancy.

We were in touch with an old friend from UCT, Paddy Lawless (Dorothy had typed his Ph.D. thesis), who was living in Pretoria. In conversation, he mentioned the Wanderers Club of which he was a member and would be only too pleased to sponsor me. I'd heard of the club but wanted to be sure that there was a football side. Once I found out that there was a Soccer Section, I joined. In fact the club ran four sides and was always on the lookout for new players.

The Wanderers Club sits astride Corlett Drive in northern Jo'burg and had many sections from soccer, cricket and hockey to snooker and even stamp collecting. The famous Wanderers Cricket Ground and the Wanderers Golf Course lie to the north and were associated to the main club. The Golf Club was almost autonomous and the Cricket Ground was where the SA Cricket Union had its HQ. There was also a rumour that the local council had to pay the club a fee so that Corlett Drive could be used as a thoroughfare.

The Wanderers became my bolt hole from life in Jo'burg. I'm a country boy and living in a huge metropolis wasn't really my bailiwick. If the club hadn't existed (or something like it), I don't know if I would have remained sane.

Jo'burg doesn't have much going for it. Its only reason for existence is gold, and plenty of it. There is no river, ford or bridge and it was certainly never a port although that changed with containerisation. When gold was discovered back in 1876, very close to where my office was, the place was a bleak, windswept grassland with some small rock outcrops (gold-bearing) and a big ridge with some infrequent waterfalls. In Dutch, a ridge is a "rand" (now the name of the SA currency) and the white water of the falls translates as "wit water". This gives the region its name of the Witwatersrand.

This desolate area was far from the diamond diggings of Kimberley and it took some time for the news to reach the people there. Some prospectors, though not all, left Kimberley to try their luck on the new diggings. However, the work on the "Rand" was much more difficult than at either the gravel or kimberlite diamond diggings. Why? The rock was much harder to work with picks and shovels but there was a one further and more important aspect of the gold deposit. The diamonds were found in river gravels, which were, to all intents and purposes, horizontal and fairly thin which meant little or no mining. Mining was required in the pipe deposits but the rock was so easily worked that it took many years before any underground mines were needed.

The Wits goldfield is unique in that the gold deposits are not like in Chile or elsewhere where they the product of volcanic action. The gold is held in sedimentary rocks (quartzites and sandstones) often described a fossil beach deposit, which, presumably, drained the surrounding gold bearing country rocks. It is not a mass of gold as in other gold mining areas but appears as thin ribbons of pure gold (reefs) or as interstitial grains in the matrix of the rock, usually too fine to be seen by the naked eye.

The initial discovery reef was a zone of natural enrichment, which was soon mined out. Then it became clear that there was a further complication. The rocks dipped at an angle of about 70 degrees from the horizontal *i.e.* close to vertical and very quickly became impossible to mine using picks, shovels and donkeys.

What was needed was heavy mining equipment and that cost money. There was no hope of raising the money in the usual places of London, Amsterdam or New York. Who would believe that the richest gold deposit ever found was just up the road from the richest diamond deposits ever found? Pull the other one! And there the story of Jo'burg may have ended but for one crucial fact.

The people controlling the diamond fields in and around Kimberley were loaded! People like Cecil Rhodes and Barney Barnato had spare cash to invest and invest it they did. Without the discovery of the Kimberley diamond pipes, the development of the gold mines would have taken much, much longer.

All in all, Jo'burg started as a mining camp and is still, essentially, one today.

Let's get back to the Wanderers. The numerous playing areas, football, hockey, cricket and rugby pitches along with tennis courts (including a lawn court) and bowling greens, were complemented by a wonderful clubhouse which had numerous meeting and function rooms with bars including one with the longest bar counter in SA. Alongside that, Saturday lunches on the terrace were a tradition but the main attraction was the first class restaurant, which served some of the finest food in town. Only members could book a table and we entertained many of our friends there. All were highly impressed.

It was an unmitigated disaster when the clubhouse burnt down in 2005. It will be rebuilt but it will never be the same.

The club badge is a chariot pulled by two horses and the club colours are black, red and gold signifying passage out of darkness, through fire and into the sunshine.

I played football (soccer) for the club for six years and in sides from 1st to 4th. I was also elected onto the section's committee as secretary, which meant keeping minutes of meetings and arranging all the subscriptions from the new players. On top of that, I was also responsible for writing the section's report, which was published in the prestigious club magazine.

I had written my monthly article and was due to hand it in within a couple of days when I watched the European Cup Final between Juventus and Liverpool, which was won, with a dodgy penalty kick, by the Italians. However, that really didn't matter. The Heysel disaster did. As I travelled into work the next morning, I mentally re-wrote the article. I was in early and wrote down the new article in about 30 minutes. It was a critique about where football was and where it was going; how we could keep the interest of kids and their parents and who cared who won the night before.

It is the only monthly article I can remember any detail of and one I was proud of. It caused two vastly different reactions. One was, "What had Heysel to do with the club?" and the other was, "The best article ever in the magazine".

Part of the problem was that the magazine always came out a couple of months after the actual events reported upon. This had its funny side as well. In one article, I congratulated one player on his recent marriage but he was divorced by time the relevant issue came out!

The club was a great social mixing pot and there were many inter-sectional events. The one that stood out was the darts competition. We won the competition a couple of times but in the first year I took part, we reached the final and were down to the final leg. The worst player in the other foursome had 93 to finish to win. Up he stepped, triple 19, double 18, thank you very much! I couldn't believe it. He couldn't hit a barn door all night and he does that! Afterwards, a 93 finish has always been a 'Wanderers' to me! I'll come back to darts in some detail later.

There were two bars. One was a 'dirty' bar which meant that people could go in casually dressed and that was where teams usually ended up after the afternoon and evening games. If the teams were playing away, they all met up back in that bar to discuss how they got on.

The Main Bar had a strict collar and tie dress code and that is where I met the famous old cricketer, Denis Compton, on one of his trips to SA.

One of the advantages of being on the section committee was that I could get tickets to the 'Chairman's Gallery' at the Wanderer's Stadium. Each section committee was given two tickets, which were usually taken by the chairman of the committee. However, our chairman, Tommy Frame, didn't like cricket and few of the other committee members did so when the subject came up, I asked to have the tickets. So I was privileged to sit in the gallery, with a jacket and tie, for all the big cricket matches, finals and rebel tour matches. I watched the unofficial Tests between SA, Sri Lanka and Australia. All the food and drink was complimentary and I enjoyed every single minute. Because there were two tickets, I could ask any of my mates to come along. One of the great pleasures in life in to sit in comfort being waited on, hand and foot, and being able to look out and notice some bosses from work sitting being fried in the summer sun.

We did have to play matches away from home but not many clubs had facilities like the Wanderers. However, one of the great treats was to play at the Rand Stadium, on the south side of the city, which was where all the local cup finals were played. We played many league games there and I played in two finals there winning one and losing one.

I've been very lucky with injuries in my sporting career. I had my nose broken once back in Scotland, I dislocated a finger playing against the Maties and I tore a muscle in my thigh while at UCT. These were the big injuries that meant I missed a couple of games. Notwithstanding all that I had a couple of injuries while at the Wanderers, the second of which really told me it was time to stop.

I was playing in a pre-season friendly and not wearing shinguards. I was kicked on my shin and the leg started to swell. By the time I was out of the shower, it was difficult to walk and it was so sore that while driving home I couldn't use the clutch to change gears. At home I found little sympathy from Dorothy who was busy preparing for a dinner party where another three couples were coming to have dinner and play 'Trivial Pursuit'. She just didn't believe that I had a problem, just that I didn't want to help. She started to believe me when I crawled out of the toilet because it was too painful to stand up!

Luckily, when the first couple arrived, the wife was an ex-nurse and immediately realised that I was in trouble. The next scene was me being helped into a car and driven round to our doctor's surgery. She checked for a fracture (!), which was negative and prescribed anti-inflammatory tablets and others. When I got back to the house, I was better received, shall we say, and spent the evening in an easy chair with my leg up on a cushion. I did go to work on the Monday but I didn't walk far.

The other injury happened in a league game, one week before a cup semi-final. I dived for a ball (I was a goalkeeper) and heard a twang. When I got up, I seemed to be fine but kicking a ball was agony. I didn't seem to have any strength in my right leg. I got through the game but, when I cooled down, walking became painful.

It didn't get easier over the weekend and on the Monday, I knew that I had to get some treatment. At this time Jo Keenan was back from SWA and his latest girlfriend was a physiotherapist. All I knew about this injury was that it was a soft tissue one. I got an appointment with her for lunchtime and limped up the road.

By this time the bruising had come out and the WHOLE of my thigh was blue-black. In fact, the physio called all her partners in to have a look, as she had never seen such a bruise. It turned out that I had torn a groin muscle, right in the cleft between my leg and hip. Sessions on every day including special strapping on the Friday meant that I could play in the semi-final, which we won. However, I never fully recovered and it was at the start of the next season's early training that I knew that it was time to stop. I was 35 and had had a great innings but I was never going to play anywhere near the top flight again. I have no regrets.

Before I leave football in SA altogether, I must tell you that I did play in some 'veterans' games where I played alongside Charlie Gough whose son Richard played for Dundee United, Tottenham Hotspur, Rangers and Scotland. Roy Bailey (ex Ipswich Town goalkeeper under Alf Ramsey), whom I had met at the Varsity tournament we had won in Stellenbosch and whose son Gary played for Manchester United and England and who is now a sports anchorman in South Africa, also turned up on the provincial football committee.

Back at Anglo, working on satellite images and air photos continued apace. I was still going to Regional Meetings as I was getting more and more work from around the country. There were two memorable meetings, one in Springbok (close to my old field area in Namaqualand) and one in Windhoek, SWA/Namibia.

The Springbok area was part of the region run from Cape Town and, usually, the meetings were held in Cape Town. However, this one was to include a fieldtrip to some of the prospects around Springbok. I had my own ideas of the structure of the area – after all, I had mapped 7000 sq kms of it – and I disagreed with some of the other workers.

There was one prospective hill with a repetitive sequence and I did get into an argument over it, which woke everybody up. I seem to remember that the phrase "structural bullshit" was uttered! The one good thing that came out of it was that people started to question the theories and so could get on with their work in a good atmosphere.

The other meeting, which stuck in my mind, was just after Dave Smith had retired (to run a wine farm that his wife had inherited – good choice!) and was held in Windhoek. Louis Coetzee had taken over and, although the SWA office had a good record of finding prospective areas, things had slipped a little. As the meeting drew to a close and everyone was about to get packed for the fieldtrip the next day, Louis let rip. He told the guys in SWA that HO was not pleased with the latest results and that they had better buck up their ideas. He was so disgusted with their efforts that he wasn't even going on the fieldtrip and he was flying back to Jo'burg that night.

To say that the evening and the drive to the prospects were downbeat is to understate the atmosphere. Funereal would be a better description and some, like Roy Corrans (who was to succeed Louis) and John Strathearn, who was the Senior Regional manager for SWA, spent a long time stating their discontent.

As luck would have it, we were on our way to a prospect called Navachab, which had some gossans but the target deposit hadn't really been delimited. In fact the grade, metals and size of the deposit were all unknown. It looked good but until the assays, from the samples that were just being collected, were back, it could well have been a dud. All geologists think that they can spot a good deposit but the chemistry decides. The area is prospective as the Rossing uranium mine is just down the road.

Anyway, the trip wasn't a bundle of laughs and we all travelled home glad that we weren't in the firing line. The news of the meeting was all around HO and was a topic of conversation for a few days but we soon moved onto other things.

The assay results could take anything from 2- 12 weeks depending on how busy the labs were and they were circulated to the Senior Regional Managers, who sat in HO, first before going off to the guys in the field for plotting and follow-up. It is extremely unusual for the labs to call up the

SRM on the phone to tell him of the results. It did happen this time and I would have loved to have been in the room when John Strathearn told Louis Coetzee that Navachab had hit the jackpot. If you put "Navachab" into Google now, you will see that it is the largest gold mine in Namibia. That lifted everybody's spirit in the whole company, whether in the field or HO.

Our workdays were broken up by lunch and Anglo had the best free canteen I've ever seen. In fact there were three, one for the hoi polloi (like me), one for senior staff and one for the upper management. You had to be careful or else you could balloon in size.

However, lunchtime was still an hour and we couldn't sit eating for that time so I usually ended up back at my desk. That changed when Dave le Maitre arrived from the Cape Town office. I had known him there and he was being groomed to take over the Admin section of the New Mining Business section. He was looking for a friendly face in the office and some advice on living on the Rand. I didn't know much except about where to live and he and is family ended up living not far from us. He also loved cricket and would often come with me to the Chairman's Gallery at the Wanderers.

Dave was also bored at lunch but he was never one to sit around moping. He played darts and managed to start up a darts school in the drawing office (DO). Derek, Peter and Paulo from the DO, Dave and I would play every lunchtime and we became quite good. In fact we won the fours competition at the Chamber of Mines Social Club after our third attempt. I got so good that I scored innumerable 180s, I finished 501 in 11 darts many times and even closed 170 once.

The darts school became very popular and some of the others on lunch would come and watch. We even let them have a go sometimes.

People at last came to visit us at Oban Ave. Jo stayed with us when he moved from Namibia before he found his own place.

Dorothy's sister, Brenda, was working in Zambia and came down to coincide with my in-laws coming out from Scotland, killing two birds with one stone. In fact, Dorothy's mum and dad came out three times and thoroughly enjoyed their holidays.

We took them round Jo'burg and Pretoria, drove them up to Sun City and even took them down to the Natal coast.

We visited a 'safari lodge' out by Halfway House, on the way to Pretoria, where there were a couple of wart hogs wandering around freely. Unfortunately, when we were there, one of them gored one of the owners, leaving him with a wound in his leg and a limp. One gunshot later, it was probable that wild boar was on the menu that night!

Anglo had an internal newsletter and within its pages were advertisements for all types of stuff from lawnmowers, cars, houses and holiday flats. I noticed one for a rather roomy flat overlooking Margate beach, south of Durban, and it was available for a week when Dorothy's Mum and Dad (Chris and Bill) were out. So off we went to the seaside. Alison and Kirsty had a great time with their grandparents and all of us had a really relaxing time. We even had time to visit another of the casino resorts, which had sprung up in the 'homelands', this time the Wild Coast resort in Transkei.

On the last afternoon, the ladies decided that they would go shopping and I decided that it wasn't for me so I went to the races. I had promised that I would pick them up at a certain time so I left the course with the first half of a double bet having won and before the second leg could be run. It was the next morning that I realised my bet had come in. The winnings paid for all the petrol costs to and from Margate.

Another of our visitors was my mother who didn't usually go far from home. One of the highlights of her trip was visiting a game park where a roaring lion appeared right outside her car window! Mum loved her holiday and really liked visiting the restaurants, especially at the Wanderers!

We also took her down to Durban while I was playing in a long weekend football tournament. She enjoyed the sea, the company and the hotel life. At around the same time, we discovered that Dorothy was pregnant again.

Alison was getting quite precocious and Dorothy thought that it would be a good idea to send her to a local nursery school before she went down the road to start at primary school. There was one a couple of streets away and every morning Dorothy would drop her there and pick her up at lunchtime.

Dorothy was a little concerned when the principal asked to speak to her during one lunchtime but it was only to ask if Alison could be put forward for auditions for a TV programme. The outcome was that Alison appeared for two seasons in a children's programme called "Zigi Zigimbot", which was set in a space station with a character called Captain Galaxy. Alison loved doing it but as she grew up she became more and more embarrassed by it.

Alison also joined a dancing and drama studio, but she soon gave up the dancing but kept on the drama.

As Kirsty started to crawl, Alison became very impatient with her and dragged her to her feet so that she crawled for about a week only before she walked!

The Cape Town regional office was run by Peter Danchin, who used to work for Union Carbide and had discovered a 'hidden' tungsten deposit just north of the Cape, and whose brother Bobby was very high up in the De Beers operation in Australia. Pete liked to think 'outside the box' and was always asking for photo-interpretations and image enhancements. This led to a couple of memorable periods in my working life.

One day I got a phone call from Pete asking if I would be interested in joining an expedition to the Richtersveld. I only asked where and when. The Richtersveld is easily located. If you check the map of the border between South Africa and Namibia, you will have no difficulty in noticing that the Orange River (which marks the border) takes a huge bend to the North and the region bounded by that 'Big Bend' is the desert mountainland known as the Richtersveld. It was underdeveloped as it was very difficult travelling country but it had always been prospective, although the only worthwhile deposits were at the Rosh Pinah mine in Namibia and the gravel hosted diamond deposits along the Orange River. Pete had decided that the best way to deal with the region was to get a team together to 'blitz' it and find whether there was anything worth following up. However the Richtersveld was still difficult to move around in and that wouldn't change no matter how many people were in the team. Pete solved that problem by leasing a helicopter (+ pilot) from De Beers. What a pleasure to do geology and prospecting without driving for hours to get where you needed to be.

A typical day would begin with different groups (of 3-4 guys) lining up to get on the chopper and being taken to an end of a traverse in turn. That trip would be about 10 – 15 minutes long and thereafter the chopper would go back to camp to collect the next group. At the end of the day the helicopter would fly back and pick up the guys, samples and all, sometimes chasing leopards along ridges, and we'd all get back to camp at teatime, not exhausted so we would all be able to discuss what we had seen during the day so that prospects could be rated in order of importance. The area had been mapped by the South African Geological Survey about 30 years before and the map (by De Villiers and Songe) was well known. John De Villliers had been the first head of the PRU where I had studied in Cape Town. They had marked mineral occurrences but had not rated them.

Some of these occurrences were in really isolated locations but the helicopter meant that that didn't matter. We were able to 'knock off' the unimportant ones very easily.

I had done some work on the images of the region and had recognised some prospective areas. Unfortunately, the best of those was on the eastern extremity and our camp was on the western sandveld near Port Nolloth. Normally the trip, by 4x4, over the well-named Hellskloof Pass would take two days. In the helicopter, it took only twenty minutes. I was taking samples in the riverbed and the pilot asked where I would like to go next. I pointed to the mountaintop, which normally would have taken hours to get to but the chopper made it in two minutes. All in all, a great fieldtrip that lasted nearly two weeks but saved months of normal fieldwork.

In February 1985, our son, Gordon, was born. He screamed the place down and he had to go to the hospital nursery so that Dorothy could get some rest. The three children had totally different reactions to being born; Alison was wide awake and inquisitive, Kirsty slept and Gordon screamed. So there and then we knew that they were going to be different characters. The girls loved Gordon from the first and we knew that our family was complete. It is a strange aspect of our family that the two spaces between our children were each 2 years and 7 months.

Dorothy was changing Gordon's clothes one day and left the room to get something leaving him on a bed. When she came back, he was lying on the floor, crying. She phoned me at work and I told her to get him to the doctor. That she did and had to go to hospital. It turned out that his skull was fractured but there was little that could be done because of his age. Thankfully, he fully recovered.

I mentioned above that Anglo had given permission for us to buy another processing system and it looked like the whole floor was going to be rebuilt. My work was going to be disrupted and I wasn't looking forward to all the problems. Two different strands came to my rescue.

Firstly, an old colleague from UCT, Bob Newton, phoned me and asked if there was any chance that I could cover his six-week lecture course while he was away on sabbatical leave. Secondly, Pete Danchin wanted me to build up a map of the Northwest Cape from all the disparate geological maps from UCT, Orange Free State University, Geological Survey and others, all of which called the same rocks different names and whose lithological boundaries could not be compared directly. He realised that I was one of the few people who had the experience to do this and possibly the only one in

Anglo. I asked if he would mind if I did this in Cape Town and he was delighted which meant that the plan would be for me to work as follows: for nearly two months I would spend mornings in the UCT geology department and the afternoons in the Anglo Cape town office.

The only possible fly in the ointment would be if I couldn't get Lillo's and Fred Cornwall's permission to do it.

However, sometimes all the tumblers fall into place and disparate 'coincidences' all come together. Because our floor was being rearranged, Pete Danchin wanted me to do some work (and had a budget to pay for it) and Anglo would get a lot of 'brownie points' in UCT, we could all look forward to seven weeks in Cape Town. The department arranged (and paid for) accommodation in the Serengeti serviced flats in the Gardens area of Cape Town, so one Friday afternoon, we loaded up our car in Oban Ave. and set off, all five of us, to Cape Town. Dorothy and I took turns to drive so we could get there without stopping, except for petrol, and we arrived in the middle of Saturday morning. We moved in and then took the kids to the beach.

Do you know what the best thing about these seven weeks? I was getting two salaries; my Anglo one and a much smaller one from UCT. I have never been so flush and Dorothy loved having the extra spending money!

We'd had to take Alison out of her school in Jo'burg (Blairgowrie Primary) but had arranged for her to go to one just up the road from the flats. They had a nursery section so Kirsty went as well. Gordon was just over a year old so Dorothy took care of him.

The next problem was that we had only one vehicle, the car we had brought down from Jo'burg. Dorothy wanted to be able to get about and quickly wore out the area round about the flats to where she and the kids could walk.

There was no use in asking the dept for a car so I asked Pete Danchin if he had a spare vehicle, which he did and I then drove around in an Anglo 4x4.

The lecture course was going well as I was able to stay ahead of the 2nd year students, mainly by preparing the next day's lecture immediately after I had finished giving the previous one. This took up the morning of every day as my lecture was at 9am, finished by 10am and I immediately got back to my (Bob's) room to prepare the next one. I was interrupted by students coming asking for clarification of some points but all in all this worked well.

I would grab some lunch and then drive off to Anglo's offices where I would continue to build up this composite geology map of Namaqualand. I knew most of the people there and my old draughtswoman, Pam Eloff, from the PRU was now working there. This was really important as she was to take my 'scribblings' and extremely bad sketches and produce a manuscript that anyone could understand.

Fortunately, the weekends were free and that meant we were able to take the kids around the Cape, visit the wine farms and take up all the invitations to braais and parties from all our old friends who still lived around the area.

I also was invited to re-join the golf "school" in the department and played all over the peninsula. One of the courses I had never played before was Metropolitan over by Greenpoint. As well as being a course I had never played before, it was the only course I've ever been robbed on. After the event it must have been when I was filling my sandbag. My wallet and watch were taken from my bag and I only discovered when I looked for some cash to buy a drink after the ninth hole. I spent the rest of the afternoon phoning banks and card companies cancelling things. Fortunately I had a couple of cheques left so we could get some cash out of the bank while it took about a week to get back to normal. I never did play the Metropolitan course again.

After the fifth week, the university had a week's break and we had booked a short holiday down at Plettenberg Bay at the Beacon Island Hotel, a really idyllic place especially with whales breaching in the bay, an annual event. We also visited the famous Heads at Knysna.

However, the lecture course was soon over and my compilation map was complete so we headed back to Jo'burg.

When I got back to my office in HO, the new computer system was in and I could get back into my normal routine. The one big advantage was that I could now process whole TM images, instead of just bits of scenes.

Because of the lack of processing power in the old system and the fact that I'd been away for seven weeks, I had a huge backlog of work but I knuckled down and gradually got on top of things.

One evening I was invited to an in-house retirement party and was talking to a number of different people when one of the head guys in the Coal Division came up and started asking about satellite images. This was rather unusual as the coal mimes were all opencast and the division usually wasn't interested in using any of our techniques.

It turned out that there was an underground fire the position of which was causing some friction over the boundary between an Anglo and another company's mines.

The short story is that I was able to superimpose the thermal data over the 'normal' image data and prove that the core of the fire, which indicated where the fire started, was over the fence from the Anglo owned property. That meant that we were in the Coal Division's good books from then on.

I was relaxing at home one Sunday afternoon when I got a call from Fred Cornwall. This was extremely unusual but there was a good reason. The chief geologist in all of Anglo was Louis G. Murray and he was missing in the Andes. Fred wanted to know if we had any photos/images of the area. Louis had gone up in a Lynx helicopter (a specially modified chopper to fly at the high altitudes) to plant a flag on the top of the world's highest active volcano, "*Ojos del Salado*" and was well overdue. LGM, as he was known, was well liked throughout the company and he had taken a keen interest in our image processing facility.

As the story unfolded, LGM's body, along with the pilot's body, was eventually found, still in the helicopter, just below the summit. The aircraft had seemingly been caught in a down draught of air as it crossed the summit and the force of the impact killed the occupants. It took a huge team of Anglo personnel to find the downed craft as it had impacted on snow free ground and so was almost invisible from the air.

Bob Lyall, from the Chile office came over to HO and gave a presentation to the interested staff on the accident and the rescue effort. It was a measure of LGM's stature that the presentation was well attended and it took a long time for Anglo to find someone to fill his shoes adequately.

Another (near) tragedy with which I was involved was when Steve and Sue, who had moved to Jo'burg, went on a holiday to the Okavango Swamp in Botswana. I only learned what had happened after the fact but they were out in a canoe when Steve decided to dive into the stream. As he surfaced Sue realised that something was wrong. In fact he had struck his head on a sandbar which they hadn't seen and broken his neck. By a fantastic stroke of luck, a ranger came up that tributary on his rounds in a motorised canoe. They managed to get him into that boat and off to Maun, the only town in the area.

When they got there, the only flight to Jo'burg had gone and they were supposedly stranded till the next day. Steve would have been paralysed if they waited that long. Fortunately, there was another plane, which was privately owned, standing on the tarmac. Sue had a high paying job so she had no hesitation in chartering it. Steve was put on board lying on a wooden door and eventually ended up in the Voortrekker Hospital in Pretoria, probably the best place for him in Southern Africa. When I saw him he had a brace round his neck and a frame screwed into his skull. He could eat and drink only with help. There is no doubt that, if Sue had not been there, he would have been paralysed, at least, and probably would have died.

Yet within a couple of years he was back playing squash, bouncing off walls and opponents!

Since we had arrived in South Africa, we had always been aware of the underlying tension created by the apartheid laws. My first winter was defined by the original Soweto riots but, all the way back to Sharpeville, the inter-racial friction was evident.

In the mid 1980s, it was painfully obvious that the ANC (and other organisations such as the PAC and SACP) were ratcheting up their anti-government campaigns. Most of the white population did not have first hand experience of "terrorist" activities but they did know about it as nearly every news bulletin seemed to have something along these lines. The international campaign affected sporting relations but on a day-to-day basis, nothing much changed.

All of a sudden, we started to hear more and more about Nelson Mandela, who was held, for part of his sentence, on Robben Island. All the native South Africans knew his story but we incomers had to be educated and, depending on who told you the story, Mandela was described as a bomber or a political prisoner. We knew more about his wife Winnie, who was always in the news breaking laws and keeping her husband's campaign in the forefront.

I can't remember when the emphasis changed but sometime around 1984/5, the ANC and its allies became strong enough and bold enough to hit the major city centres. Firstly on a small scale, for example, bombs were planted in wastepaper bins at bus stops. The bins disappeared overnight throughout Johannesburg.

One lunchtime, Phil Klinkert walked past a Wimpy bar and he was only about ten yards past when the large front window was blown out.

I was used to having guys coming in from the field to look at different images and see if certain techniques would be more helpful than others. An old friend, Heinz Fraenkel, from the Cape Town office, was due in to look at some images over the Namaqualand region.

He duly arrived just after nine o'clock, full of tales of an incident, which occurred during the night in the Carlton Hotel where he was staying. This had made the morning news but Heinz had been called out off his room because there was a bomb alert in the hotel basement garage. Heinz could talk for Africa so much of the first part of the morning was spent going over his late night experience.

When we eventually got down to looking at images, the morning passed quickly and, I think, successfully. Before we knew it, it was lunchtime so off we went to the canteen to eat and relax. It was quite tiring both mentally and on the eyes, looking at a monitor in a darkened room for hours on end. I suppose I was used to it and had some tricks to relax my eyes but I could tell that Heinz was flagging and may even have had the start of a headache, so it was time for a break.

Off we went, down to the staff canteen, for lunch and we were having some tea and coffee (Heinz never drank anything other than coffee) when we heard a muffled thump. We looked at each other and shrugged our shoulders as we had no idea what had caused it. A few minutes later, there was an almighty roar and we knew that a bomb had gone off. We went to stand on the front steps of 45 Main St. and could see smoke rising from over the roof of the Magistrate Courts to our right. As we stood there we met some people who had seen the blasts (as both noises were bombs) close up. Some were struck dumb while others were talking gibberish. All I knew was that my car was parked over there and could well have been damaged.

Smoke was everywhere and sirens from emergency vehicles were going off all around us. Work was out of the question for the afternoon. We went up onto the roof where we could see over the courts and watch a little bit of what was going on. Air ambulances arrived and left; ground ambulances went hither and thither and all afternoon we asked the question, "What happened?" There was no answer but rumours abounded. All we were told, late in the afternoon, was that the car parks were off limits and we had to find our own way home. I was fortunate that Dave Le Maitre parked his car in the basement and I could cadge a lift home and one back in the morning.

By the next day, we had found out that there had been a 'tick-tock' bomb where a small device had been exploded and when a Land Rover full of policemen had pulled up to investigate, the second charge (the much bigger one) had been exploded. It was the policemen's bad luck that they had stopped right alongside the second bomb. Many were killed and injured along with many civilians. The bombs destroyed at least 40 cars and damaged many more. My car was in a different car park and was unscathed. It was later ascertained that the bomber stood on a nearby roof and watched as the scene unfolded. These were not timed devices but set off by remote control by someone watching either with naked eyes or through binoculars.

Eventually we were allowed to collect our undamaged cars and drive home as usual. However, as I got home, Dorothy told me that she had been evacuated from a shopping mall because of a bomb scare. This was getting very worrying and, after the kids were in bed, Dorothy and I sat down and discussed what we were going to do.

We didn't want to leave but the bombs were getting too close to home and we had three young children to worry about. We decided that we had to go. Where to? A lot of our friends were also leaving, many of them to Australia, but home was calling and it was Scotland for us. It is very possible that that decision would have been different if Margaret Thatcher hadn't won the recent election in the UK. I don't think I could have taken being in a country run by Neil Kinnock.

South Africa had undergone a great deal of change in the eleven years since I had taken that long train journey down to Cape Town. In some ways, of course, it had stayed the same.

I mentioned earlier that when I first arrived, I couldn't go into a burger bar with my 'coloured' lab technician. In 1987, I could if I had wanted. Buses were segregated in 1976 then they were mixed but separate back and front and eventually totally mixed.

Areas were totally segregated all the time but there were exemptions. Hillbrow in Jo'burg was an unofficial 'mixed' area and nobody really bothered. In the old days, police used to break into flats and check if the bed was warm to 'prove' that the mixed couple had been sleeping together. Unbelievable but sex across the colour divide was totally prohibited. In cities it happened and was somewhat accepted. However, it was totally frowned upon in the countryside and towns. There the main settlement was 'white by night' as all the workers went home to the 'township' but that created embarrassing situations when it rained. Many were the times that a flash flood cut the township off from the main town. The embarrassment was when the flood subsided and the 'white' establishment men were seen sheepishly returning home as they had been marooned with their girlfriends in the townships. This separation had its tragic side when the main part of the Karoo town of Laingsburg was washed away in a flood while the township was safe as it was on higher ground.

So sex was banned across the colour 'bar' and even socialising with people of different colour was frowned upon. I was lucky as UCT and Anglo went out their ways to bend such ridiculous laws and rules to breaking point but most of our friends were not so fortunate.

But there were good things to remember about the country; spectacular scenery, beautiful weather and some wonderful people. The wildlife and the social history are rich and will always pull people to the country. Other episodes like watching Halley's Comet in 1986 stand out. Supposedly, it wasn't a great sight compared to other times it has been past the Earth but it's the only time I'll ever see it. Alison will remember going out one early morning to look at it through binoculars. Whether Kirsty will recall it is debatable as she was probably too young while Gordon slept through it all.

Before I go onto other topics, one aspect of living in Jo'burg should be mentioned. Johannesburg lies at over 7,000 feet above sea level, which is well over 5280 feet or one mile. Does this mean that Dorothy and I can be regarded as members of the "Mile High Club"? Just a thought.

So the day finally came when we were to leave. We had booked to go through Brussels as I had an interview with a company there and so we flew out on Sabena which was the only airline that flew in the daytime to Europe. All the others flew through the night so you arrived in the early morning, usually in a bad temper. I enjoyed the Sabena flight as did the kids as they were awake when they should have been. We were met at Brussels airport and taken to our downtown hotel.

The next morning I went off for my interview while Dorothy and the kids walked around the centre of Brussels. Then we got on the short flight to London where I had a car hired to drive up to Glasgow.

10

Consulting

While I was going to be job searching while doing some consulting work, we were lodging with Dorothy's sister, Brenda, in her flat in Glasgow. It was not the best arrangement as Brenda was not used to having three young kids in her home but we had no choice.

Alison and Kirsty were enrolled in the local Alexandra Parade Primary school and I went off to see what work I could get. There was not a lot of need for a gold and diamond geologist and I found that I seemed to be too old to be considered as employable as an oil geologist.

My remote sensing experience did stand me in reasonable stead, however. I picked up some contracts in Belgium, Wales and down south, working on different areas.

The contract in Brussels was to teach remote sensing, in all its different aspects, to around half a dozen Iranian students. Well, they weren't really students. A couple had remote sensing backgrounds, one was a computer programmer, one knew nothing and was bored all the time (I'm sure he was their minder ensuring that they didn't step out of line in the decadent West) and one was a borderline fanatic (or maybe not so borderline).

The course was sponsored by the UN FAO and every now and again the local representative would drop by. He was Nigerian but wasn't really interested in what the course was about and how the students were progressing. He was only interested in what was for lunch and where dinner would be with the Eurosense bosses. Not that I was ever invited!

The office was in the north of Brussels and I was given an apartment in which to live. It was close to the office and the Metro station, so I had no need of a car. Also in the north of Brussels are the Heysel stadium, where the football disaster had occurred, and the Planetarium.

The course was to last about six weeks so we had a lot of ground to cover. I was lucky because of the course I had given in UCT meant that I had a lot of basic coursework. Starting with aerial photography, we went through balloons, UV, IR, and eventually space platforms.

The students told me that they came from different ministries but I suspected that they were from the military. If I worked for the Geological Survey or the Ministry of Agriculture, I would have been interested in images of wheat fields or mining areas. They did have a passing interest but what really got their juices flowing was radar, radar images and radar theory. You're not a farmer or miner when the only really in-depth questions you ask are of details of radar and stealth technology.

Belgians are rightly proud of their culture and cuisine but they were taken aback by the Iranian 'front man' who had visited the company to inspect where the students would be taught and live. Firstly, he demanded that the two young female receptionists should not be present or totally cover up when he and/or the students were around. That produced indignation and a statement that the office was in Belgium, not Iran, and the girls were staying just as they were. Secondly, when he was taken to a high-class restaurant for dinner and he declined everything except a boiled egg. Talk about making friends and influencing people. Luckily, I never met him.

As this all took place after Ayatollah Khomeini had taken power through the Islamic Revolution and just after the Iran-Iraq war. All the students, except one, had been at the front and were obviously mentally scarred. The exception was older and had held a fairly senior position under the Shah's rule. Only when he and I were alone together would he mention those days. He clammed up as soon as one of the others appeared.

The only part of Brussels that they enjoyed was the Turkish quarter where they found halaal food and restaurants which displayed photos of the Ayatollah. Khomeini was in hospital at the time, in his final illness, and they spent a lot of money phoning to find out how he was keeping. Once they had been reassured, they phoned home to their families.

We didn't work weekends so I had a chance to see Brussels at night. Bars in Belgium sell beer and lots of different brands. The selection is far more varied than in any other country and each brand has its own glass. The reason for this variety is that wine and spirits were banned at one time in Belgium so beer became the national drink.

I was walking back to the Metro station on a Saturday night when I passed a large newspaper shop and I could see, through the window, that they sold English language newspapers. So I resolved to come back in the morning, buy a Sunday paper and sit in a café reading with a coffee and a cake. I'd be just like a local! So, I got up the next morning and travelled into the town to get my paper. As I came out of the station, I turned in the direction towards the shop and realised that I was facing a gushet or 'Y' junction. I couldn't remember down which arm I'd come so I chose the one on the left. It wasn't long until I realised that I'd made the wrong choice. I was in a street of brothels with their large front windows and strip lights. I must admit that being waved inside to one of these at 10 o'clock on a Sunday morning is not the most welcome invitation I've ever received. I got out of there; found the shop, bought my paper and then had my coffee and cake. That became a normal Sunday morning except for the walk past the brothels!

I was going to be in Brussels over Xmas and New Year so I flew Dorothy and the kids over for the week. The flat had plenty of room and I would be off for some of the time. I'm not sure that the students quite believed that they were having Christmas Day off for probably the first and only time in their lives! Dorothy and the children had a great time and got completely hooked on Brussels pate on French bread. In fact that would constitute a meal for us and they all still love it to this day. They all loved Brussels with the festive stalls, etc. in the main square (Grand Place) and the lace shops.

I can't remember what I was teaching but I'll never forget what happened. As I was talking about a slide or overhead projection when one of the students (the fanatic with the staring eyes) stood up, picked up his prayer mat, walked over to the corner of the room and began to pray. This was something that I'd never seen up close and I wasn't sure how to react. He was obviously in a trance as he prayed and the others told me to just continue and ignore him. The funny thing is that it happened only once.

Part of the course was some field work and that was to be mainly in southern Holland, around Breda, where there was a sub-office. So, just after New Year and after my family had gone home, we all travelled up to Breda to start some field investigations and visit some laboratories.

We had some fun with them in Amsterdam when we purposely drove through the canal-side red light district to hopefully make them as uncomfortable as possible as their holier-than-thou attitude was beginning to become tedious.

We were driving back to Breda one day, on one of the superb Dutch motorways, in a minibus as the sun was setting, when there was a commotion amongst the students who were in the back. I had no idea what it was all about but eventually I understood that they wanted to pray. At the time I had no concept of the Islamic prayer timetable and, if you've ever driven on a Dutch motorway in the late afternoon, then you'll realise that finding a place to stop so that they can perform their devotions wasn't easy. It was very strange to me to see how agitated they were and how relaxed they became after their prayers.

Evenings were free so I took to walking around the town as I had in Brussels. Breda is a mediaeval town and the old centre is on a hill with a ring canal defending it. The modern town has spread far beyond the original site but it's not hard to make out the historical centre.

One of the peculiarities of the Netherlands in those days was that restaurants were identified by national flags, of the cuisine inside, hanging outside the doors. Thus Thai, French, Indonesian and Indian restaurants were all easily recognised.

On the top of the Breda hill is the local cathedral and I was walking round it one evening when I passed an establishment with an Irish tricolour hanging outside. Now I can't remember ever seeing an Irish restaurant so I had to go in. I suppose I wasn't surprised when it turned out to be a pub run by a man from Dublin who had married a local Dutch girl. Apart from good beer, it also had a dartboard so I made it a habit to go in every night and play a few games.

I had been going for a few evenings and had become quite friendly with the owner, when a regular customer came in who was clearly well known to the rest of the customers. Not only that but he was a bit of a loudmouth and had a big sense of his ability with a set of darts. It was incidental that he happened to be English. The owner got a bit cheesed off with his boasting especially with him repeatedly mentioning that he had knocked Eric Bristow (the World Champion) out of some tournament or other. No doubt he did but we didn't need to hear about it all the time. Anyway, mine host was determined to bring him down a peg or two so he set up a challenge between this boaster and me. I only found out about it about five minutes before it happened but the owner was confident I could take him. And I did – by two legs to one, so I can always say I beat the man who beat the World Champion!

Eventually, the course ended and I had to say goodbye to the Iranians of whom I become quite fond over the past few weeks. I found that they did have senses of humour although they had taken me some time to find. I thought I had done a reasonable job and hoped that it might lead to further work but I was to be disappointed as none was forthcoming. So off I went back to Glasgow.

As we were coming back to the UK, one of the companies that I had as a target for a possible job, Hunting's Surveys in Hertfordshire, was closing down and there was a glut of unemployed geologists, some with remote sensing experience. I had been in contact with one of my friends (Eric Peters) who had been one of the managers there and he had picked up a position with Robertson Research in Llandudno, North Wales.

He called and offered me a ten week contract looking at some airborne images. I jumped at the chance and headed off to Wales, where I'd never been before. One of the advantages that Llandudno had over Brussels was that I could get home at the weekends, although I did so only every second week or so.

I was one of a two-man team with a young Welsh guy called Mark, geographer and soil scientist. We had been recruited to look at some images over the Sierra Guaderrama, north of Madrid in Spain, where Spanish Railways were looking at four possible tunnel routes. We were to interpret the images and, after a fieldtrip to the site, we would recommend which one of the routes would, in our opinion, be the best route for the tunnel. We had one other in the team, Jonathon, who was a hydrogeologist. He wasn't there all the time but he did go on the fieldtrip.

Mark and I met on the first morning I was down there and we were both to be put up at one of the local B&Bs. Llandudno is one of the original British holiday resorts but October is not one of its busy months. Mark's parents had visited the town a few weeks before and had dubbed it 'Geriatricville'. We discussed what we were going to do in the evenings and Mark suggested that we try to drink in every pub in town. I didn't realise how many pubs there were but I readily agreed. Fortunately, we didn't have to eat in the B&B and there were some good eateries in the town as well.

We quickly found out the good pubs and the not-so-good pubs in the town and that some of them ran quiz nights in the evenings. Also, as North Wales is just along the coast from Liverpool, we had a few bar singers on weekend nights which always led to good nights out.

We had an in-built advantage in the quiz nights as we had a few university degrees and we were up against normal working class punters. We were doubly pleased when we found that the prizes for the quizzes were beer tokens. In the eight or so weeks we entered the quizzes, we took the publicans for 85 pints!

The best pub in the town was the King's Arms, which had a fully merited entry in the Good Pub Guide. However, the most memorable evening was when the pub celebrated the arrival of the Beaujolais Noveau and the barmaids dressed up in French Maids' uniforms!

The King's Arms stood beside a local church and so it didn't open until later than normal on a Sunday evening. We either mistimed or had forgotten this and one Sunday we turned up too early. As we stood outside, Mark noticed a pub which was open further out of town and we hadn't visited it yet. So off we went to fill this space on our tick sheet. The pub sold a beer called Lees which was tasteless and awful. But one incident made the evening. We were sitting in the lounge, my back against the wall looking at one of the doors. A courting couple was sitting opposite lost in each others eyes but the man was wearing a suit, which was strange on a Sunday evening. We were struggling through our pints when the door opened and an angry young woman barged in. She stood over the other couple, said, "News travels fast, Joe!" picked up Joe's pint and poured it over his head. Then she stormed off. I burst out laughing and, because it had happened so quickly, Mark had no idea what I was laughing at.

All this entertainment didn't make us take our eyes off what we were doing at Robertson Research (RR). We were contractors so no-one had any idea who we were but then Mark found a couple of guys whom he had been at university with so we expected to be invited to some of the company's social events. But none came which didn't really annoy us as we were very busy and, although the above might give the impression that we were out every night, usually it was a couple of drinks after dinner and then home to bed.

Mark had a talk with one of his old mates at lunchtime one day and managed to be invited for some drinks with the lads that night out at one of the country pubs that dot the surrounding area. When we arrived, there was still an 'atmosphere' and, never one to just suffer, I came out and asked what the problem was.

RR was about to celebrate its 40th anniversary and the Prince of Wales was coming to unveil a plaque or something. The staff, having seen us arrive out of nowhere on a project none of them knew anything about, had jumped to the conclusion that we were Secret Service agents sent to see if there were any potential problems with the visit! It took us all evening to get them to believe that we had nothing to do with the visit. We were just fulfilling a contract. By the end of the night, I think they believed us but it took a few drinks to clinch it.

Then we were off to Madrid. The mountains lay to the north with Valladolid on the other side, which was where the track through the tunnel was headed. Valladolid's one claim to fame is that it was where Christopher Columbus was originally laid to rest.

As we were there for about a week, we had two days on each possible route. As this was the first (and so far the only) time I've been to Spain, I was looking forward to experiencing the culture. Although the Spanish enjoy their siestas, we never really had a chance to as the daylight hours were pretty short and we couldn't really do fieldwork in the dark.

We drove around the few roads that crossed the mountain range and on one of the first days we were caught in a snowstorm. Imagine that, my only time in Spain and what do I remember? Snow! At the top of one of the passes was a restaurant/café which had some skies on the wall which were once used by a Spanish Winter Olympian. We also visited Segovia with its Roman aqueduct but our most memorable lunch was one with calamari sandwiches. I'm not a fan of squid or octopus so I didn't partake but Mark did and then wished he hadn't as he was ill afterwards. We also noted that every town had its own bullring.

We visited Franco's tomb, a very impressive mausoleum although none of us were particularly comfortable standing there. Passing by one of Franco's palaces, we saw the carvings on the walls of the Roman fasces (a bundle of sticks with a protruding axe head) from where the term Fascist comes.

We couldn't stay in the car all the time so we walked traverses as well. On one such, we were passing by some government installation, when Mark realised that we were being watched by some military types. We were about 50-60 yards away but Mark was muttering that "they've got f****** guns" over and over again. We got to where we wanted to get to and back again with no trouble but it was a nervous time.

So back to Llandudno and the security had been racked up. We were re-photographed but a lot of the new restrictions were of no consequence to us as we were writing up the report and working into the nights.

After about two weeks, the big day had arrived although we were so busy finishing off we took no part in the celebrations. RR's HO was a big country house which had been added to rather indiscriminately.

We were up in an attic room putting the finishing touches and were in dire need of some more, clean map copies. The print room was the other side of the canteen which was where everybody was gathered to wait for Prince Charles so I had to wait until he had driven off. By looking out of the window, we could see the official limousines so when they moved away, I knew I could nip down to the print room.

As I approached the canteen, I could see that the crowd was still there so the Prince hadn't left after all. I went up to one of his retinue and established that he was running at least an hour late. It had started to rain so I didn't want to go back to the attic room and asked if I could just wait in the canteen. It had been a pleasant, quiet conversation and we had both been smiling so, as I turned to go into the canteen, imagine the looks I got from all the guys who had once believed I was a Secret Service agent. All their suspicions had been confirmed and it was like the Red Sea parting as I walked across the room!

That night was the company celebratory dance to which we had been invited. The next morning we left RR for good again confirming all the rumours!

While I was away enjoying myself and earning money, Dorothy was trying to get family life going. It wasn't easy for her and the kids lodging with Brenda and we knew that we had to look for our own place. Because we had been out of the country for so long, we weren't eligible for a council house so we had to look at renting privately. This wasn't easy either as I was 'self-employed' but with no real track or tax record in Britain. We were getting really desperate when Dorothy met some old workmates from her first job in a lawyers firm (Brechin Robb), who had offices on George Square in Glasgow. The upshot was that a flat that the firm looked after was available and they were looking for reputable tenants. Because Dorothy was well known to them, we got the flat.

It was in a suburb of Glasgow known as Pollokshields, in Herriet Street. A large two bedroom flat but the rooms were huge and, even although there was a dampness problem, it was to be our home for the next couple of years.

The girls had to get used to a new school but it was just up the road and, after Alison's first day, she came home to tell us that she had some cousins in her class. We hadn't known but my cousin Fiona, who was married the weekend after Dorothy and I were, lived a few streets away and her twin girls went to the same school.

ALLAH DOES NOT HAVE AN EXIT VISA

Because of the girls being pupils, I got quite involved with the school and, somehow, I ended up on the PTA committee. I enjoyed it as the area had people from all over the world, specifically the Indian subcontinent, and I needed to understand the many cultures.

One of the 'events' that we organised was a 'Photo-Night' where we arranged a professional photographer and the school kids and their families could turn up and have group photos taken. It was a roaring success and most of us were gobsmacked by the turnout of some of the families. Everybody came well dressed but some of the Indian and Pakistani women were sights to behold. I don't think I've ever seen so much gold in one place at one time. They were literally covered in it. Of course, the photos were destined for relatives back home and they wanted to look successful.

While the girls were in school, Gordon was too young to go so Dorothy looked around for a nursery school. A new one run by the Save the Children Fund was starting near the railway station and, because of the many different cultures in the area, it had been decided that the official opening would involve Princess Anne. So, in the space of a few months, Dorothy and I had been in the company of two of the Queen's children. I didn't get quite as close as she did as I didn't get to shake Charlie's hand.

My contracts were getting further spaced out and we decided that Dorothy would look for some work and I could be a 'house husband'. She got work with a company called 'Rent-a-Temp' which meant that she had to be prepared to travel to different offices all over Glasgow and the surrounding districts. It also meant that she could work or not when she wanted to if I had to go away, for instance.

We didn't have a car but the public transport system in Glasgow is pretty good so that wasn't a problem. Another of Dorothy's sisters, Kathleen, owned and ran a florist's shop over in Shettleston and I sometimes helped with deliveries on the weekend. Instead of being paid, Kathleen would let me borrow the van so that we could go for runs on Sundays and the like. It was nice to get out of the city for a while.

I had applied for a lot of jobs and had registered with a number of agencies. While waiting around I had taken advice from and old university friend, John Bremner, and looked at starting my own business in remote sensing. It was good to look at Profit and Loss, Cash Flow, personnel costs, rent and all the other aspects but I was going to be 'hock' to the banks for a lot of money and I had no collateral.

I also did some part-time lecturing and demonstrating in geology labs in my old department in Glasgow University.

One evening the phone rang and it was one of these agencies calling. They were Capital Appointments and they were acting for a company who were looking for someone to cover Scotland for them. The MD would be in Glasgow the next day and wanted to interview me. I readily agreed.

The next evening I met Mark Shopland, the MD of Ferranti Ocean Research Equipment (ORE), a company based in Great Yarmouth (GY) but who were in desperate need of someone to cover their clients in Scotland. In fact, he also wanted me to be responsible for some of the foreign reps so it looked like I was in for a bit of travelling.

The first trip I had to make was down to Great Yarmouth to see the head office.

11

The Offshore Oil Industry

My first ever visit to GY was in February, well out of the tourist season. The first time was only for a day as this was the second interview, to meet the man who was to be my immediate boss, Richard Mills, and to be shown around the facility. I was offered the position and I returned home to 'discuss' it with Dorothy but I knew I was going to accept it.

The next day I phoned Mark and told him. He told me to come back to GY on the following Monday and I would be there for about two weeks to get some training and orientation.

The job was to market the company-made equipment and support sales already made. The customers were mainly in the oil industry but also included navies, ports and harbours. This was a fair distance removed from geology, but I thought I could always go back. It was many years before I did.

It was good to get a job as part of the big Ferranti conglomerate and everyone thought I had landed on my feet as Ferranti had a great reputation especially in Scotland.

The plan was for me to have an office in another Ferranti branch (Infographics) in Livingston and share the services of a secretary and other ancillary staff.

However, that still had to be all arranged and I was trying to get my head around underwater acoustics as that was the basis of nearly all the equipment that ORE made and sold. I suppose that acoustics underwater can be thought of as similar to radar in the air. Apart from the technical aspects, I also had to learn about selling because I hadn't sold as much as a tin of baked beans before.

GY in February is not a fun place. I had asked about the nightlife but everywhere was empty. It's a depressing feeling when you walk into a cavernous bar and they switch on the piped music because they've actually got a customer.

ORE had a portfolio of acoustic gear such as side scan sonar, sub-bottom profilers and beacons. Their biggest seller was an acoustic tracking system with the jazzy name of Trackpoint II. This system worked by listening to a beacon with a pre-determined set frequency and repetition rate. The 'listening' head, or hydrophone, had an array of sensors which gave an azimuth and range to the location of the beacon. The beacons were small (a cylinder of about 30cms with a diameter of 6-7cms) so they could be attached to a variety of things underwater either stationary or moving. The data coming out of the surface console could then be imported into any navigation system on board.

I was busy trying to understand all this with the different menus and settings when Richard Mills asked me if I had a passport. Of course I did and he went back to his phone call. When he finished he came over and told me that I was going to India in about 2 weeks!

The Indian Water Affairs Dept had bought an ROV (underwater vehicle) with cameras to inspect dam walls and they had bought a Trackpoint system to track it while it was working so they would know which part of the wall they were looking at. Anyway, all our field engineers were unavailable so I was the sacrificial lamb.

I did have one problem, though. There was no way that the Indian Embassy would issue me a visa as my passport was full of South African stamps and this was still in the days of apartheid. I would have to get a new second passport and , thanks to a letter from the company and a helpful passport office official, I duly did get another passport and I still run two to this day; a great help when I'm travelling and need to get a visa for another upcoming trip.

My passport was not the only issue. I had to get a number of injections and tablets and my rear end felt like a dartboard must!

Before I left, and while my passport was in the Indian Embassy, Richard and I went to visit some customers in Aberdeen. I must admit that I had never been to Aberdeen before but I was to get to know the city pretty well in the next few years.

So all the paperwork, passport and medical aspects were completed so off I flew to what was still called Bombay in these days. I had been told that I would remember India by the smell and I had mistakenly thought it would be the smell of curries and the like. How wrong I was!

157

As I got off the plane at Bombay airport, which had recently suffered a fire and so was not a pretty sight, I realised what had been meant. The hot, fetid stench of sewage is what assailed my nostrils. It's true that first impressions stick and that smell is still what comes to my mind when anybody discusses India. Also on the plane was John Leslie from Deep Ocean who was to be a great help on the trip but, of course, I didn't meet him until we were both on the ground.

We had an immediate problem, or rather John did. The Indians had ordered a top-of-the-range underwater camera, one that the Indian Customs had never seen before. The Customs were, for some reason, suspicious even although the camera and everything else had been bought by the Indian government. The camera was not in the original delivery as it was deemed as fragile so John had hand carried it. Anyway the customs wanted their 'pound of flesh' and John had to stay behind an extra day to sort out the paperwork. It was my first brush with Customs around the world but it wouldn't be my last!

As we were driven through the crowed streets of Bombay to our hotel and later to the railway station, we could see all around us the evidence of the poverty that we, as westerners, usually only read about.

The untold beggars and the fact that people lived beside open sewers were a couple of the scenes that appalled and repelled us. The Indians that we were dealing with seemed totally oblivious to all this suffering or perhaps they were just used to it all.

One part of Indian life that works and works extremely well is the railways. The following morning I was off to the station to catch the train to Surat, a trip of four hours. Surat became infamous a few years later when it was the centre of an outbreak of plague.

As the train pulled up at Surat station, it was obvious that there was a welcoming party and then it was obvious that it was for me (and John who was still back in Bombay, negotiating with Customs). After the formalities were over, we still had a two hour drive to get to where we were staying so off we went down the access ramp. Halfway down, we passed a bundle of rags lying at the side of the ramp. After we had passed it by something made me turn round to see a pair of feet sticking out the bottom. We had just walked past a dead body! And no-one seemed to be bothered! Another one of the culture shocks I had to get used to.

When we got to the guest house where we were to live for the next week or so, I entered a world very close to what life must have been like during the days of the Raj. Mosquito nets, air conditioners (don't think they were around in Clive's time!) and servants for everything abounded. My major worry, apart from hoping that I could get the Trackpoint kit to work, was drinking the local water. I had some water purification tablets with me but, as the days went by, I used them less and less. It became obvious that I wasn't going to become ill and it was probably all due to the fact that we were close to the headwaters of the local river. All habitation and its consequent pollution were downstream so no nasties were in the water we drank. Believe it or not, there was no bottled water available.

The dam was in the state of Gujarat, where Ghandi was born, and, as a mark of respect, no alcohol was available so we had to make do with India's equivalent of Coke, a brand known as "Thumbs Up".

As John was still down in Bombay, I had to start the training course on my own to some disappointment on the students' part as my 'bit' was by far and away the less exiting of the two components. Anyway, I started to give them some insight into underwater acoustics and how the Trackpoint system would help in their investigations. Here I must tell a story which rather embarrasses me.

Indians have a way of rocking their heads to signify 'yes' which is alien to a westerner. In fact, if you don't pay attention, or have never seen the gesture, you can mistake it for the normal shaking of the head meaning 'no'. So, I would ask the class if they understood what I had been explaining and they would rock their heads. So I, having taken it as meaning 'no', I would explain it again. This, of course led to some confusion until it was all ironed out by one of the organisers, who realised that I had got things all back to front!

Then John arrived with the camera and we could start the training course in earnest. The first thing to do was to unpack all the gear and explain what each part did. And then we had to launch the ROV which we did to great excitement.

The dam lake was a local tourist attraction and there was a little motorboat which took parties out on tours round the lake. The jetty that the boat used was also from where we launched and demonstrated the ROV. Most of the time, there wasn't a problem but, if the ROV was in the water and the boat was approaching the jetty, we had to beach the ROV quickly so that the umbilical cable wouldn't get snagged or even cut by the propellers.

159

My father had been in India, Ceylon and Burma during WWII and he probably learnt a few of the local words (most of them likely unrepeatable) but the only one he ever used when we were young was the Hindi word "Jildi", which means 'hurry up'. It was part of my vocabulary, so, when the labourers were being a bit slow in pulling the ROV out of the water one day, that was what I said, quite unconsciously, to get them to get a move on. In fact, for a moment, it had the opposite effect as they all stopped and looked at me in some consternation. I could see them all thinking the same thing. Horror of horrors, he speaks our language! We'd better be careful and get this machine out of the water smartish!

The course was going quite well, with some usual hiccups, when we got another surprise. The class we were teaching was only half of the total students. The other half was due down in about a week's time and we were required to stay a bit longer. This was a problem as my ticket needed changing and I would have to change some more travellers' cheques.

I would need to phone Bombay but the phone system where we were staying had only local access. I would have to be driven two hours to, believe it or not, a local railway station master's office from where I could call the airline in Bombay. But I couldn't do it immediately as arrangements had to be made with the stationmaster and the local bank so that they could change my US Dollars travellers' cheques on the same day. I think, although it wasn't said, that the stationmaster had to be present while I made the phone call and a certain bank official had to be around to sign some paper or other when I cashed the cheques.

Eventually, it was time to go back to Bombay and catch the flight home. When I checked out of the guest house the manager was very apologetic that he would have to charge me extra for some laundry that I had done as I ran out of clean clothes when I had to stay longer than planned. The pile of laundry was a good 18 inches high and cost 40 rupees. As the exchange rate then was 25 Rupees to the pound, I wasn't greatly bothered. Then I was driven down to Surat where I couldn't get a 1st Class ticket so had to sit in 2nd Class with chickens, goats and the like. Getting to Bombay, I grabbed a taxi to one of the airport hotels to get a decent meal. The guest house food had been OK but rather monotonous.

After my meal, I went off to the airport to check in to find that the flight was delayed from 0100hrs to 0700hrs the next morning. Bombay airport, especially after the recent fire, was no place to sit and waste 6-8 hours.

Eventually the plane arrived and we boarded. Now Bombay to London is a 10+ hour flight and I can't actually pinpoint what caused the problem but I spent the whole trip either in the toilet or queuing for it. My suspicion is that either one of the drinks or the snack I had while waiting in the airport was the problem but, whichever it was, it gave me the worst flight experience I've ever had. The irony is that for the almost two weeks I was 'up country', I was fine but the "Delhi Belly" got me right at the end.

One last effect of the trip was still to come. As I had been in a rush to get to India, I hadn't had all of the injections I needed. Specifically, the anti-cholera course was two jabs, of which I got the second after I got home. If you want any advice, try to avoid that course of injections. I've NEVER been that ill and this was the prevention/cure! I spent the Good Friday of 1989 switching from burning up to freezing cold and driving my family ill with worry.

I had survived (just) the trip to India but I had a lot to learn so off I was back to Great Yarmouth.

As soon as I was back in GY, I met up again with Richard Mills and Dave Hampshire whom I had briefly met on the day of my interview. The next item on the sales team agenda was an exhibition called 'Defence Oceanology' which was to be held in the Metropole Hotel in Brighton. I had never been to Brighton, had never stood on a vendor's stand and didn't know anybody who might turn up. The industry ran another exhibition called 'Oceanology' every two years at the same venue so this one was really to fill in the empty year.

What it did give me, apart from the realisation that guys at exhibitions love to drink and party, was an idea of what kind of industry I was getting into. The other bit of good fortune for me was that people came from all over the world to this show and I made a lot of contacts which I kept up all the time I was in the industry.

As soon as the exhibition was over and everything packed away to go back to GY, I was off home to Glasgow.

Dorothy and I had decided that we had to get out of rented accommodation and buy a house of our own, so much of our weekends were taken up with driving around looking at properties.

But, before we did that, I had to move into my new office in Livingston. There had been an agreement, at a much higher level than I was ever at, that I would occupy a room in the Ferranti Infographics building in Livingston and would have access to all the communications facilities (phone, fax, copying, etc) and share a secretary when required. As I had never been in Livingston in my life before and hadn't a clue how to navigate around the many industrial estates, we took a trip one Sunday so I could locate the office on the Monday.

So I turned up nice and early to introduce myself and settle into the office. I met the various bigwigs and my new secretary, Carol Wardropper. I'm not sure that she was entirely happy with having another 'boss' and especially one who didn't belong to the company she worked for. I think we sorted things out and I think she appreciated the little souvenirs I would bring her back from my various trips.

My title was 'Export Sales Engineer' and my brief, apart from looking after the Aberdeen side of things, was to liaise with our various representatives and agents around the world. Mainly our patch was Europe but we also took in Africa and the Middle and Far East excluding Japan.

So here I was travelling more than I thought I ever would do. I was to go on trips around Scandinavia, Germany, France, Netherlands, Italy and Greece plus a visit to China and one to South Africa.

On top of that I was on boats in both the Firth of Clyde and the Firth of Forth, a fly-ash dumper out of Blyth in Northumberland and suffered the fall-out of one of the biggest scandals ever to hit the British defence industry.

But first our new home was to be in the small village of Glenmavis, just outside Airdrie, quite close to where Dorothy's parents lived. We settled in pretty quickly with Alison and Kirsty going to school at the local primary. Gordon was still under school age so he was at home most of the time. The advantage of Glenmavis was that it was easy to commute to Livingston from there, the main road to Aberdeen was just down the hill at Cumbernauld and I could get onto the M74, on my way to GY, with little effort.

It was a little way from Glasgow or Edinburgh airports but, as the flights I caught were usually early in the morning, that wasn't a great hardship.

Dorothy and I had been thinking about our family and we had decided a few years ago that three kids were enough. Dorothy had been on and off the 'pill' nearly all through our married life. Up till now she had had no adverse reaction but the doctor was getting a bit leery of her continuing. I suppose contraception is nearly always the woman's responsibility although it shouldn't be so (this is going to sound really noble so I apologise) I said that I would have a vasectomy. There was little or no great thought about it. One minute I just said, "OK, I'll organise it".

Glasgow Health Board had a dedicated clinic up near Park Circus and the doctor got me an appointment. The first (of two) was so the clinic doctor could go over all the pros and cons in case we didn't understand the implications. Needless to say, we had done some research so I was ready to go for it. Anyway the rules were that I had to go away and have a week to reflect. A waste of a good week but I turned up on the Friday evening, shaved and ready. As an aside, that's the one and only time I've shaved my genitals and I don't think I'll be doing it again, especially as my hands are likely to get more shaky as I age! The op was done under local anaesthetic while the doctor asked me about my job and life history. About half an hour later I was ready to go home. I've heard many stories from other guys who've had the 'snip' and some are horrific but mine was fine and I was back at work on Monday morning and I never did have any ill effects.

I was soon off on some more travels again.

My first trip was to Norway, Sweden and Denmark to visit our agents in those countries. A couple of days spent in Bergen were uneventful as was a day spent in Gothenburg which I found rather sanitised. I then drove to Copenhagen using the Helsinor/Helsingborg ferry crossing. As I approached Copenhagen, a traffic information screen told me that the temperature was 33deg C and as I got near to Nyhavn where my hotel was, it was clear that the town was on holiday and innumerable sidewalk bars were being set up to slake the thirst of the populace.

I had a lunchtime appointment with Commander Willy Lars Nielsen from the Danish Navy whom I had met in Brighton and who used our Trackpoint System on his minesweepers. Willy was most apologetic that Copenhagen had run out of draught Tuborg because of the weather and we had to make do with the bottled type.

It was on that trip I realised that personal relationships were key to having a successful career in the oil industry.

Due to the tax regulations, I had to fill in a form every month stating how much business and personal mileage I had done. I'm sure someone in Personnel/Admin checked up on mine because I drove a lot of miles and 90% on business. One month I did over 8000 miles which certainly rated a phone call. Let me explain.

I was down to demonstrate a piece of kit to the French Navy in Brest. I drove from Glenmavis to GY to collect the equipment and then onto London to pick up Dave Hampshire. Then we boarded the ferry at Dover, after the customs had checked the paperwork (this was before the customs regulations were dropped), got off at Calais and then drove across the north of France to get to Brest. After the demo, I had to retrace my steps all the way back to Glenmavis, although we crossed from St Malo to Portsmouth. As an aside, military historians amongst you may be interested that the scars left by the bombing of the submarine pens during the Nazi occupation are still visible as are the pens.

It so happened that we were down to attend a big exhibition in Hamburg ten days later. Richard Mills decided that he didn't want to go (I think he had a local golf tournament to play in) so he sent me and Dave again. There are perks to being a boss. I originally thought that I would fly but then I was told that I had to transport some kit, again! So I drove to GY (again), picked up the kit and caught the ferry from Harwich to the Hook of Holland. You're probably not interested in this but I like to drop snippets of information. Hook here is not 'hook' as in English but '*hoek*' as in Dutch which means corner.

Then I drove across the Netherlands into Germany and onto Hamburg. One thing I should say about Autobahns. Everything you heard about the speeds is true! I set up the stand and drove back to Bremen where we were to stay. No hotel rooms were available in Hamburg. I told you it was a big show. Bremen was where our agent was based and the hotel was the Queen's Hotel. Not a 5 star but it did have one claim to fame. When I was checking in I noticed that there was a pennant hanging up behind the desk. A Celtic one! They had played Werder Bremen in a European competition the year before and they had stayed in this hotel.

Fortunately I didn't have to drive to and from Hamburg every day. The train stopped right outside the show hall. Which was just as well otherwise my mileage would have been even higher.

However I was knackered. The show ran to 8 pm every night and I hadn't had a decent rest since the Sunday when I left Glenmavis. So when Dave and I were having dinner I told him that I wouldn't be on the morning train. He didn't protest as he could see that I was having trouble not falling asleep in the soup. So, for the one and only time I can remember, I hung a "Do Not Disturb" notice on my door and slept until I woke naturally.

On the Wednesday night we went to the football to see Bremen beat Bayern Munich 1-0 with one of the best long range goals I have ever seen. Dave is a rugby man but even he was impressed. He was even more impressed by the beer on sale on the terraces which you don't see in the UK.

Once the show was over, Dave and I packed up the kit and headed home. We made the Dutch border and stopped for the night in Enschede where we dined in a restaurant which served the best *"Rystafel"* I've ever had. Then we were off to the Hook and Harwich. Dave jumped on a train to London and I headed to GY to drop off the kit and head home. That month's return was the largest I ever did.

I want to take you away from tales about my travels for just now. I'll come back to similar stories later but for now I'd like to show that I did have to stay in Scotland some of the time.

Nowadays it may be difficult to believe that the Global Positioning System (GPS) didn't always exist but in the early 1990's it was very much in its infancy. So there was a time before GPS but people still had to know where they were. If you had a map and compass, things on land weren't too difficult, and, believe it or not, you can still use the techniques today. However, it was a whole different ball game at sea. Techniques had moved on from the days of Harrison's clocks to determine longitude and with the advent of radar and electronic charts ships were a lot safer.

There's always some discipline that isn't satisfied with whatever is available and in the offshore oil industry the driving force for more reliable, accurate and up to the second positioning it was the surveyors.

We've now got a huge number of artificial satellites orbiting the Earth, some of them geostationary ones i.e. they orbit at the same speed as the Earth rotates so they appear to be at the same position in the sky. However, before they all appeared the industry had to rely on land based, radio dependent systems which triangulated the position of the user utilising chains of known base stations. A whole industry grew up maintaining these stations and selling the radio signals. There were systems used along the coast such as the Decca chain and longer range systems such as Syledis, which had base stations positioned on some of the oil rigs.

Ferranti ORE quoted and won a contract to supply Marine Position Recorders (MPRs) using the Decca Chain to the UK government environment department following an EU edict. These units had to be installed, maintained and inspected on any vessels which legally dumped material into the sea around the UK.

If you're reading this while having your breakfast, I'd advise you to stop one of the activities as what follows is not compatible with eating.

I suppose that not many of us give much thought as to what happens to what gets flushed down our toilets. We've heard of the sewage pipes and works and we may even have watched a TV programme or two on water treatment, but I'm sure that it's not a subject that we discuss over coffee and a biscuit. Well, now I'm going to tell you what happens to it, at least in Glasgow and Edinburgh.

Once all the treatment is done, the solid residue, known as sludge, has to be disposed of. Some places burn it in incinerators but Glasgow and Edinburgh dump it at sea. There are two sludge-dumpers on the Clyde, named the *"Garroch Head"* and *"Dalmarnock"* and the marvellously named *"Gardyloo"* out of Leith.

The Garroch Head berths at Govan, while the Dalmarnock comes out of Clydebank. Both ships are of a fair size and they both go off down the Firth of Clyde every day Monday to Friday except public holidays and travel down to the location where ALL of Glasgow's sewage sludge has been dumped for over 100 years. That is OK but the regulating authorities wanted to make sure that that was where they actually did go there every trip hence the MPRs were to be installed. The units were attached to the bilges which opened to dump the sludge and recorded when and where that happened. The first time I saw it I was really impressed. Not just that the machines worked but as the ship dumped the sludge, it slowly rose out of the water as its load reduced. The Clyde boats dumped as they went in a U-turn and then we watched as the local fishing boats moved in to catch the fish which were known to feed on the sludge!

On one trip, the captain switched on the ship's echosounder to show me the sea bottom. After over a hundred years, one would expect a seamount of sludge but although there was as slight rise, it was much, much less. The Firth of Clyde is tidal and self-cleansing so that sludge is dispersed into the open sea. I had to do multiple trips as the MPRs were known to 'hang' and it was always the same fault which just required the unit to be reset. The Decca chain relied on 'lanes' and sometimes the unit 'refused' to come out of a lane so the position information became faulty. I kept the keys to the units so the crew couldn't interfere with them meaning that when anything went wrong I had to go on board and reset the unit and also sail so I could check that the unit didn't have any further problems.

One morning I turned up to go on an inspection trip on the Garroch Head and was greeted by the sight of a double-decker bus drawing up and a load of pensioners going up the gangplank. It was a lovely summer's day and they were off for a trip down the Clyde! As they stayed in the galley (for lunch) and on the back deck, they never got anywhere near the 'business end'. Not that they would have smelled anything as I never did.

Well, that's not strictly true. On one trip, one of the sluice doors stuck open after dumping and so the sensor wasn't properly engaged and the MPR unit showed a fault. The tanks were almost empty but there was residue. One of the crew had to go down and unblock the door and I, as the 'inspector', had to stick my head in to see that everything was OK. That was not the most pleasant experience of my life!

The name Gardyloo comes from the shout in old Edinburgh (and probably in other towns and cities) of "Guardez L'eau" (Look out, water – actually sewage) given when depositing the contents into the streets of the chamber pots from upper windows of the town dwellings. Not very hygienic by today's standards so it's a little ironic that the Edinburgh sludge dumper has this given name. Perhaps there was a bureaucrat with a sense both of history and humour.

If I had to choose which of the three boats I'd rather go on, I'd have to pick the Gardyloo. Just a lovely boat, well run and the crew were great fun. They also had the more beautiful run. The dumping ground was NE of Dunbar in the North Sea and was much bigger than the one on the Clyde so they would run straight through. But the best parts of the trip were the views of the Bass Rock and other islands in the Firth, North Berwick and the coast along the south shore of the Firth of Forth.

The Gardyloo had a framed saying hanging outside the galley from Manny Shinwell, the famous old politician. It read, "Water borne sewage is the first sign of civilisation."

Leith Docks are totally different to the ones on the Clyde. The Clyde is tidal but the Leith is too small a river to accommodate boats of any size without help. So the entrance is controlled by a huge lock and that keeps the water level within the docks at a usable level.

These three boats were my usual beat but I had to install and de-install an MPR on a boat that was dumping old ammunition from Irvine and go down to Blythe to maintain and inspect the MPR on the fly ash dumper from the power station.

I also had to go to Belfast to check on the sludge dumper from there which dumped just off the mouth of Belfast Lough. The fun bit of those trips was the flight into and out of Belfast City (George Best) airport which is situated in the old Shorts site in the Belfast Docks.

Try to imagine this scenario. You're driving to work on an ordinary Friday morning, listening to the news on the car radio when an item catches your attention. When the item states that the shares of the company (Ferranti International) you're working for have been suspended from trading on the Stock Exchange, you almost drive off the road.

Getting into work, everybody had heard and work was of secondary importance. Basically, the company couldn't trade so we couldn't work. Obviously, the phone lines were buzzing and we were told to wait for an announcement. That didn't come until late in the day so we went off back home for the weekend still wondering what the future was of the company.

The weekend papers were full of the 'scandal' but they just skated around the matter. Ferranti was one of the biggest employers in Scotland and this was important. It was obvious that the whole future of one of the major defence companies was in jeopardy.

I'm now going to lay out the history as I understand how it panned out.

In the mid to late 1980's, the board of the then Ferranti company realised that it was just the right size for a hostile takeover from a larger company. To protect themselves and the company, the board decided to look around for a similar, or slightly smaller, company to merge with. After some searching, they discovered a company in America called International Signal run by a Paul Guerin. It was a perfect match especially as the companies weren't in competition and even chased different markets.

There was one very small fly in the ointment. International Signal had 'secret' arms deals on their books with countries (Pakistan was mentioned) that the countries didn't want revealed. The Ferranti board (plus lawyers and accountants) took Paul Guerin at his word and believed that the undisclosed sales were true and the balance sheet was valid.

Guerin was made of a vice-chairman of the new company, Ferranti International Signal (FIS), and everything was hunky-dory for about two years. Guerin then declared that he was tired of business and had decided to retire. On his retirement he sold the shares in FIS that he had been given as the price for his old company (for USD$200 million +) and went off to his condo in Florida.

About 6-9 months later, one of the top financial guys in FIS was doing his job, perhaps one that he should have done sometime sooner, when it became obvious that something wasn't right. When he began delving some more he realised that none of the 'secret' International Signal deals was anything more than paper. NONE of them existed and Ferranti had bought a shell, an empty one at that.

Read through the last few paragraphs and think about the size of the swindle that had been perpetrated on an unsuspecting company. I must admit to having a sneaking admiration for Guerin's incredible nerve in waiting so long before cashing in his shares. Every unexpected phone call at the office or at home must have brought him out in a cold sweat as he dreaded being found out before he was ready.

The hole in the FIS books was about USD$350 million and Ferranti had to fill it in or go broke. The company started to sell of some assets but that was just papering over the cracks. Eventually, it became clear that they would have to sell the Defence Systems group (the jewel in the company crown), based in Edinburgh, to save the rest. GE Systems bought the group for around about USD$350 million but it destroyed the structure of the whole group and foreshadowed the inevitable demise of the brand.

The authorities tried to get Guerin but he was safely in his Florida condo and never did face the music as far as I know. However, there are thousands of ex-Ferranti people who would willingly stomp on his face for what he did. The final consequences of the fraud took over a year to take effect but nobody who worked for the company would forget that morning radio announcement.

We (ORE) had had a company meeting and had been reassured that we were going to keep trading and working as before. Our books were good and there was no need to change anything we were doing. So off I went back to my travelling.

I travelled almost continuously and Dorothy only had one complaint. She didn't mind me being away during the week but she did like me to be home at the weekends. She did, however, concede that if I was on a foreign trip, I sometimes had to stay for up to 3 weeks.

My trips fell into two separate categories. One was purely sales where I would visit people in their offices to see what we could do for them. In the UK I would be on my own but abroad I would be with our local rep as strategic support. The other trip would be to demonstrate or commission some piece of kit and these were the trips that lasted the longest. Most of the time I was on a boat and the boat had a schedule to keep.

I usually tried to start my trips on a Monday morning so giving me the best chance of finishing by the Friday. Before I stepped on a plane, I would have a schedule of meetings in my briefcase.

Off I went to Rome one day and I knew that it would be a relatively short trip as we only had a couple of customers in the area. So I flew to Heathrow and on to Rome. I must admit that Rome's airport is one of the nicer ones in the world. I met the local rep and off we went to his office. One thing about Italians is that they never seem to stop drinking coffee and espresso at that. That is in the mornings. Afternoons appear to go a bit slower and coffee is less apparent. Also the traffic is horrendous in Rome, far worse that Paris and that's saying something.

We had our meetings and I was dropped in my hotel in the middle of Rome, not all that far from the Vatican. After I had dinner, I decided to go for a stroll around the area. It was a lovely balmy evening and I must admit that I was looking for a comfortable bar or cafe where I could spend an hour or so. I was looking into a shop window and a man started to talk to me. It took me a little while to realise that he spoke in English so something in my manner or look must have told him that I wasn't a local Roman. He said that he would show me a 'nice' bar so off we went round the corner. It wasn't until I went down the stairs with nude murals on either side that I knew I was in a brothel or as close to one as not to matter. I had one thing on my side. I hadn't had a drink so I was going to have to think quickly to get out without the 'gorillas' who were hanging around practicing their boxing skills on me.

The staff went into a well practised routine. I was 'allocated' a pretty young lady who led me to a booth and then a waiter appeared with a bottle of 'champagne' for my companion. Not being drunk, my first question was, "How much?" This was in the days before the Euro and the Pound/Lire exchange rate was a joke. Not only did it fluctuate but it was around 7,000 lire to the pound. As I wasn't befuddled, when I was told that it was the equivalent of about 80 pounds, I told him to take it away as I didn't have that kind of money on me. That didn't go down very well and I could see the gorillas getting interested. The establishment took credit cards as if I was going to let them get their hands on any of my cards. I told them that I'd left my wallet in my room so I only had some change, enough for a diet coke and a glass of 'champagne'. By the way, if that 'champagne' had ever been anywhere near France it must have been lost. It looked like some fruit juice but, as I didn't taste it, I'm not sure. Of course, the young lady then went into her routine. Some small talk followed by wandering hands and I must admit she was lovely. As I was sober, I wasn't subject to her charms but I can understand what could happen to guys whose brains were a bit befuddled. I'm sure that through the back there were what were called 'cribs' in the Wild West saloons but she was asking to come back to my hotel. I always thought that that was what the 'punter' suggested so she must have been desperate. I've just had a thought that perhaps she was going to get into trouble with the gorillas if I didn't play ball. Anyway I put her off by telling her that my wife was back in the room with our young baby whose crying had driven me out of the room in the first place. I didn't know I could lie so convincingly. In the end she gave up and I could leave. As I climbed the stairs, I could feel the gorillas' eyes boring into my back and I didn't breathe until I reached the sanctuary of the pavement.

As I flew home from Leonardo de Vinci airport, which is one of the most pleasant airports in the world, I thanked the stars I got out of that place undamaged.

When I was in Rome, I walked past the Vatican City. Some people say they feel close to God when they're there but I can't say I felt like that. Perhaps being a Scots Presbyterian doesn't help!

I went back to France again but not to Paris. Richard Mills phoned me one day and told me that we were off to help the French Navy find a torpedo they had lost in the Mediterranean. We had to fly from London (where I met up with Richard) to Marseilles and on to St Tropez where we met our French agent, Claude Pacheco. We spent the night in a small hotel but were due to be picked up by the navy in the morning. As we boarded the big catamaran I promised myself that I would have a look at the boats tied up in the marina when we got back. After a couple of hours sail we reached the approximate location of the torpedo and started the search.

The torpedo was emitting a 'ping' with a certain frequency, which we could listen to and track with Trackpoint II, but the onboard battery had only a certain life hence the urgency. It didn't take us too long to pinpoint the torpedo and send the navy divers down. They managed to get ropes around it and get it lifted back on board. When that was done, they couldn't get us back to St Tropez quick enough. Perhaps they were paying by the hour. Anyway it gave us a chance to wander around the marina where every yacht was grander than the one before with flags from every country you could think of, even Scotland.

However we had to get back to Marseilles as we were on a very early flight the next morning and staying another night in St Tropez was out of the question. A pity as I would have liked to have seen the nightlife.

Richard and I ate in the hotel and wandered through to the bar. Richard was never a big drinker and we were about to go back to our rooms when Claude turned up. He had gone to another meeting from St Tropez so we didn't expect to see him again. He was insistent that I should go along with him to a club downtown. I protested that I had to be on an early plane but he wouldn't take no for an answer. So off we went down to the Old Port area where the club was nowhere to be found. It had closed or moved so I was ready to go back to the hotel. But Claude was determined that we were going to have a drink. We ended up in "Le Café Americaine" which, as quickly became obvious, was a brothel. Are you beginning to see a trend here?

I only realised where I was once I was inside where I was immediately accosted by one of the girls. She obviously had only a limited exposure to male occupations as she never did grasp that I wasn't a sailor! However, I couldn't take my eyes off the lady behind the bar who was obviously the 'madam' of the place. Grotesque is a word I use rarely but it certainly described her. She had dyed blonde hair down to her shoulders but a face with the heaviest, almost white, make-up I have ever seen on any living being. She put white faced clowns to shame. To emphasise that her mascara was as black as soot and thickly applied. Her dress was low cut, half-exposing the biggest bosom it has ever been my privilege (?) to see. To top it all, her voice was gravely and could have been a man's!!!

The night was going along alright – we were talking and drinking – when another, obviously regular, customer came in. There are some affectations in dress that instantly tell you something about the wearer. A bikini top on a woman out in public probably means that the wearer isn't a nun while a suit, tie and bowler hat on a man don't usually indicate a rock 'n' roll star. My assumption when I see a man wearing a coat without his arms through the sleeves and only hanging over his shoulders cries out "Spiv, Wide Boy, Crook" to me. Perhaps I'm prejudiced. This guy was thus attired and I didn't like the look of him at all, especially when I saw his companions – two more gorillas. Another trend seems to be appearing.

He 'collected' his usual girl and went off through the back to one of the cribs. It didn't seem long but he was soon back again and stormed off out the door accompanied by his gorillas. Then we heard the sobbing and the young girl came back to the bar holding her face after being given a beating. You never know what happens behind a closed door even in this case but she must have displeased him somehow. Was it from a previous night? Or perhaps she wasn't being faithful (in a brothel???). Or perhaps he couldn't get it up and blamed her.

The rest of the girls, including her from behind the bar, started to console her clucking like so many chickens so I grabbed the chance to leave and fairly pushed Claude out the door. I had a plane to catch in a few hours. Thank goodness for air travel. It allows you to catch up on sleep you otherwise have missed.

I would hate you to get the impression that I spent all my time gallivanting about the world. I did actually spend a lot of time in the UK, especially Aberdeen. I got to know that road extremely well and rejoiced when I could drive there and back on dual carriageways.

My mundane duties were to visit those people in the industry who would need to use our kit and make sure that we got a chance to bid on any tenders that were coming out. The city was booming with lots of new companies starting up, especially in the rental sector. So I had quite a few potential clients.

Every two years or so, there was a huge exhibition called Offshore Europe, which was held in Aberdeen and took over the town. People came from all over and hotel rooms were at a premium. In fact, Aberdeen has had to build more and more hotels because of the success of this show.

As Ferranti ORE, we attended only one of these shows, when Dave and I were detailed to man the stand. With Ferranti, we didn't have to do anything other than turn up. Usually we had to set up, get the demos going and dismantle the stand afterwards. But Ferranti had a department to do all that. We had only a small corner as Ferranti had taken a large booth to showcase other wares.

I found that most of the guys from other parts of Ferranti didn't like to mix with us "oil types" which didn't bode much for their success at this show but our mood was lifted when we realised that the two girls who adorned our stand were not Ferranti employees but local models hired for the occasion. They also found the others a bit stuck-up.

Any show is a time for socialising but the oil industry takes it to extremes. Companies threw parties and one stood out. The Bennico bash became famous (notorious?) as people were found the next day sleeping behind desks and taxis refused to pick people up late in the evening.

On the stand, we had a visit from the then Defence Secretary, Malcolm Rifkind, which was the highlight of the week as I had a 'go' at him over the much-discussed 'Peace Dividend' that was supposed to appear now that the Berlin Wall had come down. That single event has been talked about by much more erudite experts than me but, to me, it showed that all the years of waiting and hoping for a socialist utopia (as we had all been told was on the horizon) had just been wasted. As the truth from behind the wall came out, it showed that the economies there were so bad that only government fables gave them any credence at all. As Billy Connolly once said, "Any system that has had every chance to work and doesn't, probably was no good in the first place." I've no doubt misquoted him but the sentiment is there.

After the show, we didn't even have to dismantle the stand like every other show I've been involved in. The Ferranti Show Department took care of that so I was able to get away quite sharp and off back down the road.

Although I was away a lot of the time, I did have most of my weekends free, especially when I wasn't travelling. We always tried to do something together as a family but not always. It so happened that one of the guys, who worked for Ferranti Infographics, where I was squatting, was on the committee of Aberfoyle Golf Club. When I learned this and talked to him about it, he told me that they were looking for members and, as I had a link to the area, I would get in no problem.

So off I went to Aberfoyle one day with my family and duly signed up. As they enjoyed the run, it wasn't totally wasted and we spent a pleasant day. So that was my Saturday summer mornings taken care of. Up with the larks, I'd make a 7.30am tee-off time, play 18 holes in a medal and be home again just after lunch. I was a bit surprised when Gordon asked if he could come along. So I'd wake him up just enough for him to grab some breakfast and jump into the car where he would sleep till we got to Aberfoyle. He had an ulterior motive. His deal was that he would pull my caddy cart (i.e. be my caddy) and I would buy him lunch in the clubhouse and he'd be due 10% of my 'winnings'! The medal competitions would have prize money (about 30-40 quid) and we also ran a magic "2s" sweep so that anyone who scored two on any hole, (e.g. a birdie on a par 3) kept the money. If you were the only guy then you could get over 50 quid. So Gordon was on a bit of an earner and the worst he could do was to have a hamburger and chips and a coke after the round.

One day I was sitting in my office in Livingston when the phone rang. It was Richard Mills from GY asking me if I could send my passport down so as to get a visa for China put in it. Yes, I was off to the Orient. We had sold an underwater acoustic ranging system to the Chinese Oil Company and I was off to commission it, with the help of one of our field technicians, Barry Fogg.

The visa application took about a month and Richard, Barry and I all met up at Heathrow Airport. We were booked on a Cathay Pacific flight to Hong Kong and then into the mysterious 'Red' China. This was a long time before China became open to western businessmen. You can now buy a visa on arrival, for example.

The flight made a refuelling stop, in the middle of the night, in Bahrain so we got off to stretch our legs. That was my introduction to the Middle East and I had no idea that I was to get to know the region pretty well in the future.

I must comment on the cabin crew on the flight. They were all very beautiful oriental girls who couldn't do enough to make you comfortable and with a terrific attitude. They put the normal stewards and stewardesses on European flights to shame.

Then we were coming into land at Hong Kong. This was at the old airport and the approach path took you through some of the high-rise flats. In fact I could see ladies hanging their washing out on their balconies as we were on final approach. It was quite hair-raising!

After landing we were transiting onto a China Airlines flight to Canton, where we would catch another flight to Zhanjiang, our final destination. It was alright until we reached Guangzhou (Canton) but from the information on the monitors, Richard could tell that our fight was delayed for about six hours. Now there was not a lot to do in a Chinese airport of that vintage so it was just as well that we had some books to read. One other aspect of Chinese airports then was that the toilets had no paper but Richard had been there before so had some in his hand luggage!

Our plane eventually turned up and we arrived tired but relieved after the relatively short flight. We were staying in a guest house but it had hot and cold water and telephone with a reception area so it was like a one star hotel, really.

The next morning Richard, Barry and I turned up for breakfast to meet our local rep, Dr Dao, who also acted as our translator. Someone had obviously told the cooks that Brits liked ham and eggs for breakfast but the instructions had got mistranslated as we were presented with a fried slice of something like Spam and a hard boiled egg. Have you ever tried eating a hard boiled egg with chopsticks? Probably not. That brought us to the next problem. Although I had no trouble with chopsticks, I had been using them for years as I used to cook Chinese dinners for the family and Richard had travelled many times to the Far East, poor Barry had never used them before so he was to be pretty hungry for a couple of days. However he became very adept by the time we left China.

After breakfast we had to go and meet with the local oil company reps and plan the commissioning trip. We were to go out on one of their boats and trial the system. The underwater beacons would be placed so that we on board could measure the relative separation using our equipment and then the divers could go down and physically measure the distance between the beacons.

It took a few days to get the boat ready so we spent them alongside the quay mounting the over-the-side pole, running cables here and there and making sure that the equipment was up and running OK. It had been shipped out separately so we first had to locate it and unpack it. This all went smoothly and Richard, who had to go off to Korea, left us in a good frame of mind.

These few days allowed us to wander around the town in the evenings which let us see a bit of the real China. I was standing at a crossroads one day, looking at the huge amount of bicycles filling the streets. I wondered about the congestion if they all were ever able to afford cars!

There was one other mode of transport which almost defies description. It was a one-man motorised cart/tricycle which was used to carry any type of produce. The engine was a (I think) two stroke machine which was fuelled by any organic material which happened to be available. It made a terrible noise and belched a horrible exhaust all the time. I was reminded of these when the car in the "Back to the Future" films was being refuelled.

So off we went into the near reaches of the South China Sea. By this time we had been joined by a squad of young Chinese lads some of whom were to be trained in the use of our kit and others were just observers. One of the lads spoke very good English and was, in fact, a second translator. Our trip was only a few months after the incident in Tiananmen Square and when we asked him about it, he said, "Oh, you mean the massacre!" I'm sure he got into trouble about that.

Food is something very important to the Chinese. I've already told you about our breakfasts but we also had to undergo the traditional banquet which is just an excuse for the local dignitaries to get smashed and show us 'big noses' up. Well, of course, we held our booze better than they did but I don't think they remembered too much about it afterwards.

On board, we were fed fantastic meals, much better than what the crew got. One night Barry (whose chopstick prowess was coming along in leaps and bounds) and I had eaten our fill when a lovely whole steamed bass was brought in. Barry and I picked at it but really it was too much. Dr Dao asked if we had finished and then proceeded to eat the head! All that was left were the skull and jaw bones. I looked at Barry and we both had the same reaction. We needed some fresh air!!

After a couple of days shaking down the kit we were ready to deploy the underwater beacons. Being used to the way the western oil industry worked, both Barry and I were a bit frustrated at the attitude to time. We thought that we would be on the boat for 2-3 days but that had come and gone and we didn't seem to be getting anywhere fast. However the beacons were in the water and we were ready for the final test. As described above we were measuring the beacon separation.

Then we hit a problem. We had up the equipment so that all the students had to do was hit one button on the keyboard and the measured separation would come up on the screen. However, the students started a long discussion over something or other. It was all in Chinese but it went on for such a long time that the captain walked of the bridge in disgust. Barry and I were looking at each other and I was getting just a touch exasperated with the whole thing. You have to be nice to customers but this was stretching things a bit. And I was running out of clean underwear as we had been on the boat about four days longer than originally planned.

This discussion was going on far too long and somebody had to do something. Was this prevarication a Chinese trait? I don't think so as it didn't gel with other Chinese I've met through the years. They all seem to be great decision makers. I put this down to the communist upbringing that the students had had. They had been taught that a superior should always take the decisions so when it came down to them hitting that button, none of them wanted to or could do it.

So I reached out between all the squabbling lads and pushed the said button. The readout on the screen said so many centimetres so we could now send the divers over the side. These divers had been sitting around for day, drinking tea and playing cards so it was good to see them earning their keep.

Up they came with a string almost exactly the same length as we were expecting so we could now all go home.

Back on shore we got ready to go home after the compulsory farewell banquet when all the Chinese bosses proceeded to get very drunk. So the next morning we were up ready to go to the airport but the farewell committee of about half a dozen was late. I wonder why?

Barry and I were sitting in the foyer of the guest house when we witnessed one of the great linguistic feats ever. A tall Australian walked in to the foyer saying "G'day, mate" as he walked to the desk. He then talked to the girl behind the desk in, what sounded to us as, perfect Mandarin/Cantonese. He then picked up the house telephone, asked the operator for a number and carried on a conversation for several moments again all in the local lingo. I had used the telephone to call Dorothy back in Scotland so I knew how crackly and old fashioned the system was. This was really impressive. Unfortunately our bus and committee arrived and we had to leave. I would have liked to find out more about our Australian but it wasn't to be. So Barry and I were back on CAAC to Canton and then Hong Kong where we would catch our return flight to London. It was a really memorable and unforgettable trip.

Sometimes I went on trips that I really didn't need to but Richard thought that two were better than one on occasion and that certainly applied when I accompanied Dave Hampshire on one of the most bizarre trips either of us would ever make.

Dave had been talking to the Geophysical Department of one of the German Universities when he was asked to bring the kit along on one of their cruises into the North Sea. He, of course, jumped at the chance and Richard told me to tag along. We flew to Hamburg and then onto Kiel where we were meeting the "Planet", the research vessel which was to be our home for the next couple of weeks.

Although the boat was a research vessel, it was manned and run by the German Navy so it was very efficient. We slept on board when we first arrived so that we didn't miss the sailing. At EXACTLY 8.30 a.m. we cast off. That set the tone for the whole trip.

So up we went round Denmark, which looks pretty uninteresting from the sea. Flat lying and dull, it's no wonder the early Danish Vikings left for greener pastures i.e. Scotland. Up the Kattegat, round the top of Jutland and into the Skagerrak below the southern bulge of Norway, we sailed heading for the northern North Sea but close by the Norwegian coast.

As we sailed into the open waters, we hit a Force 4 gale. Not really too bad, or at least that's what I thought but enough to put everyone who was not a sailor (or me) in bed with seasickness. In fact it was so bad that I didn't have anyone to talk to for two days. I've never been seasick in my life and couldn't understand how it could affect everyone else so much. Eventually the weather subsided and we went on our merry way. The trip's prime job was to lay seabed seismometers and the set off depth charges and record the effects. Not too controversial you might think. That was not what the Norwegian Government thought!!

Our initial plan was to be dropped off in Norway and then fly home. However, as the first charge went off, the Norwegians told us to stop as we would be 'damaging' the salmon hatcheries. We'd already 'crossed the Rubicon' so the next message from Norway told us that if we docked in Norway, the vessel would be impounded and the crew, including us, arrested. So we had to change our return plans!

We had a lot of free time on board so we talked a lot and got to know the students fairly well. The bar in the mess was run on an honesty basis and we would tally up at the end of the cruise. One day Dave and I were chatting about nothing very much when he said that wasn't felling very well. I thought he was being seasick again but the sea was like a millpond so that was out. He'd had a hard couple of months. Just before this trip he'd been to Taiwan and before that we'd both been at OTC in Houston. I thought he might be just tired but he told me about jagged lights in his eyes and other queer symptoms.

I'm not a doctor but I do recognise when someone is worried. Luckily the boat had a medical orderly and well stocked medical room so I sent Dave off there. He did know the orderly as he was the one who had handed out medicine during the seasickness episode but I doubt if Dave was paying much attention at the time.

A few minutes later, Dave came back with a worried look on his face. It turned out that the orderly did some tests and realised that Dave was more sick than usual with a crewman. Luckily, for Dave, we had a Consultant Surgeon on board! Within the German system, doctors were supposed to do tours in the Armed Forces and this one had won the Lottery! He used to sit out on the back deck reading a book and we couldn't work out what he did. We never asked as it wasn't our business. All of a sudden, his two week 'cruise' was turned upside down. Dave was primarily suffering from high blood pressure, dangerously high, with high cholesterol and a few other things related to rugby injuries. He had to have diuretic pills and drink plenty of fluids. Not a great burden if you've ever seen Dave drink beer!!!! But he had to have daily checks on his blood pressure. In a quiet moment, the doctor told me that if we'd been back on shore, he'd have hospitalised Dave immediately!!!

We got to 64 degrees 30 minutes north, the furthest north I've ever been and in June, the Sun hardly dips below the horizon. As a Scot I'm used to light summer evenings but this was ridiculous. It was light at 3 in the morning, and it's extremely difficult to go to sleep when the Sun's still high in the sky!

On the night before we turned around we had a barbeque and beer party on the back deck and I was feeling a bit sore the next morning. Just to get his own back, Dave organised for me to get a visit from the full medical staff just as I was getting ready for breakfast! Just my luck, there were no pretty nurses!!!!!

So we then had just over two days sail back to Kiel with nothing much to do. I like being on a boat but you have to have something to do or it gets very tedious especially when the weather is benign.

When we docked Dave and I went up to say goodbye to the captain. He and the rest of the crew had been really good to us during the cruise and it seemed only polite to wish him good luck and farewell. On our arrival in his cabin, he immediately took out two bottles of whisky (one Scotch and one Irish) and he wasn't going to let us go until they were finished. At least we could call on the students to help out but there were a couple of self inflicted wounds by the end of the session. One of them was the captain himself but he was collected by his son. One or two of the students were in a real fix but Dave and I seemed OK although I wouldn't have driven a car or operated machinery!

We were dropped at Hamburg airport by the university bus and off home we flew.

12

John Smith

I'm now going to tell you a story about a local and national politician which, as far as I know, never made any newspaper.

We were living in the little village of Glenmavis and our local parish church was New Monkland, a name which was taken over for local authority and parliamentary boundaries. We worshipped there on a regular basis and it became part of our life.

As an aside, the Communion traditions in the church hadn't changed in many a year. The elders all had to wear morning coats, tails and all and the communion wine was served out of goblets not the normal small glasses used in other churches nowadays. However you didn't drink directly out of the goblet. You used a long (6 inch) curved silver spoon to which there was a certain technique. I've seen a few wine stains on shirts and blouses after these services!

The church was built at the top of the hill; in common with many churches as that land was usually some of the worst land for agriculture having the driest and the thinnest soils around.

One of the elders decided to write a book on the history of the church going back to the Reformation and the Covenanters. He called it "The Auld Grey Kirk on the Hill". Not the catchiest of titles but he wasn't aiming at the bestsellers list. When finally the book was finished and published, it was launched, to great fanfare, in the church itself. Copies would be available for purchase and the author would sign your copy if you wanted.

The church was packed, much fuller than during a normal service and our local MP, John Smith, would be the main speaker. This was the same man who would become the Leader of the Labour Party but died in 1994 before his party regained office. He then became known as the "Best Prime Minister Britain Never Had".

His speech was relatively short but towards the end, he wanted to whip up some enthusiasm for the book so he said, and I quote, "The book costs only three pounds fifty, so you can buy three copies and still have change out of a tenner." There was a deathly hush as the audience could all add and multiply and they knew he was as wrong as he could be.

Mr. Smith MP had a puzzled look on his face as he was expecting either a gentle laugh or even applause but certainly not silence. The minister (who could also do mental arithmetic and was a close friend of Mr. Smith) got up and whispered in his ear.

The embarrassment was obvious but he came back with the rejoinder, "Perhaps that's why I'm only the Shadow Chancellor!" That got a nervous titter and we could then get down to buying the book.

Can you imagine what harm that could have done to his reputation in finance if that made the tabloids?

It never did.

13

Back to Offshore

Ferranti ORE won a long-term contract from the Royal Navy to add the Trackpoint system to the Single Role Minehunter 'Sandown' class vessel. As with nearly everything the MOD requests, the system had to be modified even although the Trackpoint II (in its civilian guise) was a well tried and tested system.

As the 'Military' Trackpoint was a modification (and I'm not going to bore you with the details), the Navy demanded sea trials. The MOD runs an underwater acoustic test range in the waters between Applecross and the Isle of Skye; so that was where I had to go. The initial trials were aboard a civilian vessel called the Northern Horizon which had been chartered from the oil industry. On board were the normal crew, some Royal Navy observers, me and a bunch of young boffins (boys with beards) from GE who built and ran the 2093 sonar which the Trackpoint would track.

The trial lasted a few days and we were lucky with the weather. The Navy types seemed pleased and the GE lads were happy that the system performed well. I had an easy time as the Trackpoint never had a problem.

About six months later, Les Ford, who was our technical manager, phoned me to tell me that we were on our way back up to Kyle of Lochalsh. My question was "When?" The answer was second week in February. To which my comment was, "Are they mad?"

February in the northwest of Scotland is not the time of year to do sea trials. The weather is foul and the daylight hours are still short. But, surprise, surprise, the range had a free week then! I would not have been surprised if the range had had a free three months!

But we had to do as the Navy wanted so I picked up Les at Glasgow Airport and off we drove to Kyle. This time the boat was the H.M.S.

Sandown – single role minehunter – the first in the class. She was a fiberglass catamaran and apart from Les, me and about six of the GE boffins, all the crew was Royal Navy.

When I visited clients I usually wore a jacket, shirt and tie but on trials jeans and pullover/jersey were normal. On going aboard Sandown for the first time to meet the GE guys (some were the same lads from the Northern Horizon) and the captain and officers, I was wearing a Scotland rugby top. No big deal, I thought, but David Sole's Scotland team had just beaten Will Carling's England team to snatch the Grand Slam the previous weekend and the wardroom was full of England rugby supporters so my welcome was less than cordial. Some of the seamen were Scots and they loved me for putting certain noses out of joint so I had no trouble getting help throughout the trip.

The weather on the first day was pretty calm but the forecast for the rest of the week wasn't good. Anyway off we went to the range and started checking the equipment. It all seemed to be working fine but as we headed back to Kyle for the night, the wind picked up. By the next morning, the winds were howling and Sandown was struggling as we headed back to the range.

Let me explain the geography of the area. Kyle of Lochalsh sits at a narrows between mainland Scotland and Skye (Kyle is from the Gaelic for narrows) and is sheltered from westerly gales by the mass of the island. So the harbour is a safe haven during storms. The new Skye Bridge lies just to the north of the town where it uses a small islet to stabilise its span.

However, sailing north to the testing range, the topography of Skye lessens and flattens out so south to southwesterly winds have nothing to stop them until they hit the western cliffs around Applecross.

By the time we reached the range (a lot later than we planned) the ship was being tossed all over the place and the captain was having trouble keeping it on the course required for the trials. The trial lines were such that if he kept to them the winds were hitting him broadside and the ship was rolling back and forth. Now this didn't bother me much as I'm not prone to seasickness but everybody else who wasn't a professional sailor was suffering. This meant that the trials were going nowhere fast. Well, not quite. Because I was OK, I was able to 'run' the Trackpoint system and the performance was first class. However, although the sonar was deployed, what was being displayed on the screen was taking second place to trips to the heads.

The captain was wearing a worried expression all day and in the late afternoon, as the sun was setting, he called us together and told us that he was not going to risk taking the ship back to Kyle he would be head on into the, by now, Force Ten gale. He would ride out the night under the lee of the Isle of Rassay but he didn't have enough bunks on board for us to stay. He called up a MOD tender/tug, a couple of which helped maintain the range and were stationed in Kyle, which would take us back to land and pick us up in the morning.

Hands up those of you who have trans-shipped in the middle of a Force Ten gale? Not a lot, I suspect. Well, I've done it and a terrifying prospect it is but I must say the professionalism of the RN seamen made it a doddle. The trip home was a nightmare, into the teeth of the gale, rain and darkness. The tender was being rocked through 60 degrees and again I was the only non-seaman not being ill.

By the next morning the only change was that there was daylight and the trip out wasn't too bad as we were running in front of the winds. The storm wasn't abating and the forecast had it continuing for the next few days. Again the trial (which was due to end the day after) was a waste of time. Sandown had to be somewhere else by the Saturday so it was decided to cut our losses. I never did discover which cretin booked that week but I've got a feeling that it was one of the RN observers who kept very quiet all trip!

I used to fly down to company meetings in Great Yarmouth sometimes. There was a 'red eye' flight from Aberdeen which stopped at Edinburgh and went onto Norwich arriving about 10.00 in the morning. Someone from the office would collect me and drive the 20 or so miles to the office.

I was on that flight one morning when the captain announced the news that Mrs. Thatcher had resigned. There was a stunned silence broken by only one cheer (cut short by looks) out of the 90-100 people on board. That was the sole topic of conversation and when I got to my hotel that night the staff were all wearing black armbands!!

I was always getting phone calls to go here or there and off I'd go. Some of these came from GY and some from clients. Sometimes the visits were courtesy calls or to speak to people in their offices and some were requesting demos of equipment. Taking kit around the UK was easy and, even into Europe, we could use Carnet documents.

However, some trips needed long term plans. Kit had to be freighted and fairly rigid timetables adhered to. This was certainly the case when I got a call from the Racal Survey office in Cape Town, inviting us down to demo some kit to De Beers, the SA Navy and other interested parties.

They principally wanted to see the Trackpoint system but would consider any others as well. Dave got to hear about this and decided he wanted to come along with the seismic processing workstation that he was promoting at the time. Richard wasn't so keen in sending two guys but Dave had a trump card. His wife worked for BA so he could get a ticket to Cape Town and back for just 10% of the normal cost. That clinched the deal so both of us ended up going. By the time all the kit had arrived and cleared customs, it was early December so we left the cold and wet of the UK in winter behind, arriving in the Cape at the height of summer.

Paul and Aubrey, from Racal, had arranged a boat in Hout Bay to carry out the demos. When we saw it, I nearly burst out laughing. They had told us it was a fishing boat but this was a floating gin palace! Its real job was to take guys out deep sea angling but the guy had a free week available.

The demos went really well and before we knew it the weekend had arrived. We always planned to stay for one weekend and it gave me a chance to show Dave round my old stamping ground. I arranged that we would meet Keith and Judy Martin, who were still living in Cape Town, at their house for an afternoon braai. That gave me a chance to take Dave on a sight-seeing trip round the peninsula. He wanted to visit a wine farm as well but, because he has always been late for everything in his life, we wouldn't get to Stellenbosch, so we would go to Constantia instead.

As we drove along the west coast road past Clifton and Hout Bay down towards Cape Point, we stopped at one of the many roadside stalls. Dave was drawn to the range of seashells. His wife collected them and he had his eye on one which was about three inches long but had a spine of the same length. I told him he'd never get it home in one piece but he was adamant. It was his money and wife, after all.

Arriving at Groot Constantia, I was struck by the changes in the place. It had always been a government-run experimental wine farm, where, at one time, you could only buy wine on Wednesday afternoons or Saturday mornings. Now it had become totally commercial with a visitor centre, restaurant and a gift shop. After the obligatory wine tasting, Dave and I went to the shop. He was immediately interested in the 800ml wine glasses. They hold a bottle of wine each! A perfect gift; one for him and one for his dad!

We were back to discussing whether he would get them home in one piece but again he wouldn't be swayed. I had my doubts but he did get both the glasses and the shell home unbroken which I think was remarkable.

I bought a souvenir corkscrew, the type known as a waiter's friend. It certainly was my friend as I threw it out only in 2007 as the corkscrew part had become uncoiled. It had opened a lot of wine bottles!

On the Monday, we had the last of our scheduled demos and we were both booked to fly home on the Tuesday afternoon/night. Then Paul got a call from De Beers Marine saying that they wanted to trial the Trackpoint on their own vessel later that week.

The Monday after was Christmas Day and I had no intention of spending it away from my family. So we timetabled Wednesday as the preparation day and Thursday as the trial. Dave flew home on time while I phoned GY and got them to change my ticket. I got booked out on the Friday night.

Off we went to the De Beers Marine quayside on the Wednesday morning to oversee the mounting of the hydrophone on a pole which was going to go down a moonpool. It doesn't sound much but most of the day was taken up with hole drilling, bolt sourcing, cable running and power checks. But we got it done. De Beers had built their own tow body which they used for underwater mapping but they had no idea where it was in relationship to the towing vessel. That was what they hoped Trackpoint would solve.

I must admit to being a bit nervous as we cast off. I knew some of these guys from my Anglo days and I didn't want to look a fool in front of them. They had seen the demo on the 'gin palace' but this was for real. The trip was out into Table Bay and the views were spectacularly beautiful. I could have stared at them all day but I had other things on my mind. We had fitted a beacon to the towfish and as soon as it hit the water, the Trackpoint picked it up so my first worries were over.

The system had a few different screens and I could navigate around the menus fairly expertly. I'd been doing this for nearly two years so it was almost second nature. From one screen it was clear that the towfish was stable and was following directly behind the boat.

The trial had one other purpose. It was to check that the data coming out of Trackpoint would interface with the De Beers software programmes. This would allow the operators not only to see the relationship between the boat and the tow body but also to locate it in a geographical co-ordinate system.

Another of the screens I could bring up showed a list of the X, Y and Z positions of the towfish relative to the hydrophone and these were the measurements that were being fed into the De Beers package.

I could see instantly that while the X and Y measurements were fairly stable, as in the previous screen, the Z component was all over the place. It's difficult, from a column of numbers, to visualise what's actually happening but I soon realised that the towfish was undulating up and down in the water in a wave-like motion.

I broke the awkward silence that had fallen in the room by saying, "Do you guys know that your fish is moving up and down in the water column?" All of a sudden everyone was talking. They had suspected this for a while from their sonar records but had had no proof. Here it was in front of their faces. What a relieved bunch of guys I had all around me. It was a really great feeling.

Believe it or not, I now had another problem. De Beers didn't want to let the system off the boat. It worked so they wanted to keep it. That wasn't the way things were done but they were insistent.

I had to get on the ship's radio and talk to GY. It was decided that De Beers could hire the kit on board on condition that they placed a purchase order within a week for a new system and the two systems would be exchanged when the new kit arrived. That made everybody happy.

So I was a happy chappy when I got on the plane for home. It had been a successful trip, I'd met up with some old friends and I'd been back to Cape Town. I was even happy after the overnight flight came into land at Heathrow. A film had shown the new procedure for being able to drop your luggage at Terminal 4 after clearing customs and you would next see it after your connecting flight landed, in my case in Glasgow. Great, I thought, I don't need to lug these cases around.

Clearing customs and passport control was a nightmare. It seemed that everybody in the world had just landed and was trying to get into Britain. It was 6.30 in the morning and I'm not my best at that time. So I got out into the arrivals hall to find that the baggage drop wasn't working. Another notch on the temper meter racked up. I then had to drag my bags onto a bus in the freezing cold wind and rain and sit on it for over twenty minutes while it drove to Terminal 1 from where my flight to Glasgow left. I could hardly get into the building, there were so many people trying to get on flights. It had to be the busiest day of the year and it wasn't 8 o'clock yet.

After I'd fought my way through to the shuttle desk, I found that there were only two manned check-ins. The other four were idle. We were forced into a queue like you get in a bank and the exasperation quotient was reaching boiling point. I vowed there and then that I would fly any long distance flight through Amsterdam after this. Eventually I checked-in and the staff didn't seem to think anything was amiss. Everybody then had to go through a couple of security checks. This was the time of the Troubles in Northern Ireland and, at last, I made the sanctuary of the lounge where I could get a cup of tea and a newspaper. As I sat down, a middle-aged lady with a clipboard approached me saying, "We're doing a survey of customer satisfaction with Heathrow. Could I ask you a few questions?" Sometimes fortune smiles on you. It was a very chastened researcher who left me about ten minutes later. I enjoyed getting it all off my chest!

About a month after getting back from South Africa, it was clear that Ferranti ORE had not escaped the fallout from the Guerin fraud. As a successful part of the main Ferranti Group, we were not going to be closed down or suffer a slow death like the Infographics business in Livingston but we were up for sale.

The management group in GY had put a proposal together which would have meant that the structure would have basically stayed the same but there was a counter-proposal from the old MD, Dave Stone, which would mean that the company would be cut back to the GY facility.

Obviously, I wanted the present management team to succeed as otherwise I was facing redundancy. As the process progressed, Richard called to tell me that I had to get to GY on a certain date. From the tone of his voice, I could tell that the news was not good. So I flew down and we were told the bad news. Dave Stone's offer had been accepted and Ferranti ORE was no more but would reappear as GeoAcoustics.

As the 'satellite' offices were no longer required as costs were to be cut, I was handed a redundancy package which, I admit, was reasonable but nothing actually helps when you lose a job, especially one that had been so much fun. Of course I'd worked hard and had learned a lot about the offshore industry but the two years had flown by.

Dave Hampshire was in the same boat and we talked about doing something together but nothing ever materialised. Because of the redundancy money I had no immediate need to find another job but I had no intention of sitting around. Luckily for me the next Brighton 'Oceanology' show was just around the corner and it would be the perfect opportunity to circulate my CV and 'network' with potential employers.

Before that though, I had the chance to spend a bit more time with my family. Both Kirsty and Gordon were in the local primary school and Alison was now in Airdrie Academy. She started to play the flute which she continued throughout her school career. Dorothy was keeping the house together but she was glad to both have me home for a while and to be close to her, now retired, parents who lived in Coatbridge.

Dave and I had arranged that we would attend the Oceanology show together and go round the stands to see if anyone was hiring. Everybody that we talked to told us that we had the best chance of finding new jobs there, or at least starting the process.

We both had a number of people to speak to and we were getting nothing but encouragement. Dave was eventually to get a job in the Racal organization and I was offered a position as a salesman in a company based in Aberdeen called Positioning Resources Ltd (PRL).

In hindsight, I should have looked a bit longer but my excuse is that I was unemployed and I jumped at the first offer which came along. The job was only to last six months but I learnt a great deal about GPS and its ramifications during that time. I think that was the only saving grace.

The company was run by two guys – Colin Pike (P) and George Ritchie (R) – whose business relationship was heading towards the rocks but I didn't know anything about that until I was caught up in it a few months later.

George was a car fanatic which meant that I was to find myself with him at the car auctions near Edinburgh Airport to find me a company car. Large companies usually give all their guys the same car and there are certain cars which appeal to those fleets – the Ford Mondeo comes to mind.

The outcome was that I drove away in a beautiful Rover 820 in British racing green. Both my wife and I loved that car and it ranks as probably the best company car I've ever had.

Another 'tool' I was given was a mobile phone. You must remember that this was in the early nineties so the phone was not one you could slip into your breast pocket. This was a brick with a cord-attached handset and one you couldn't carry around for any length of time. In fact it only left the car when either I got home or to my hotel.

To give PRL their due, they did send me on a couple of courses which stood me in good stead in jobs and years to come. The Global Positioning System (GPS) was a closed book to me and was in its infancy both on and off shore. PRL was involved in rig moves throughout the North Sea and also were reps for Magellan GPS who produced the first handheld personal GPS unit and this was the unit I was tasked to sell.

The first course was down near Jodrell Bank, south of Manchester, where GPS was one of the satellite-based surveying techniques discussed. Not everybody was convinced that GPS would take over as completely as it has done.

The second one was at the University of Nottingham and was run by one of the early doyens of GPS research, Prof Ashkenazi. That three day course has been the basis of my GPS knowledge through the years.

So, inexorably, the day that I knew was coming eventually arrived when PRL and I parted company. It was done with tact although I didn't enjoy the feeling of being sacked. Little was I to know that I wasn't the only oil employee feeling like that as the industry went into a slump.

So I entered the longest period of unemployment that I have ever suffered, nearly eighteen months. In one thing I was fortunate. I had an insurance policy that would pay my monthly mortgage for 24 months. This meant that I had no need to grab a menial, relatively low paid job to get by. In fact, the terms of the policy forbade any such job as I needed a monthly stamp from the Unemployment Office confirming that I was still unemployed. I suppose I could have become one of the 'black economy' and worked for cash in hand but that was somehow repugnant and I would surely have been found out.

Dorothy went back to working, firstly for an agency and then fulltime for a printing supplies company. She enjoyed the work and the money that she made so much that she stayed there even after I went back to work. She didn't earn nearly the same as what I had been earning but we kept things afloat.

The Unemployment Office was never really going to be of any great use but they did have a scheme where the long term unemployed (and I qualified after six months) could go to a separate office and use facilities such as phones, faxes, newspapers and the jobs database. It was something to get me out of a rut and I went willingly. In fact, it was from there that I got my next job but more of that later.

I met people of all sorts from all over the town. Some I even helped write out application forms and letters. One chap was convinced that the letter he wrote under my direction got him a delivery driver's job. It may have helped but he got it on his own. Anyway he brought me some cakes (he was now working for Dalzeil's – the local bakers) as a 'thank you' which I took home to the family. I had stopped eating cakes and I'll tell you why later.

We saw a lot of different people in the 'office'. Some got lucky and were there only a short time but it perked everybody up when someone got a job. Some were there for the long haul and some were just playing. We had one young lad who just didn't realise that he was going nowhere fast. He'd come in hung-over, he wouldn't put the hard hours in writing letters, scanning newspapers and filling out application forms. All he wanted to do (if Celtic wouldn't have him – yes he did write to them!!) was to play pool and hustle punters. He was still, nominally, there when I left but I never heard of him as a pool player. Perhaps he went the way of all hustlers and met his match or hustled the wrong guy like Paul Newman did in the film of that name.

It was my (mis)fortune to be in the company of some characters, although I'll tell of only one more. This man was a nice enough chap but his language was atrocious. I kid you not but every second word was a curse and his favourite word was one of the versions of "Fuck". I was astounded at first, and I've heard a few swearwords in my time, but gradually became immune. In fact, even now, that word has little or no effect on me. It certainly doesn't shock me.

I had written umpteen letters, filled out numerous application forms and made innumerable phone calls but to no avail. I must say that Dorothy was never one to grumble about me not working but I could see she was worried.

Then one morning, the phone in the office rang and it was for me. An agency in Aberdeen had an interview lined up for me with a large company in the town. Could I get to Aberdeen for it? I was ready to go that afternoon! In the end, the interview was in a few days and I had plenty of time. The company was Marconi UDI in Bridge of Don and after one interview I was hired as a salesman promoting their in-house designed and manufactured underwater sonar.

So I was off to Aberdeen again but I must tell you of a couple of other things that happened during my unemployment period.

Dorothy and I have always had a very healthy marriage. Lovemaking was high on the agenda and I'm convinced that sex is the glue that binds any marriage. If that's OK, everything else falls into place.

This sort of crept up but I became aware that my foreskin was painful. At first it wasn't too bad but it gradually worsened. I went to the doctor who called it some condition with an unpronounceable name and gave me some cream. That worked for a while but the symptoms returned. Back to the doctor who told me the only cure was a circumcision! That took the wind out of my sails. I could be fitted in about two weeks later. Would that do? I was unemployed so the timing was no problem. It was just getting my head round a circumcision!!! The doctor assured me that this would cure my problem so I agreed.

When I told Dorothy, I was surprised she took it so calmly. It was going to be an overnight stay in the hospital and a few weeks of rest and recuperation.

The day I was due in came around very quickly so into hospital I went for the one and only time in my life. I'd been in Outpatients before but had never spent the night.

A very kind junior lady doctor was the first to come and see me. She asked if I knew what I was in for (in all meanings!) and then got me to sign the consent form. She then gave me another one which was so they could take some bone marrow from my hip to include in some leukemia research. She said that it would be painful afterwards but, to be truthful, it never was.

One funny moment happened when they staff gave the gown that I was supposed to wear during the op. It was so small it wouldn't have fitted around my leg so I had to call them back. That was the last time I laughed during my stay.

Then it was time to be wheeled to theatre where I met the surgeon for the first time. As we had a chat, someone filled me full of anaesthetic and the next thing I knew I was being bundled back into my bed, with an oxygen mask over my face. I was told to go back to sleep and doctor would be round to see me later.

So I flitted in and out of sleep for a couple of hours, never quite sure if I could discard the oxygen or not. The surgeon came and inspected my wound, declared himself pleased and I never saw him again. I must have been full of painkillers as I didn't feel any pain in my most delicate place. I'd also been left a supply next to my bed as if the dose I'd had would wear off. After a few hours I was wide awake still feeling no pain and reading the book I'd remembered to bring when one of the nurses asked if I'd been to the toilet. I hadn't but I was told to let them know when I did. I didn't know that operations often delay urination and sometimes catheters need to be used. As the nurse was leaving she told me that they'd found elevated sugar in the earlier urine sample they'd taken. That was the least of my worries.

Around about midnight, I was still awake reading. Well, I'd been asleep (induced) most of the day when I realised that I would have to use the toilet. Nothing, but nothing, prepared me for that experience. When the acid of the urine hit the wound, I nearly hit the ceiling! I have never felt pain like that and I never want to again. Of course the staff all knew that was in store for me so I had to get it over with. As the days went on, the pain gradually got less and less until my toilet functions no longer had me screaming.

I've never been embarrassed by my body. I'm no Adonis and I don't tan well but the bits that make me up are all natural. So it didn't bother me in the least when the nurse took me into the bathroom so I could soak off the operation bandages and she could put a new dressing on. She did, however remark that some of her younger nurses would run a mile if that had been on their agendas!

So I went back home and start the recuperation. I had to wear loose trousers (tracksuit bottoms were ideal) and make sure I didn't drop anything on my lap.

Apart from Dorothy and the kids, the only person I told about my op was my Mum, who blithely told me about the mass circumcision that the Israelites underwent which is chronicled in the book of Joshua. Well, if anyone is interested in drawing timelines through the Bible, they can take it that the Israelites rested for a month before being able to move as that's how long it took me to recover.

During that month, I had to visit the doctor even although the district nurse came by to check on my supply of painkillers and bandages. I'm not brave enough to have gone through those days without any help from analgesics.

So there I was sitting in the doctor's surgery, discussing how I was recovering when he dropped a bombshell. He told me that it looked like I was suffering from diabetes. I had to go and take a test in the hospital when I was well enough. I really didn't need this. I took the test (drink a bottle of Lucozade and get urine and blood samples taken every 30 minutes for 3 hours) to be told that I was borderline diabetic but the only treatment required for the time being was to watch my diet.

I was devastated. I thought it was a death sentence. I suppose being unemployed, just having undergone surgery and then being told this was just too much. When I told Dorothy, she just told me to never mind and just to get back to looking for a job. Trust her to get things in perspective.

The NHS is very good with diabetics. I watched some instructional videos and thought it was great that I wouldn't need to inject myself (Huh!). Diabetics also get free prescriptions for life so that was a boon. As time has gone by my condition has steadily worsened and I've graduated to tablets and finally insulin. However, I've never let it rule my life. I watch my blood sugar and my diet and even although it is a chronic (incurable and lifelong) condition it hasn't stopped me living my life. Insulin injections are just like brushing my teeth and the only inconvenience is making sure I have all the medicine I need when I go somewhere.

Marconi UDI was an underwater survey company heavily involved in the North Sea oil industry. Situated in its own warehouse and offices in Bridge of Don, it had a very good reputation in the industry.

Apart from supplying offshore survey services from boats, it ran its own DGPS correction service and supplied offshore cameras and sonars. UDI had made sonars for both the oil and military markets for many years and the in-house engineering team was always trying to improve the technology. They had come up with the new Sonavision 4000 imaging sonar which used new techniques and ceramic technology to give greater accuracy and more detailed imagery.

My job was to try and sell this to the water industry around the UK. This was to include port, harbours and water boards. Needless to say this was going to involve a lot of traveling. The job got me back into the industry and I was able to re-acquaint myself with some old friends.

I had one major problem, though. The company was expecting me to relocate to Aberdeen but there was a housing slump and we had been caught by unemployment before while trying to move while I was with PRL. The fallout from that was still going on.

However, one of the guys, John Pears, in the UDI office offered me a room in an old farmhouse he shared with another 3 guys, all of whom worked offshore. It was a farm called Butterywells in the area of Banchory-Devonich, which lay just south of the River Dee and was about 3-4 miles outside Aberdeen itself.

The lads rented the house so it wasn't in the best of repair. It was cold in winter as it had no central heating or double glazing but was fairly pleasant in the summer. Because I was only there through the week, I got the box room which was OK for me. It was the other lads' base so they were entitled to have bigger rooms. So I settled into a routine of going up to Aberdeen on a Sunday night, working all week and then going back home to Glenmavis on a Friday evening. Then again I spent some considerable time visiting potential clients and I would try and time these visits so that I would leave from home on the Monday and arrive home whatever else on the Friday.

It was fun but a little strange sharing a house with lads young enough to be my sons. The only people I'd ever shared a house with before were my family either when I was growing up or after I was married. The guys worked for different companies so all had different rosters. So the house was either full or empty. It was a bit creepy when you were there alone but it was chaos when everybody was around.

John fancied himself as a bit of a cook so he was always trying out new recipes. Some worked, others didn't. I arrived back one Sunday night and walked into the kitchen by the back door. We hardly ever used the front one. It was like walking into a wall of garlic. He'd tried a "Floyd" recipe where a chicken was roasted with a kilogram (!!) of garlic. It took days for the reek to dissipate!

Like all young guys they drank a lot of beer and the bills were getting slightly ridiculous so it was decided that we would take turns at brewing our own using the store bought kits. Little was I to know how I'd use this skill later. Well, it was something to do during the long evenings.

The other thing the lads were into was 'pot'. No, I've never tried it. I've never seen the point. However the lads used quite a lot and even had a wild plant growing in the garden. They must have thrown some away and it sprouted. I must admit that it didn't seem to any lasting or prolonged effect on them. However, there was one evening when one of their girlfriends (they kept changing and I could never keep up) was sitting in the kitchen looking rather distressed as she had run out and needed to buy more supplies. She was as nervous as a kitten and kept asking for one of the lads who would take her down to meet the supplier. At least she wasn't stupid enough to go by herself. Normally she was a happy laughing girl but that night she was haggard, strung-out and extremely tense. I only hope it was dope she was after and nothing stronger. Have you ever wondered why it's called 'dope'? I'll leave you to ponder that one yourselves.

UDI was run by Jim Couser and Graeme Kidd and nobody really liked them. The company was part of the large Marconi conglomerate and a lot of the problems were caused by Marconi not understanding how the oil industry worked. That stemmed from the fact that Marconi was a defence contracting firm in the main. Jim and Graeme however had to follow the procedures laid down from above.

One example of this was the attitude to weekends. At UDI we had technical staff who worked a Saturday roster and even some who would be in on Sundays. Our HQ in Waterlooville in Hampshire didn't understand why and wanted to stop the practice altogether. (It was well known that you couldn't find any one in the office at HQ after 4.30 on a Friday afternoon.) It never crossed their minds that the oil industry is 24/7/365 and if a part has to be on a helipad at 0600hrs on a Sunday morning, it had better be there then, not on the Monday morning. They were basically told to go away and stop bothering us.

It was a good experience being part of a large organization again. Apart from the work support, there were plenty of social activities such as golf days, barbeques, Christmas lunches and general getogethers in the pub.

The sales team I was in was headed by Bill Austin who was an enthusiastic fisherman and Guthrie Robertson who had been with UDI almost since its inception. Bill came from the north of England and was almost as new to UDI as I was and he was having a few run-ins with Jim and Graeme. It was to his credit that he kept a lot of it away from Guthrie and me so that we could get on with things.

Guthrie, on the other hand, was a local boy and he taught me a great deal about Aberdeen and the way the local oil industry worked behind the scenes. As he was almost 'in with the bricks' at UDI he had a lot of opinions on the direction the company was headed and he wasn't slow in letting those opinions be known. Very level headed and full of common sense, I learnt a lot from him.

Apart from running around the country visiting clients, I also had to man stands at exhibitions including a couple of times in Stavanger, Norway at Offshore Northern Seas. My Viking heritage was confirmed as the locals usually started talking to me in Norwegian as they took me for one of their own.

One of my more memorable visits to a client was to the port authority of Barrow-in-Furness. They looked after the locks and docks for the atomic submarines which were built and maintained there. We thought that they would be a potential client for the sonar as they would want to know if there were any obstructions. In the end they didn't buy any units but I did get to see my first Trident submarine. They are huge! There are films about them cruising about on the surface but nothing to give you the scale of the boat. I must admit that they are pretty impressive.

Another memorable visit was to Hartlepool where I was to demo the sonar on a boat out of the new marina there. Hartlepool is an old industrial port and has been rundown for many a year. The marina and the accompanying shopping centre have tried to turn that around. I was absolutely starving when I got off the boat and the only place to get some reasonable food was in one of the pubs in the centre of town. That was where I tried the local brew, Cameron's Ruby Red Bitter, which is one of the best beers I've ever tasted. It doesn't 'travel' very well so you can find it only in the surrounding district.

For those of you who don't know, the nickname of people from Hartlepool (including the football club) is the "Monkey Hangers". I'm now going to tell you why. During the Napoleonic Wars a French Man-O-War was wrecked off the Hartlepool coast. All the crew was drowned but there was one survivor, the captain's pet monkey. The locals had never seen a Frenchman (no 24 hour war reporting in these days) and they assumed that the monkey was a Frenchman and he was speaking French. So they hanged the monkey. Thus if you ever see a pub called the Noose and Monkey or a variant on that, you can be sure that the owner is from Hartlepool.

Another funny story about Hartlepool concerns Peter Mandelson, the MP for the area for a while in Tony Blair's Labour government. Mr. Mandelson was visiting some of the local businesses and stopped in a Fish and Chip shop to have a fish supper. When he was ordering his supper, he pointed at the mushy peas and asked the server if he could have 'some of that guacamole (!) '.

Dorothy was working in a company of printing supplies. One of the problems with any small company is getting paid. It so happened that the company had sent some supplies to a customer in Aberdeen and hadn't been paid even after several reminders. As I was away in Aberdeen during the week, I tried to slip away in the late Friday afternoon so I could get home to spend some extra time with the family. When Dorothy told me the story about the debtor, I volunteered to see what I could do. The following Friday was a really hot (for Aberdeen) sunny day. Hence I was wearing my sunglasses as I pulled up at the shop. I'm a big guy and I had to stoop to get through the door which wasn't very wide either so my bulk dramatically blocked out a great deal of the sunlight streaming into the premises. The owner looked up to see this big guy with sunglasses on in his doorway. When I told him I was there about his unpaid bill, he paled and started to stutter and stammer. Dorothy had told me that if I couldn't get the money, then I could see if I could take goods *in lieu*. So while the owner spluttered, I cast my eyes over his shelves. Try to imagine the sight the owner was seeing. Here was this big guy asking him to pay his debts, blocking his doorway, wearing sunglasses with his sleeves rolled up and looking around the shop as if he might take it into his mind to destroy the shelves. The shop was isolated so he couldn't shout for help. After blurting out that he had cashed up for the week and taken his takings to the bank, I asked him that perhaps he had the money in the till. Would I sign a receipt? Of course, I would. So then I walked off with the payment. And that's the only time I've ever acted as a debt collector. Dorothy and her whole office couldn't believe that I'd actually got the cash. When I told her the full story, she couldn't stop laughing.

UDI were trying to attain a quality control certificate know as ISO9001 which would help a great deal in securing contracts but meant that the staff had to re-learn a lot of procedures that seemed to us pretty pointless. However, we had to comply otherwise the whole effort would have been in vain.

On top of that, there was a rumour flying about that there was a takeover in the offing. Aberdeen lives on rumours so some people dismissed this one out of hand. We were more astounded when Jim Couser announced, about 2 months after UDI got the ISO9001 accreditation that he was leaving as he'd had enough of the oil industry.

Again the rumours started to fly around but I was more concerned when the factor for Butterywells turned up one day to tell us that the house was being sold and we had a month to move out. This was a bit of a blow as we all now had to find other accommodation. A couple of the lads decided that it was time to buy a place while one lad said that he was going to take some time off to travel. I, of course, didn't have those choices and had to look around for some other place to rent. I had no illusions that I would find somewhere as cheap as Butterywells but I got somewhat lucky as one of the young surveyors, Ron Dickie, in UDI had recently bought a flat and needed a lodger to help him with the mortgage. So I approached him and there I was in a much more convenient mid-town location.

Then came the day when the rumours were confirmed. We were the subject of a takeover from the Dutch company Fugro who were in the midst of buying up any small survey company around the world. UDI wasn't small but Marconi probably wanted rid of us so we didn't have any corporate back-up, we weren't huge and Fugro could probably afford us. By this time, Graeme Kidd was in charge and he reassured us that if the company was sold, there would be no job cuts.

Let me say that it's no fun working in a company that is up for sale because that's all people talk about. I'd experienced it with Ferranti ORE if only on the periphery and there was a nasty surprise at the end of that, so I took the company line with a pinch of salt. One of the worst things is the waiting. It took 5-6 months before the deal was actually struck and it's very difficult to dredge up much enthusiasm during that wait. About the only thing that does flourish is several forms of gallows humour.

So the day dawned finally when we were going to be told our fate. The deal had been done and we all gathered in the canteen to hear from our new owners. Again reassurances were made and we drifted back to our offices. About fifteen minutes later, I was summoned to Graeme Kidd's office and, as I sat down, he wordlessly pushed a brown envelope across the desk to me. I didn't need to be a brain surgeon to know what it indicated. There I was redundant again. The reason was that the sales force was being cut back and I was the first to go. I should have asked about all the reassurances regarding jobs but I wasn't in the mood. Kidd also asked me to clear my desk and leave immediately but I protested that that was impossible to do before end of business. I would do it in the morning. Kidd agreed but that didn't stop him earning the nickname of 'Rottweiler' from me, a name that stuck, at least in some people's heads.

So a couple of days later, after a farewell drink with work mates, I moved out of the flat and went back down to Glenmavis. Poor Ron was offshore so I had to leave him a note explaining what had happened.

14

Saudi Arabia (Part 1)

There I was unemployed again. The financial settlement was reasonable so immediate worries were calmed. In the past, I had been worried about where I was going to get a job but for some reason, I was relatively unconcerned this time.

It's amazing how much you can find to do in the immediate aftermath of redundancy. There the signing on at the Unemployment Office and, because Dorothy was working part-time, I fed and watered the children when they came home from school plus all the things that needed doing around the house.

About a fortnight had gone past when the phone rang. On the other end was the personnel manager, Beverley, from UDI giving me a phone number to call. She explained that the number was for some recruitment company who had called UDI looking for me but company rules did not allow her to give out my number even although I was no longer employed there. She had promised that she would pass on their number to me and I could make contact if I wanted to.

I've found that you must never assume what people will do or think. I could easily have dismissed the whole thing as a 'wind-up' and thrown the number in the bin. However, that was for the guy on the other end to show whether it was or not. So I called.

As luck would have it, there was a company looking for someone who knew something about GPS and had experience of Ferranti ORE/GeoAcoustics equipment. I must admit that I fitted that bill fairly well. There was only one surprising element in all this – the company was in Saudi Arabia!

We ascertained that I was interested so the agent went away to sort out interviews and the like. However, I've also been of the opinion that chickens are not for counting before hatching. There was an exhibition in Aberdeen (Offshore Europe) where I could hand out my CV to potentially interested companies. So while the agent was busy, I headed off to Aberdeen. I still had some friends in UDI and one of them, Mark Murphy, had offered me a bed for the night if I was going to be up for OE.

I wandered round the show and dropped off some CVs but I could see that there wasn't much enthusiasm from the receivers. Then, on the second day, I heard a rumour that a company called TSS (based near Oxford) was recruiting so off I went to their stand to talk to their Sales Manager, Charlie Foll, to confirm the rumour and hand over my CV. Charlie seemed interested enough and promised that he would let me know. I had done what I could do so I went back home feeling pretty confident.

Then came the waiting. There is a fine balancing act to be performed when in such a situation. I never had any compunction in phoning a recruitment agency every two days or so but that certainly is not the thing to do on a direct line to company personnel like Charlie. However, it was OK to phone every week or so.

Two or three weeks went by before I got two calls. One was to say that the boss of the Saudi company would be in London the next week and would be able to see me on the Thursday which was followed a few hours later by one from Charlie Foll asking me to come for an interview the following Friday. Things had fallen into place and all I had to do was make sure that I got one of the jobs.

The interview with the Saudi owner was to be held in the Grosvenor Hotel, just off Hyde Park, where he was staying. Rich Arabs like staying there as it is owned by the Sultan of Brunei who is also a Muslim.

So I flew down to London, stayed with my brother and met up with the agent who gave some more background to the company. Off I trotted to the hotel for my 11 o'clock interview to be told by the reception desk that Mr. Al Misehal had left instructions not to be disturbed. This threw me a bit but it was my introduction to the different Arab attitude to time and timekeeping.

I phoned the agent who told me to come back to his office and we'd wait there for instructions. In the end, I did get to meet Adil in the middle of the afternoon where it was fairly obvious that he had been partying the night before and his heart wasn't really in it. After a few perfunctory questions, he told me that his GM, would phone me on Saturday to interview me further.

I was a bit confused as I went away not really knowing where I stood. Anyway, I had to get my head ready to meet Charlie Foll the next day.

The TSS offices were in Weston-on-the-Green just off the M40 near Oxford. A few years later, there was another famous inhabitant, Tim Henman. Being in the countryside, it was a totally different experience being interviewed in an industrial unit from the Grosvenor Hotel. At the end of the afternoon, I thought I had had a pretty reasonable interview so I drove away pretty happy with myself.

Back home that night, I suddenly had a thought. I hadn't established what time the call from Saudi would be. Saudi Arabia is three hours ahead of GMT (two hours ahead of BST) so I thought that I would have to forego any thought of a long lie and get up pretty early (for a Saturday morning) and wait for the GM to call.

Hanging around waiting is probably the least favourite way of passing time, I find, especially when you can't move very far from a telephone.

So it was after midday when the phone eventually rang, roundabout the end of business in Saudi. It was rather strange as Glenn Pearson, the GM, kept telling me all the duties I would be responsible for and never really asked me any questions. When I came off the phone, it was to tell Dorothy that I thought I had the job.

On the Monday morning the agent called to ask how things had gone. When I brought him up to date, he promised to get in touch with the Saudi end and move things along.

About a week later, I received a draft contract and suddenly it became obvious that I had got the job. Dorothy and I had to talk about the prospects. I wasn't uncomfortable in going to Saudi but Dorothy wondered if working for TSS would be better. That seemed a good idea so I called Charlie Foll and asked him what my chances were. When he told me that TSS weren't going to be making any decisions until the New Year (this was in October), I had to tell him that I was going to accept another position as I couldn't wait that long.

So I signed the contract and I was off on another adventure.

Firstly I had to get a work visa which meant I had to travel to Harley Street in London for a medical. Seemed to me a waste of an air ticket but the Saudi Embassy recognised the Harley Street clinics only. When all that was going on I also went off to Great Yarmouth to see GeoAcoustics as they had just sold a unit to Saudi Aramco through Almisehal and then to Hook in

Hampshire to see Trimble Navigation who were the main company that Almisehal represented. We were in the midst of delivering over 1200 GPS units to the Saudi Arabian National Guard (SANG).

In Hook I met up with Bob Lee, from Edinburgh, who was also joining Almisehal as the Technical Manager. Bob had been out to Saudi before as part of the British Aerospace Al Yamamah project so was able to fill me in on some things I could expect.

Eventually I had my visa and air ticket and I was off to the Middle East.

Ah, Saudi Arabia! For those who've never been there, it's from a different planet. Unlike most countries, it is defined mostly by what is forbidden rather than what is allowed. Everybody has heard of the country's oil reserves but there is a lot more to the place than that.

So what is forbidden?

Alcohol, even though it is a word derived from Arabic, is forbidden in all its forms which gives medical staff and high class chefs problems.

Driving, if you're a woman, is not allowed. Saudi is the ONLY country in the world not to allow women to drive. Hence there is a whole employment class of 'Driver' who can be anything from taxi drivers to chauffeurs.

Pork is banned which means that one of the great breakfasts of 'bacon butties' with HP sauce is off the menu. You can buy a substitute of 'beef bacon' but it's not the same.

There is NO social mixing of the genders in the society. This extends even to weddings where the only man and woman to actually meet (sometimes for the first time) are the bride and groom. There are two receptions which are separate 'stag' and 'hen' events and it is not unusual for them to be held on different days.

All of the above derives from the fact that Saudi Arabia society is totally Islamic. Everything that goes on is tested against the template of whether it is Islamic or non-Islamic. This is all pervasive and governs all aspects of life. As the place where Islam started and the site of its two holiest sites, Mecca and Medina, it is not really surprising that it is controlled by the tenets of Islam. So that will run through all of what follows.

So, do people mange to get around the restrictions? Some people do manage to get bacon into the country, usually for their own consumption, especially in the Eastern Province where people go over to Bahrain and bring it home in their cars. However the driving ban on women is, to all intents and purposes, total.

Social mixing is another matter. The Saudis decided a long time ago that the ex-pat western workers would be housed in compounds. These are of all sizes and are usually very comfortable. They are surrounded by high walls and have gates manned by security personnel belonging to the compound. Inside is a little bit of western life. So there are parties and social getogethers where you wouldn't know you were in Saudi Arabia. Women dress normally and don't need to wear the all-encompassing black *abaya*, which they are required to wear outside the compounds.

I would expect that many people have heard of the Islamic prayer call which happens five times a day. In truth, only four impinge on a daily life. And there are actually six prayers. The time of the prayers vary against the clock as they are determined by the place of the Sun in the sky. The earliest is one and a half hours before sunrise, which implies that the ancients must have had a great understanding of the solar day. After all they were predicting when the Sun would rise. The second prayer (which is never called) is at dawn. The next is at local noon, followed by the mid-afternoon prayer when the Sun is halfway to the horizon. The last two prayers are at sundown and then an hour and a half later. Everything closes at prayer, shops, petrol stations, restaurants and some offices. All this means that it is necessary to print the local times of these prayers in the papers to give people some help. There are additions to these times during the month of Ramadan and Friday prayers (with sermons) last longer than on other days. One of my pet complaints is that although the times of the beginning of the prayers are known, no-one seems to know when they finish.

I have a theory of how the times were decided and it all comes from the days of the camel caravans. This may get me into trouble but what the heck. The caravanners would break their camp in the hour and a half before dawn and would be sitting on their camels waiting for the dawn light. They would then stop when the Sun was overhead and rest during the hottest part of the day i.e. the early hours of the afternoon. They would then travel along until dusk and their camp would be up and ready an hour and a half later.

This story may be apocryphal. A western businessman (Swedish in the version I was told) was in Saudi for some meetings and was staying in a hotel. Unfortunately for him, his room was right next to the local mosque. Nobody had warned so when the early morning prayer call went off, he got the shock of his life, jumped up and looked out the window to see what the commotion was. He saw a few people wander into the mosque, realised that there was nothing to worry about and when back to bed. When he got into the office later in the morning, he was asked if he slept well. He told the story and the locals guffawed as they explained about the prayer call. The incident was forgotten as the day went on but the next morning he was disturbed again. When he got to the office, he asked if this prayer call happened every day. When he was told that it did, he asked if the racket was actually necessary when only a few people attended. Couldn't the imam just telephone them?!!!!

Just to confuse things, although the prayers are determined by the position of the Sun, Saudi uses the lunar Hijra calendar. It runs alongside the 'normal' (Gregorian) calendar and, although day to day everybody uses the Gregorian calendar, anything official or governmental uses the Hijra calendar. The calendars differ by 11 days a year so the Islamic events, holidays and months get earlier by 11 days in the (Gregorian) calendar. In 2008, there were three Arabic years. Jan 1-6 was in 1428, the bulk of the year was 1429 and the last few days were in 1430.

Hijra means 'flight' in Arabic and the calendar started when the Prophet Mohammed was expelled from Makkah, as the Meccans didn't take kindly to being told what to do, and fled to Medina from where he began the religion we now know as Islam.

The ninth month of the Hijra year is Ramadan which is celebrated by fasting. It signifies the time that Muslims believe Mohammed spent receiving the Koran from the Archangel Gabriel and/or Allah (depending on the source).

During Ramadan, Muslims should refrain from eating, drinking, smoking or having sex during the daylight hours. Although this is a personal thing, in Saudi it controls everything. What the locals do is change the days round so that they sleep all day and party all night. That's an oversimplification but, believe me, it is strange going to the bank at 2 a.m. It is also an indisputable, ironic fact that during this month of fasting, most of the population gain weight. Working/school hours are reduced which had the consequence that all I remember from our first (and only) family Ramadan was early morning sex and plenty of it!

The one area of 'forbidden fruit' that is most commonly circumvented is around alcohol. There are no public bars, nightclubs or off licences in Saudi so where do people get their booze? They make it. Alcohol is not difficult to make if you have a rudimentary grasp of chemistry. Although alcoholic wine and beer are not allowed, all the necessary ingredients are available.

Let's take wine. Grape juice is available (even in wire topped bottles) as is sugar (in 25kg bags!), water and yeast. If you were shopping in the UK for yeast in Tesco or Asda, I'd bet that you'd be hard pressed to find any yeast at all. However there are whole sections given over to yeast in Saudi supermarkets. Perhaps the locals bake a lot of bread at home.

Beer is even simpler. 'Near beer' (non-alcoholic beer) mixed with sugar and yeast yields a very strong brew. If you then dilute the resultant concoction with near beer, it is very palatable.

There is one other alcoholic drink which is made locally. There are two versions, one called 'arak' which is made (from a date base) and consumed by non-westerners, and 'sid', a favourite tipple of the western ex-pats. 'Sid' is short for 'siddiqui' the Arabic for friend as that was its original code word. You would be invited to a barbeque or party and be asked to bring your 'friend' along. Sid is a spirit made from a simple mash of water, sugar (remember the 25kg bags) and yeast. It requires distilling (at least four times) and the initial quantity reduces by about 90%.

The 'cooking' process also produces an unmistakable aroma which has led to many an illicit still being discovered by the authorities. The outcome of all this is that nearly every ex-pat home has wine &/or beer bubbling away with the makers vying with each other as to who makes the best. So parties always have suitable lubrication.

On the other hand, Sid is usually made by one or two people to whom you are introduced after you have been suitably vetted. The spirit is sold neat which is cut 50-50 with water or in some other suitable ratio. Saying that there are/were some industrial scale stills but every now and again they get raided and the entire product destroyed.

There is one other aspect of alcohol in Saudi – "real stuff". This is mainly whisky, in reality "Johnny Walker Black Label" which is smuggled into the kingdom. There are rings which bring it in and they have obviously paid some people to turn a blind eye. Hence it is expensive and litre bottles sell for the equivalent of USD$150-300. It is said that there are top Saudis have a taste for Black Label and a commonly stated statistic is that Saudi is one of the top export markets for Johnny Walker! Other spirits such as rum, gin, vodka are also available but are much scarcer.

What all this has taught me is many sided.

One aspect is that the desire for alcohol is deep seated within the human race. Obviously there are people who react badly to it by becoming addicts or overly aggressive. But many people enjoy its social effects and like the way it makes them feel.

Secondly, even if it was banned everywhere, people wouldn't take a blind bit of notice. Remember Prohibition in the USA?

Thirdly, the Saudis are missing a fantastic way of raising taxes. That may be frivolous as they've got all that oil but it is a fact. Of course you wouldn't want anybody in Saudi drink driving as the driving is so bad that you would think that they must have been drinking anyway!

When I first went to Saudi (in 1993), the country was still very repressed. TV and radio were strictly controlled as was the press. You could get foreign magazines and papers but they had been censored to remove any 'Un-Islamic' content. Seemingly there warehouse of people going through every publication with a pair of scissors and a black marker pen. So you would buy a Weekly Telegraph with missing articles and pictures of women showing hair and bare arms blacked out.

The country was also still recovering from the after-effects of the 1st Gulf War. The US and Coalition Forces had been based in and around Dammam, Al Khobar and Dhahran Airbase. Stories of that time abound. I have a couple of favourites. One is that the old-age Saudi custom of not allowing women to drive came under serious threat. Not only were there women tank drivers and pilots in the coalition forces, the women who fled Kuwait as the Iraqis invaded also drove. Some Saudi women decided that they would drive through Riyadh. They were stopped and detained (notice that I didn't use 'arrested') and their "responsible male" was told to attend the police station. When they got there the women were turned over to them but before they left the men were told that if this (the women driving) happened again, the men would be serving time in prison!

Every woman in Saudi has a "responsible male" and that is her father, uncle, brother (older or younger) or husband. This injustice perpetuates Saudi society and is perhaps the main example of the 'backwardness' of the whole country.

The other story is an example of what happens when cultures collide. The incident happened just after Al Khobar had suffered a missile strike from the Iraqis so people were a bit skittish. One of the female US Marines was walking around the town. Dressed in long trousers and a T-shirt, she seemingly had her shirt sleeves rolled up to her shoulders. This is regarded in Saudi as almost being naked so a local Mutawah took it upon himself to berate her over this. However, as befits a religious fanatic, he didn't think ahead. The Mutawahs' usual opening gambit was to either poke or hit a woman with the ubiquitous short stick. They don't want to contaminate themselves by actually touching a woman. This particular Mutawah made a couple of mistakes. His first was to come up behind the Marine and the second was to use his stick to prod her. As I said everyone was a bit skittish and when she thought she was being attacked she let her training take over. As she turned round and hit him with a karate chop, he got the biggest, but unfortunately for him also the last, surprise of his life. He dropped to the ground, dead. The Marine was out of the country that night and the Mutawahs realised that these women were not the usual docile ones they normally dealt with.

I'd better explain what the Mutawah are. They are the religious police and they belong to the Commission for the Advancement of Virtue and the Elimination of Sin (CAVES). Sometimes the English transliteration is slightly different but I like the idea of them coming from CAVES as it fits. Their job is to make sure that no-one sins in Saudi Arabia. Unfortunately, sin has a much wider definition in Saudi than elsewhere. This leads to them interfering in everyday life. Ordinary Saudis have a dislike for them because of the interference and the ex-pats detest them. Known by some as the MB's (the B can stand for anything you like), they are best avoided or ignored.

The MB's are the front soldiers of the system of Islamic Sharia law which is the legal system in Saudi. It is NOT the fairest system in the World especially if you happen to be female or a non-Muslim. It still uses capital punishment for murder, rape and drug dealing. In fact the landing card one fills out when arriving in the country has "Death to Drug Trafficker" highlighted in red ink. These death sentences are carried out in public, usually after Friday prayers. All Saudi cities have a 'Chop Square' and no; I haven't been to a public execution. It is not my idea of fun.

The recovering from the first Gulf War and the after-effects were seen all over. Not only did Saudi have to pay the Americans for saving their country, there were still physical marks of the war that hadn't been cleared up.

One of my customers was the Arabian Oil Company (AOC) which was an anachronism left over from the establishment of the two countries of Saudi Arabia and Kuwait. In the beginning there was some confusion over where the border lay and, if this was a problem on land, it was much more at sea. So the Arabs came up with a compromise. Until these issues could be resolved, there would be a "Neutral Zone" (NZ) between them which would be jointly run. That would have been fine except that the NZ had both onshore and offshore oil deposits. So somehow Shell got the rights to exploit the onshore oil while the AOC was set up by both governments to exploit the offshore deposits. AOC was the one company which flew both nations' flags. A further twist was that the Japanese (!) also had a financial interest in AOC. In fact the company represented the only foreign source of oil that Japan 'controlled'. Japan's interests were such that the whole of the technical staff were Japanese who formed their own little ex-pat community.

AOC was headquartered in a town called Al Khafji, just south of the Saudi/Kuwait border, the only town on Saudi soil which was occupied by the Iraqi forces of Saddam Hussein. It was the occupation of that small town which scared the hell out of the Saudis and others because the vast Saudi oil fields were only a few hours drive away. When I first went there, the evidence for a fairly heavy battle was all around. Bullet marked walls and burned out windows were all along the main street but the biggest single trace of the battle was the water tower in the centre of town.

The water tower had been where a couple of Iraqi snipers had taken refuge and were wreaking havoc on the opposing ground forces. At the meeting of the coalition forces, the Saudis volunteered to take out the snipers. However, two days later when the snipers were still there, the Americans told the Saudi to step aside while they dealt with the situation. A couple of Blackhawk helicopter gunships left the tower smoking and the snipers dead. When I got there, the tower was no longer smoking or functioning but had a couple of holes that a double-decker bus could have driven through. It took the Saudis a few years to get round to fixing the town but if you go there now there is a new water tower and all the scars have been cleared up.

AOC is an oil company but it (along with nearly every other oil company) is dwarfed by the Saudi Arabian Oil Company, commonly known as Saudi Aramco, or just Aramco. The figures are staggering but suffice to say that Aramco controls at least 25% of the world's oil reserves. It is the basis of the Saudi economy and no-one works in the Eastern Province of the kingdom if they don't work for or with Aramco.

The Eastern Province oilfields are based around the three towns of Dammam, Al Khobar and Dhahran, all three of which used to be separate entities but now they are almost one large conglomeration. Dammam is nominally the administrative and government centre of the area while Al Khobar is where the main shopping centres and ex-pat compounds are. Dhahran consists of the airport/airbase, King Fahd University for Petroleum and Minerals (KFUPM) and the headquarters of Aramco. The Aramco HQ is not just the offices, etc., but also a medium sized town where the 'normal' writ of Saudi society doesn't run. Not only does Aramco have female secretaries, women can drive within the Aramco compound.

As vitally important to the ex-pats in the Eastern Province as the oilfields, is the small island Emirate/Kingdom of Bahrain. Up till 1984, the island could be reached only by ferry or infrequent flights but then the Causeway opened. Built by the Dutch firm of Ballast Needham, the causeway changed the way of life of the whole region. Suddenly Bahrain with its forbidden fruits of bars, nightclubs and general freedom was within easy reach. There was still the bureaucracy of the border (built on an artificial island halfway across) but that was just something which had to be borne. Depending on the day of the week and the time of day, you could be in Bahrain in about an hour or it could take you 4 hours. Somehow it always seemed less crowded coming back!

There is something else that is different about Saudi. It is extremely difficult to get into. There are no tourist visas (or weren't until fairly recently -2008- and then only under strict conditions) and business visas require a 'Letter of Invitation' from a Saudi firm and an involved application process. To get a work/residence visa is even more complex but, once you have it, life is so much simpler. However, even after that you have to get an Exit-Reentry visa stamped in your passport so that you can leave the kingdom. Each stamp lasts for six months but can be either for a single trip or multiple trips. So you need a visa to get OUT of the country! There are other visas for pilgrims but that never really bothered us. In the old days, you had to be at a certain level of importance to get a multiple and wives of the ex-pats got only a single shot visa. That's changed now and it seems every ex-pat has a multiple.

You might ask why does this happen. You must remember that there are literally millions of labourers and unskilled workers in the country. All of these go on holiday so they get a single run visa. While they are in kingdom, they don't get to go over to Bahrain to enjoy themselves, they have to stay in Saudi. It seems a bit excessive as their employers apply for the visas on their behalf and, in any case, all ex-pat passports are held by the employers with the employees carrying their Iqamas or ID books/cards. It's all about control.

I was the Sales Manager of the company which meant a lot of traveling and visiting clients. The company (Almisehal) was run by two brothers, Adil and Adnan, and a British GM, Glenn Pearson. Glenn did most of the day-to-day work but Adil was the entrepreneur and the driving force behind the company.

Almisehal was a company which represented overseas businesses in Saudi. Usually these were exclusive agreements which meant that we got a commission on any sale of the equipment whether we had sold it or not. This may be hard to believe but one enterprising Saudi businessman traveled to Japan where he negotiated such a deal with an unheard-of car company. He became the exclusive dealer for Toyota and died a very wealthy man.

Anyway, we were known as dealers in high-tech electronics and our main brand was Trimble GPS. There was one slight problem. GPS was actually illegal in Saudi at the time. We could sell it only to a government agency. For some reason, GPS was classified as a "radio" and came under the same strict regulations as UHF/VHF radios.

In reality, our biggest clients were Aramco and the National Guard (SANG). The Survey Dept. in Aramco was changing over to GPS and we supplied them with a lot of gear. Their first big job using it was laying out the route for the Saudi E-W Pipeline from Abqaiq to Yanbu on the Red Sea. They, of course, were interested mainly in the high end (expensive) surveying tools.

SANG, on the other hand, needed GPS navigation. Their preferred option was a piece of kit called the Trimpack which was rugged, easy to use and, most importantly, had an Arabic language display. It also showed the direction of Mecca from anywhere which was a great selling point.

In the end, SANG placed an order for 1200 Trimpacks along with a contract for installation in their Light Armoured Vehicles (LAVs). As our office was in Dammam and the SANG headquarters were in Riyadh, I got to know that highway pretty well.

Since I arrived in Saudi, I'd been constantly shocked at the standard of driving. It was (and still is) abysmal. This is as much true for the locals (and you can't blame women drivers in Saudi!) as for the many thousands of immigrant workers from mainly the Indian subcontinent. Perhaps that's not so surprising as I would reckon the last time they actually drove anything before arriving it was a herd of goats, sheep or cattle. Perhaps this isn't wholly accurate but I've experienced driving in India and it's much the same.

212

Anyway, I was so shocked that for the first few days I was in Dammam and being driven around, I shut my eyes most of the time.

One of the incidents which made me jump was while I was driving back from Riyadh on the highway. It was dark and the highway is a lonely place as habitation and lights are few and far between. I was well away from any civilisation when suddenly this car switched on its light and overtook me! It had been following me 'lights out' for I don't know how long (saving his battery!!!!) but he obviously thought I was going too slowly so decided to go on his way. I then knew what people meant when they said "jumped out of my skin"!

I spent my first three months 'on probation' to see if Almisehal liked me and I liked them. I was quite happy doing what I was doing (and Almisehal seemed happy too) so I started organising to get my family out to Saudi. The only real problem was that my three months ended just as Ramadan started so that put the whole thing back by over a month. I lived in one of the flats the company owned (the Tabaishi building) but I had found a great four bedroomed villa in a small compound which was ideal for us.

We had sold the house in Glenmavis and Dorothy and the kids were staying with Torquil while the visas were being processed. At long last they were on the plane and I was at Dhahran Airport waiting anxiously for them. So we had one night in the flat and then moved into the new villa.

We then hit our first major problem. The education for western kids in Saudi Arabia in 1994 stopped about age 14. The Saudi didn't want hordes of western teenagers running around with hormones raging all through their veins. Alison was older than this so we had to think of something else for her. Kirsty and Gordon were younger so we enrolled them in Dhahran Academy situated in the grounds of the US Consulate. We looked at the possibility of her going to school in Bahrain but that would be really too much hassle. So in the end, we had to look at boarding schools back in Scotland. It was something that neither Dorothy nor I had ever contemplated for our kids. We always thought that they would be home every night.

We looked around and decided on the Wellington School in Ayr, a boarding school for young ladies. During our holiday home in the summer, we went down and had a look around. It seemed just what we were looking for and Alison also was happy with the choice. Although it must have been quite an upheaval for her, she coped very well after the initial three or so weeks. Her time there taught her self reliance and gave her the confidence she needed when she went off to university and the world of work. She would travel back and forth to Saudi on her own with no problems. In fact, after a while, she became very annoyed that she was an 'unaccompanied minor' as she believed that she could handle the traveling on her own.

Going back to driving to Riyadh, I'd be up before sunrise and drive to a 9 or 10 o'clock meeting, have some lunch and drive home again. This was routine and I did it almost on a weekly basis.

Driving in town and on the big highways differ immensely. Let me say that accidents on the highways result from one of the following – excessive speed, tiredness (falling asleep at the wheel), bad maintenance of the vehicle or hitting stray animals (usually camels and usually fatally).

On this occasion I had a meeting in the OPM-SANG (Office for Program Management – Saudi Arabian National Guard) building in the centre of Riyadh. The meeting took a couple of hours and although I'd had a couple of cups of coffee, I was feeling pretty tired. It was really hot and my car had been out of any shade for hours. I drove out of the car park and was thinking about lunch when I hit a parked car. My fault, I admit it!

We'd been told never to leave the scene of an accident as that compounds the offence so I sat there waiting for the traffic police to turn up. I phoned my office to tell them I might be in some bother. I'd keep them up to date with what happened as and when I could.

Eventually a Traffic Cop did arrive, took down my particulars and invited me to sit in the back seat of his car. He then proceeded to drive me around Riyadh, stopping on the way to chat with some of his colleagues. Eventually we pulled up at the Traffic Police HQ and again he politely invited me (by gesture as I didn't understand his Arabic) to accompany him into the station where he showed me where to sit while he went off to fill in the paperwork. A pleasant guy, fairly short (+/-5ft 4in), he sported the ubiquitous black moustache and beard. I remember he smiled a lot but I'm not sure if that was at my predicament or life in general.

My friendly cop then left wishing me farewell and leaving me in a bit of limbo as I wasn't quite sure where I was or what was happening.

It was quite confusing as the passing parade in the open foyer area continued and I didn't understand any of it!

The next thing I knew, I and a couple of other miscreants were being marched up a walkway at the end of which we turned to see the cells! "Wait a minute; I'm not going in there, am I?" I thought. Oh, yes I was! First I was asked to leave all sharp objects in a tray so I handed over my pen, penknife and then we were all taken over to the door. Let me tell you that the 'clang' and 'clunk' of the door closing and being locked behind you are the most depressing and distressing sounds anyone can ever hear.

So what's the first thing a jailbird thinks about? Let me tell you, it's how am I going to get out of here? A quick scan of the communal cell showed that there was a little shop and a coin-operated telephone. I always carried cash with me in Saudi in these days as credit cards didn't work in most places.

Apart from giving change, the shop sold sandwiches, sweets (candy), soft drinks and water. NO diet drinks and I'd been diagnosed diabetic a few years before. What is it with Saudis and the over consumption of sugar?

So I changed five Riyals into 10 halalah pieces and called the office in Dammam. You've never seen coins disappear so quickly into a telephone in your life but the short conversation told my company where I was and I was assured that I'd out as soon as they could manage it.

The cell had about 40 people in it with space for plenty more. But 40 were plenty as far as I was concerned. Cleanliness was not paramount; no more so than in the toilets. OK for peeing but there was no way I was going to squat. One of the many reasons I wanted out!

After that there wasn't much to do although my colleagues in Dammam paged me a couple of times to keep themselves amused and increase my misery. The gaol was split in two. The side I was in was for perpetrators of accidents while the other side was for traffic offences like running a red light. The different parts and the front were separated by ceiling to floor bars and each side had an entrance to a prayer room also walled by these bars. My side of the gaol had many more people than the traffic offence side. I wonder why?

Although the punishments change from time to time, just at that time, running a red light was punishable by 24 hours in gaol and a SR500 fine. A Filipino driver had been caught and put in the cells for just that offence but after the 24 hours inside his sponsor/employer had refused to pay the fine so the police just kept him in. He had already been in 20+ days when I was there.

I talked to some of my fellow inmates but I was the only westerner and most didn't have a lot of English. I did talk to another Filipino who had been driving the middle car of a five car pile-up and was the only one to be incarcerated but he was pretty philosophical about it. Many of the others felt sorry for me as my office was in Dammam and here I was in gaol in Riyadh.

A young Saudi on my side of the gaol had knocked down and killed a youngster. He had been in that cell for four years and may still be there as he had no way of paying the 'blood money' to the child's family. He was only in his early twenties.

All through that afternoon, guys were being let out. A guard would open the door and shout out not the name but the nationality of whoever was being let out. One of the two men that accompanied me didn't have time to sit down before he was called. Lucky so-and-so!

There were only one or two Saudis in there. It seems that most of them can talk their way out of incarceration for things like speeding and accidents. Most of the inmates were ex-pat Arabs or Filipinos (plus one Brit!) and many slept a lot. There was a TV mounted high on the wall but it was tuned to Saudi 1 and seemed to be broadcasting from Mecca all the time.

As time went on (dragging as it did so), I quickly became bored. A feature of the prison was the runners. If you wanted anything like cigarettes, say, you gave one of these guys some money and off he'd go bringing you back the goods and change but probably keeping a fee for himself. Another extraordinary sight was the delivery of mattresses and bedding to the inmates as those weren't provided by the prison. You just found a place on the thin carpet and lay down.

There were communal meals which were pretty dreadful so nobody would actually starve. Of creature comforts there were none unless you could get someone to bring them to you. I never saw a lawyer and the only other visitors, apart from people bringing bedding, etc., were the guys springing the inmates.

By the end of the afternoon, I was getting pretty despondent and was reduced to hanging onto the bars looking out at the free world wondering if I was ever going to get out. I was resigned to spending the night inside when I caught sight of someone whom I thought I recognised. I dismissed this as the man whom I thought it was lived in Bahrain and worked for the Saudi Embassy there. He was a friend of my Saudi bosses and I'd met him socially. Anyway, the light was fading and, as he was in a thobe and gutra, I couldn't really be sure it was him as I hadn't seen his face.

So imagine my surprise and delight when he turned the corner about twenty minutes later and told me that I would be out as soon as he signed a couple of documents. You can't imagine the relief and I was so glad I didn't have to partake of the communal meal which was just arriving.

So the cry of "Britanni" from the door signalled that I was out. I must say that I never did get my pen back. It must have been taken by someone freed earlier. Well, what do you expect from a bunch of prisoners?

The guards were all full of smiles and good wishes. They seemed almost sorry to lose me but I couldn't get out quick enough, back to my car and drive back to Khobar where my wife and kids were waiting and were worried sick. Alison was back in Ayr and she was pretty upset when she heard that her dad was 'inside' but I'm sure that was just a feature of her loneliness.

Soon after we moved into the villa, Dorothy met our neighbours across the road. The compound had only 14 villas so it was a small community. Our neighbours were a South African couple, Impey and Roy, so Dorothy had no trouble breaking the ice. Roy was in insurance but Impey was a lady of leisure. She spent her days shopping so in that regard she wasn't all that different from nearly every other woman in Saudi.

However, Impey and Roy had a hobby – booze. They used to have about half a dozen large Winchester jars bubbling away making wine but they also had a home still where they made Sid. They never sold it so it stayed relatively secret and their parties were legendary.

So Dorothy and Impey would play some tennis and then adjourn to the bar which is where I would find her when I came home from work. It became a regular occurrence.

We used to go to a weekly quiz night and the deal was that if you won one week, you set the questions for the next week. Our team did win and all the rest of our team announced that they wouldn't be around the following week which left Dorothy and me to do it all by our lonesome. However a few weeks later we got our own back as again the team won the quiz but we were able to tell all the others that we wouldn't be available the next week as it was our wedding anniversary and we'd be out for dinner.

Dorothy assumed that we would be going somewhere local but I had a secret plan to take her to Bahrain. I told her to be ready when I came home from work but when I turned up she wasn't in. Kirsty told me that she had been playing tennis which meant that she was, right at that moment, sitting at Impey's bar drinking a glass of wine. I went over and there she was with sweat drenched hair not looking like she was ready for dinner. Impey's excuse was that she needed some wine as she wouldn't be getting any at the local Chinese. Nosey as ever, she asked where I was taking her but I wasn't going to spoil the surprise.

I almost dragged Dorothy out of there and told her that she had about half an hour to get ready or it would be too late. I must admit that she got ready in record time and we were off. Dorothy seemed a little surprised as we drove towards the causeway as she hadn't packed her passport and visa, so I had to break it to her that I had arranged a visa and had her passport in my pocket. It was a very good night.

It may sound that I did nothing but work all the time but we did have weekends off. They were Thursday afternoons and Fridays. That takes a bit of getting used to. Gordon started to play some kids football on Friday afternoons and I was asked to help out. So I started to referee the games and thoroughly enjoyed it. The kids came from all nationalities and I was standing beside the parents of a child who played alongside Gordon when the local imam was preaching over the mosque's loudspeakers. As fate would have it, the mother was a Syrian American who spoke fluent Arabic. Out of interest, I asked her to translate what the imam was saying. She said that he was urging his congregation to have nothing to do with Christians or Jews as they were infidels and should even be killed. This was in 1995!

I was doing a lot of driving, mainly to Riyadh and Bahrain but I also had occasion to drive to Kuwait City. The road goes past Al Khafji to the border where the formalities were never as slick as those on the causeway to Bahrain. The other major change is that the road became an eight lane motorway from a two lane road in Saudi. I went to Kuwait a number of times but the first time was an eye-opener as burned out Iraqi tanks were scattered around either at the side of the road or in the central reservation.

Before I knew it, I was back in the UK, this time at another Oceanology Exhibition. One my first night in the hotel, I phoned home to be told that my mother had rung wanting me to call her. That was unusual to say the least so I called to be told that her sister, my Aunt Cathie, has passed away. Cathie had been childless and I had always liked her probably because we shared the same date for our birthdays.

I dropped everything and travelled up to Morpeth in Northumberland to handle all the funeral arrangements. It was the first time I had ever done anything like that and it is much more complicated than you would ever believe. One of her friends and neighbours had given the authorities the wrong middle name for the death certificate. It is a VERY complicated procedure to get a death certificate changed even though it is wrong.

I also told the local vicar that I would say a few words at the funeral and it was only when I stood up that I realised that it would be one of the most difficult things I have ever done. I have said earlier that I am quite comfortable with public speaking but that 'eulogy' had a lot of emotion wrapped up in it.

We would get requests for quotations (RFQs) all the time but one from America was unusual. It was asking for prices of logistic support in case they won a contract to work in the Middle East. We replied and promptly forgot about. About a year later we received a fax telling us that the contract had been won and our support was required. Laidlaw Environmental was a company based in Minnesota who specialised in clearing up after the US Military. The military had based scattered around the Middle East from Egypt to Cairo. For some reason Laidlaw had decided to base their guys in Saudi. Perhaps it was because their knowledge of the region's geography left a lot to be desired. They certainly didn't get the political boundaries right as they thought UAE was a town in Saudi! So one of their first lessons was on the region's the different countries. I met the first four guys in Bahrain and drove them across the causeway to Saudi. Two were going to stay in Saudi and the other two were a lawyer and the overall boss. I later learned that he had grown up in Cedar Rapids, Iowa that town I had visited so briefly years before.

I had to escort them round the region to UAE, Bahrain, Qatar, Kuwait and Oman as well as round Saudi. On the first trip to Dubai/Jebel Ali, we went to see the US Aircraft Carrier "Abraham Lincoln". That's a BIG boat. I can't remember the size of the crew but it's basically a floating city. The Emiratis are never ones to miss a commercial opportunity so at the bottom of the gangway (which seemed about half a mile long to me standing on the dockside) was a congregation of fast-food stalls including McDonalds, KFC, etc. It seemed as though Dubai was bring a touch of home town America to the US Navy.

Our area of responsibility covered Saudi, Bahrain and Qatar for some products and the whole of the Middle East (ME) for others. This meant that I travelled a fair bit. Bahrain wasn't a big market but did have a good airport and places to socialise in. We did have a couple of good clients there but mainly we went there to enjoy ourselves.

We were contacted by people in Doha, Qatar who wanted to buy some GPS gear so off I went. Qataris never wasted my time and I could say every time I went there I sold something. On one occasion we demonstrated the capabilities of the system to the Qatari military and were way out in the desert when I noticed some local in a small hide/cave. I asked one of the officers what was going on and he told me that the man was training his falcons.

Falconry is still very popular in the ME and once when I was flying between two Gulf states I was astonished to see that one passenger had bought two business class seats, one for himself and the other for two of his prize falcons hooded and sitting on a cross pole!

In 1995, the whole region was rocked by a *coup* when the nephew of the Emir of Qatar overthrew his uncle. This showed how unstable the region could be. The new Emir has been very progressive and has allowed Qatar to flourish spending its huge gas revenues to modernise the country. As an example, Qatar Airways is now one of the world's best and Doha has become a sporting destination of choice, rivaling Dubai in that regard.

Shows and exhibitions are held all over the world even in the ME and we were attending one in Abu Dhabi. Staying in the Sheraton Hotel, we had arranged to meet up in the bar before going out for dinner. Propping up the bar alone, I started to talk to a guy who was looking lonely. I quickly established that he worked for Racal in London and he was out in the UAE visiting the local office. I knew Rick Gore who ran the office in Abu Dhabi so we exchanged business cards. When he saw my name Gary said, "You're not the famous Allan Jack, are you?" Slightly surprised I asked why he recognised my name and it turned out he shared an office with Dave Hampshire whom I had worked with at Ferranti ORE. Dave was never shy in telling stories and it seemed as though I featured prominently in a lot of them.

One of my colleagues met and fell in love with a nurse. He was a Brit and she was Finnish. They were living together (totally illegal in Saudi) and were being hassled by the local cops when they were out in a car together (also not allowed in Saudi). The relevant laws are 1) No sex outside marriage and 2) If a couple are in a vehicle together they must be married OR be relatives that can't marry i.e. siblings, mother and son, aunt and nephew, etc. Needless to say a great many ex-pat romances hit the same problems. Our couple decided that, seeing they were in Saudi, they would get married under Sharia law. Every time I tell this story, people ask why they did it that way. I've got no real answer. Perhaps just to be different and/or experience something totally different.

This plan got them out of their immediate problem because they could get a letter from the nurse's employer saying that they were 'engaged' and so were allowed to drive around together unsupervised. However, the plan had other associated problems.

In Saudi Arabia, EVERY woman has a man who is responsible for her. This leads to hilarious consequences. For instance, a lady was flying from Riyadh to Dammam and wouldn't switch her mobile phone off as the plane was landing despite numerous requests from the crew. On disembarking she was detained while the authorities established who her responsible male was. He was in Riyadh so he had to get on another plane and on his arrival in Dammam, HE was arrested and she let go! But I digress.

Our bride-to-be's father lived in Finland and he wasn't going to fly out to Saudi so a 'surrogate' father had to be found. Guess who got the job? Yes, me! Somewhere I have a document (in Finnish with an English translation) transferring the father's right to hand over his daughter in marriage to me. It has innumerable stamps from every conceivable government department both in Finland and Saudi. That solved that problem.

Next problem was that we had to get an appointment with a local judge. Weddings in Saudi, although the celebrations can be extremely lavish, are not held in the mosque. The couple actually goes to court to have the licence drawn up. However, nothing is ever simple and we had a couple of false starts. On one occasion, we were told that the judges weren't 'doing' weddings on that particular day; they were only doing murderers and rapists! We were standing in the bleak corridor waiting for this news when the door of one of the courtrooms along at the end opened and two prisoners walked out in chains. Obviously, they had been found guilty and they shuffled along in their shackles. A couple of aspects of the scene struck me. One was that they were going to be executed the following Friday, for certain, and that gives one a very peculiar feeling at the back of the neck and secondly, the guards never laid a hand on either prisoner. They knew that they would take their time but the guards had all the time in the world.

This postponement (again) had created another problem as we had been assured that the ceremony would take place that day and the (now not so) happy couple had laid on a big party for all their friends. The still not married bride was in floods of tears as we drove away from the court and she was inconsolable. To be honest, none of us was particularly happy as we went home at the end of the day.

Imagine my surprise when the phone rang and the groom told me that the party was going ahead. Then he asked me if I had a bible. Bibles are banned in Saudi and many have been confiscated at the airports. However Dorothy had brought a small Gideon New Testament and he asked me to bring it along.

When we arrived the party seemed to be going along nicely and the mood had certainly lifted. I was dragged into the kitchen and asked if I knew the marriage ceremony. Stunned I replied that I thought I could remember it. Right, now I was going to 'marry' them in a totally unofficial ceremony. Coupled with readings from 2nd Corinthians about two becoming one and love is ……, I acted as a minister. They even exchanged rings. Everybody had a great time and it certainly boosted the atmosphere.

A few days later, we tried again at the court and this time we were taken into the anteroom of the judges chambers. His assistant, a Mutawah, was extremely pleasant and spoke remarkably good English. A scribe faithfully noted down all the terms for the marriage. Then, for the only time in the whole procedure, he turned to the bride and asked her if there were any conditions to the marriage. Both bride and groom just wanted to get on with it and shook their heads, However, I realised that this was the only chance a Saudi bride has to put her stamp on the relationship. She can ask for anything and the groom can like it or lump it. So I put forward that the contract should have that she would be allowed to work. I didn't want her to get into any trouble at her hospital. Eventually the contract was finalised and we all signed it. Then we went into the courtroom to see the judge. His first remark was for the bride to cover her face so she sat through her very brief wedding ceremony looking through a black curtain. As the judge spoke only in Arabic we couldn't really follow what he was saying but he inspected the documents we had brought along and asked the groom and me to shake hands. This signified that I was handing over responsibility for my 'daughter' to her husband. I still have a copy of the contract and I was told that the heading on it doesn't say 'Marriage Certificate' but 'Licence to Fornicate'! Nobody ever said that the Saudis don't get to the heart of the matter!

I'd always stayed in touch with the alumni associations of my old universities and I received, through the mail, a copy of the alumni magazine from UCT. The latest edition announced that the Geology Dept. would be celebrating its hundredth anniversary.

It was probably very selfish but I decided to go down for the celebrations and I couldn't even say that it was business. It was during school term time so I had to go alone. I thoroughly enjoyed my few days, staying with Jo Keenan, and seeing a lot of my old mates at UCT.

When I got back, we were closer to having to make a decision over Kirsty's schooling. She was getting to the age when she was going to become too old for the local school (Dhahran Academy) and, if the family was going to stay in Saudi, she would have to join Alison at Wellington School in Ayr. However, there were a number of reasons NOT to do this. The first was financial; it would be an intolerable strain on my wallet. The second was that it didn't seem sensible to have half the family in Saudi and the other half in Scotland. A further reason was that Kirsty wasn't really cut out for boarding school even if she would have an older sister there.

So, what should we do? There never really was a choice and, even although I love having my wife and kids around, they were going to have to go back. Once the schools were closed for the summer and Alison was back with us, Dorothy went off to Ayr to look for a house. We had decided that she would rent a flat at the start and then go round the estate agents.

I had the kids to myself for about six weeks and then we were going to all go back. It was great fun as they played in the compound all day and the girls would cook dinner for me coming home.

Dorothy found a flat near the river and kept us up-to-date on the house hunting. We'd decided to keep Alison in Wellington School as a day pupil as she was coming up for her Standard and Higher Grade exams. Kirsty and Gordon would go to the local schools.

Eventually, it was time for the kids to bid farewell to Saudi. By a stroke of luck, when I booked the flights home, KLM offered us a weekend's FREE stay in an airport hotel for us. The kids loved it as we went on the canal boats and visited art galleries, museums and take-away restaurants.

All too soon, it was time for me to go back to Saudi and we still hadn't found a house though that wasn't for the want of trying. However, I would be back at Christmas.

I was soon back in the swing of things although I was a bit lonely in the big villa that seemed so noisy only a few weeks before. In fact, the company soon put our new accountant in to share with me. The weeks rattled along and before I knew it, the Christmas holidays were upon us. I had used so much of my leave that I could go back only for eight days and as I wanted to spend New Year at home, it meant that I would fly home on Christmas Day night arriving back in Scotland on Boxing Day.

I nearly always flew KLM which usually flew out of Bahrain rather than Dammam. KLM would put on taxis to take the passengers over the causeway to the airport. I had to use that facility as there was no-one willing to give me a lift across, not on that date anyway!

It turned out that only one other chap was traveling across the causeway with me so only one limousine was required. He was an American but very quiet which was unusual. We had to stop on the causeway as in those days Americans were required to buy visas to enter Bahrain. Even while we were waiting for the driver to get the visa organised he was extremely taciturn. Because the roads and the causeway were very quiet, we arrived at the airport well in time. In fact the booking-in desks weren't even open. The airport itself was quiet and so we started up a conversation. He asked me what I did in Saudi so I told him and then I asked him what he was doing over there. You could have knocked me down with a feather when he replied, "I'm a Catholic Priest!"

I knew that Aramco had their own Catholic and Anglican priests but this guy was extra. He had been between parishes in the Chicago diocese when the archbishop had picked him out to give help to the resident priest over the Christmas period. Practicing Christianity (or any religion other than Islam) is banned in Saudi although many people of faith do so in the secrecy of their own homes. A great proportion of the Aramco workforce comes from the Philippines and a lot of the nurses employed in the Aramco hospital are Irish. Both communities are mainly Catholic and there is a number from the Protestant faith also. Attending Midnight Mass on Christmas Eve was a VERY popular event and help was needed on the priestly front. So here was my traveling companion heading home at the end of his stint.

I wondered how he was described on his visa application as 'Priest' probably wasn't mentioned! It seems he came in as a 'Special Teacher'.

Although this story took some time to relate, the check-in desks were still not open so he asked me what I got up to in Saudi when I wasn't working. I don't know what made me do it (probably his story) but I told him the saga of the Saudi marriage. He then asked me a strange question. Was I a member of the church? I told him that I wasn't a Catholic but a Scots Presbyterian. Was I baptized? I had been. Then came the next jaw-dropping statement. Well, in the eyes of God, I married them!!!!

That I couldn't believe. It just shows you never to joke about things you may not fully understand.

Some of the guys had been suffering from bad colds when I left the office and I had a feeling that I was about to come down with it as well. When we landed at Schipol airport I was feeling rough. This wasn't helped by the fact that we were told that the temperature at Glasgow Airport was -19C!! Flying in everything was white and the temperature didn't rise as I drove down to Ayr. My teeth were chattering by the time I'd walked from the car to the flat's front door and I was feeling so bad I went straight to bed.

Not really the best way to start some days off but it was good to be back with the family again and the weather did improve slightly before I left to go back to Saudi.

A lot of things were happening including Dorothy eventually finding a house in Ayr. So it turned out that I bought a house without ever seeing it!

I've already mentioned that Almisehal represented a lot of foreign companies. One of these was a Danish company called Reson who made and sold high quality multibeam echosounders (MBES). They (and we) had sold a system to the Hydrographic Section of Aramco and Reson sent one of their engineers out to discuss the delivery, mounting and installation of the unit. Richard Lear was his name and he was the head of the Reson office in Aberdeen.

Part of my job was to accompany him to these meetings and on the way back to the office we started to chat. I asked how things were back in Aberdeen where I still had a lot of friends and Richard told me he was actually being transferred to Reson's facility in Santa Barbara, California. That was interesting but not as interesting as his next statement. He told me that he had been asked to find his replacement and he was going to recommend me! Needless to say I was stunned. I told him that I couldn't say yes or no until I knew more details. He understood and said that he would ask his boss Claus Steenstrup to talk to me. As another Oceanology was due in about a month and I was going to be there. That would be an ideal opportunity to discuss the position.

By the time I got to the Brighton show I had heard nothing further so I thought that they had talked it over and thought twice about it. I wasn't overly concerned as I was quite settled at Almisehal and Reson hadn't made any type of offer.

It so happened that the first person I recognised when we were checking into our hotel was Richard Lear. We said hello and he asked me if I'd heard anything and I told him I hadn't. He promised to have a word with Claus.

225

I still hadn't any expectations when Claus sat down at my table when I was having breakfast the next morning. To be concise, he offered me the job and we discussed salary and conditions. I was never one to say yes to something I didn't have in writing. I asked him to send me the offer by fax to a number I'd give him later. It wouldn't be the office fax!!

A couple of weeks later and back in Saudi I still hadn't heard anything so again I was sure that Claus had had second thoughts. But no, the offer came through and I spent about an hour on the phone with Dorothy talking it over with her.

In the end it was no contest. I would be home with my family and I wouldn't be in Saudi. So I just had to time my resignation. Reson wanted me in Aberdeen at the start of August so I would resign at the end of June.

Believe it or not, one of my last sales was of a Reson multi-beam sonar to the Arabian Oil Company all of which meant that I knew that I would be back, albeit on the other side of the desk/fence.

Is it only me that has regrets after making momentous decisions like resigning? Moving from South Africa all those years ago sometimes felt like we'd done the wrong thing but it worked out in the end. I must admit that I was feeling just a touch worried but then something happened to put my mind at rest.

I decided that I was going to resign on a certain Saturday morning. The week before we had been called up by a Government Ministry asking us to quote and demonstrate some GPS equipment so off we toddled to Riyadh to give the demo. We'd already sent the guy the quote so he knew what the equipment cost. After a day driving around the country outside Riyadh, we got back to the offices to discuss how many he would want. By the way, we were using GPS equipment in our vehicles ten years before SatNav became all the rage.

After talking for an hour he hit us with the bombshell that he had a budget which would pay for about a third of one unit. That was the last straw and suddenly all possible regrets disappeared. My colleague couldn't understand why I just stood up and started to pack all the kit away. It was probably rude but I had stopped caring. We had just wasted eight hours of driving to Riyadh and back and a day demonstrating high-tech equipment to someone who couldn't buy it!

My resignation was a bit of a shock to a lot of people both in and out of the company as I hadn't let on to anyone. Then came the job of packing up and I was on my way home.

15

Return to Ayr

Reson was a family run firm with an HQ in Denmark and offices in Aberdeen and Santa Barbara, California. Three brothers, Claus, Jens and Per Steenstrup, ran the show with their father, Hans, although retired, taking an occasional interest. Jens ran the office in California while Claus was based in the office in Slangerup, a small town a few miles north of Copenhagen. Per ran demonstrations all over the world and sometimes it was a bit difficult to keep up to date with his movements.

Although nominally the office was in Aberdeen, it was actually a few miles north just outside the village of Methlick. In my opinion it was not in the right location and one of my first decisions was that we would have to move much closer to Aberdeen.

Reson Offshore (as the office was known) had recently changed its business model. For years it had run a rental pool of the MBES units but had sold the used units and now was to concentrate on selling units. Aberdeen is full of companies renting out gear and there was a lingering resentment from some that only one of them had fallen heir to all of the Reson kit; so one of my first tasks was to go around these companies smoothing all the ruffled feathers.

A couple of weeks after I joined Reson, it was decided that I should go to the Slangerup offices for some 'initiation' and training. It also allowed me to meet the many people in that office I would be dealing with.

The day was going along with little drama when a conversation I was having with Claus was interrupted by one of the staff with a message of some importance. They were talking in Danish but even I could make out that there was some emergency. It turned out that a tender had not arrived at its intended destination and seemed to have been lost *en route*. Things were complicated by the facts that the tender had to be in Constanta on the Black Sea coast of Romania at noon the day after next. This is where I made a contribution that I came to regret. I said that the only way that the tender was going to get there in time was if someone hand carried it. Claus gave instructions (in Danish) and our time was effectively over. This took precedence. I was left to my own devices for a time so I could wander round and ask questions. A couple of hours passed and then Claus sought me out and handed me air tickets and a large envelope with tender documents in it. My advice had been taken to heart and I was the only one available. I was on my way to Romania!

The flight was from Copenhagen to Bucharest via Frankfurt. I had to catch a train to Constanta as there were no flights available. However I did have a flight booked from Constanta back to Bucharest. Although this was all after the Berlin Wall had come down, I wasn't expecting too much. As you may remember, dear reader, I had been to Czechoslovakia in '75 so I had some experience of Eastern Europe.

The flight landed at Bucharest and there ensued a mad scramble to get the visa stamped in the passport (only US Dollars taken!). Then a taxi ride to the rail station with a driver who had pretty good English. I'm sure we went the long way round but he did take me past the White House where the Ceausescus had been shouted down by the crowd/mob. He was hanged a few days later.

I had to buy a ticket when I reached the station. Unfortunately, there were no first class seats left. I didn't really believe that. I think the ticket man just wanted me to ride in second class. I suppose I could have offered a bribe but I don't do that. Anyway the ride was an experience. It took about four hours and I must admit that riding with chickens, ducks and assorted bags of vegetables gave some local flavour. I'm sure there was even a goat for part of the ride.

The track crossed the great Carpathian Plain and then followed the Danube until it reached Constanta. Romania, at that time, couldn't feed its population which seemed far fetched when it had such vast areas of fertile ground. The only farmers who did make ends meet were those fortunate enough to have small market gardens along the canalised sections of the river. Another feature was the villages of gypsy tents, which looked like North American Indian teepees.

Constanta was a port town and its infrastructure looked pretty modern.

The hotel was simple and the weather was warm. I went out for a stroll after dinner and was approached by two youngsters. After a few words, they picked my pockets and ran off. I tried to chase them but they were too quick and they knew all the back streets. Apart from the embarrassment, I was more concerned that they had got away with all my 'hard' currency. I had a suspicion that the hotel didn't take credit cards and I had no more cash.

The next morning, true enough, the hotel told me the bad news. However, they did tell me that I should be able to get some cash from the bank up the road. After a few anxious moments, I did get some cash, enough to pay for the hotel and the taxi to the airport which lay a few miles outside the town.

As I climbed into the taxi, I heaved a sigh of relief as surely nothing else could go wrong. Could it? The taxi diver didn't speak much English so conversation was limited. He dropped me at the airport and drove away. The fact that there didn't seem to be any aircraft at the airport did raise some worries but, hey, I had a confirmed ticket, didn't I?

There wasn't a great deal of activity but I tracked down some people in an office. I showed my ticket to be told that the flight had been cancelled! So there I was stuck in a small airport with no taxis and no flight out. I must admit that even the staff at the airport understood my predicament and offered to arrange a lift back into town.

However I had one more task. Remember the tender I had to deliver? The arrangement was that the local agent would collect the documents from me at the airport before I flew out. That arrangement still stood – except for the flying bit! So after the initial panic faded I thought I'd still be OK when the agent turned up. That was, of course, IF he turned up. I hadn't spoken to him; the arrangements had all been made by someone in Reson HO. How did I know if he was a good timekeeper?

I'm not a worrier by nature. I've always thought that it didn't seem to have many advantages. But I must admit that sitting/standing in that office I began to worry.

The meet was scheduled at noon and at five minutes to the hour this big burgundy coloured Mercedes pulled into the parking area. The driver helped his stiff backed passenger out of the front seat. This was my contact right on time!

At last control returned to my situation. Firstly I handed over the tender documents and then I was driven back to town where they organised another

229

train ticket, this time back to Bucharest. The difference this time was that the 'locals' managed to get me a First Class ticket.

While we were standing on the platform, we were hassled by young gypsy beggars much like I was back in India all those years ago. My Romanian friends chased them off and then the train arrived.

Back in Bucharest another taxi ride took me to the airport. At the time western mobile phones didn't work in Romania. In fact the only place any mobile phones did work was in the departure lounge at the airport but the kicker was that you had to hire one from a desk in the lounge!

Checking in with the office in Denmark, I got no reply. No-one had bothered to tell me that this was the day when ALL of Denmark closes down at noon for Monarchy Day. I did get an answer from Reson in Aberdeen so at least someone knew I was alright.

I flew back to Copenhagen via Vienna (the only time I've been in Austria – so far) and then home. Let's say I was glad to be back at my own hearthside and it was going to be a long time before I went back to Romania or volunteered for anything.

Back up at Aberdeen, I spent a lot of time going round existing and potential clients. The office was in Methlick as I mentioned before, in what had been the Laundry House for Haddo House. It was an isolated place but how isolated never really struck me until one evening in November. The clocks had gone back and darkness fell in mid-afternoon. I was alone in the office and ready to go back to Aberdeen to my hotel. I set the burglar alarm and then put the lights out just before I locked the front door. I turned round to total pitch darkness. I couldn't see my briefcase never mind the path to the road. I could only tell when I was at the road was because of the surface difference. I was glad when a car came along because its headlights showed me where my car was. It was right there and then I decided that we would have to move. It was also a fact that when Claus or someone else came to visit clients, they didn't have time to come out to the office which didn't really help the morale all that much.

So we started to look for a new place and eventually settled in a building close to the airport; a much more satisfactory location.

The oil industry was in crisis (not for the first or last time) and this manifested itself as the oil price being down at US$10-11 a barrel. Even the Saudis were hurting and it cost only +/-US$5 to get a barrel out of the ground there. What this meant was that investment (looking for new fields) didn't get any money and so spending was down and people weren't buying new kit. So the atmosphere wasn't great but Reson were very strong in selling to the marine and defence industries.

Part of the social life in Aberdeen was to attend evening meetings under the auspices of one or other of the local societies. Sometimes it included dinner and usually a presentation from some company or other. I gave one on behalf of Reson. The most memorable one was given by an economist up from London in front of an audience (which included me) of "oil types". The oil price was around US$11 a barrel at the time and we were all anxious to hear any encouragement this economist may have for us.

The short version is that there was NO encouragement. In fact, he told us that the oil price was never going to be higher and we really should be looking for jobs selling insurance or the like. This annoyed me somewhat as he seemed to think that the oil industry was of no use and we all were wasters. I stood up and asked him what would happen to the price if King Fahd died during the night. He scoffed and implied that King Fahd (who was very ill at the time) was immortal. And people wonder why I'm a skeptic!!!!! In the end, it was the Emir of Bahrain who was the first to pass away of that generation but the point was still valid and the US$140+ barrel price showed that he was talking absolute rubbish!

Not only was the health of the local 'monarchs' of concern, there was another even greater threat which was raising its ugly head. About a month or so after I left Saudi, there was the bombing of the 'Khobar Towers'. These blocks of flats, built to a design that wouldn't have looked out of place in a run down suburb of Moscow or in Easterhouse or Drumchapel in Glasgow, were originally to house the local Bedouin in the Saudi cities. Every city had some. As an aside, I would have loved to have met the salesman who sold the idea to the Saudi Government. There was a movement to move the 'backward' desert folk and change them into town dwellers. Of course, the Bedouin took one look, said, "Thanks but no thanks" (or the Arabic equivalent idiom) and went back to their camels, pickups and tents. The towers were lying empty and the growing American military presence needed somewhere to house their staff and use as offices and the like.

The Towers were ideal as they were basic and didn't need much upgrading to make them ship-shape. There were concrete bollards and barriers but determined suicide bombers can usually find a way in. Perhaps the security wasn't as tight as it should have been. Anyway this truck bomb was so big that the blast rocked the villa I used to live in and knocked my colleague, who now occupied it, off the sofa onto the floor. And the villa was several kilometers away! Of course the authorities claimed that it was an isolated incident, the perpetrators would be rounded up (some were) and dealt with (executed) and it couldn't possibly have been planned and carried out by locals. It must be due to foreigners, possibly Iranian or even Mossad! One might be able to discern the beginning of a theme here.

Saudi was still part of my brief so, after a suitable period of quiet, I went back out. There was a very good reason for this as one of the last things I did for Almisehal was to sell a Reson SeaBat to the Arabian Oil Company in Al Khafji. I was in constant contact with my replacement in Almisehal. This sale actually led to more sales, this time to Saudi Aramco but that is for later. I was trying to get the Port Authority and some construction companies interested in the technology and they seemed impressed. The construction companies didn't want to spend the money but the Ports actually did buy systems but nearly ten years later. One must persevere in the Middle East! I also sold a system into Bahrain to a dredging company.

There was another incident which caused newspaper headlines in the UK. An Australian nurse was murdered in a hospital compound. At first a lowly male worker was suspected but it was quickly established that two of her fellow nurses (both British) were responsible. I knew another nurse who worked with the three of them. As the details emerged (the Australian was an unofficial money lender and one of the British nurses had been 'struck off' back in Dundee) it was obvious that there were many nefarious activities going on. It was a *cause celebre* in the UK newspapers and, of course, they took the viewpoint that the British girls couldn't possibly have done it. However, all the local ex-pats thought they were as guilty as sin. Being found guilty, they were due for the 'chop'. The Saudis weren't keen to have two western women executed (in public) and fierce diplomatic efforts finally got the two released.

Another area that the head honchos thought I should look after was South Africa. I suppose they had an idea I would know something about the country. Not only did I but I actually knew some of the principal players. However, many of them wanted to rent a system (from the local agent who had one in his rental pool) to try it out but Reson had signed a worldwide agreement with Ashtead Technology that Reson wouldn't rent any more systems which stymied this at birth. I filled in many Sales Visit Reports and put this to Claus but either he wasn't listening and/or didn't read the reports. This would have consequences in years to come.

One may get the idea that I did a lot of traveling and one would be correct. As I've said before I used KLM a great deal and eventually attained their Platinum Frequent Flier status. However, long before that I was getting sick and tired of sitting in the awful plastic seats that airports use. In one of the in-flight magazines, I came across an advert and application for a lounge pass. Get the card and gain access (at a cost) to airline lounges all over the place. It sounded like a good idea so I wrote off to them. My next long trip was to our offices in Santa Barbara, California and this card arrived a day or so before I went. I didn't have time to use it on the way out as I had a short connection at Schipol but I was determined to use it on the way back.

These trips to Santa Barbara were the yearly sales getogethers of the company and were really the only time we were all in one place at the same time. The office was in a suburb called Goleta (second line of "Hotel California", anyone?) and had one of these small local airports just across the street. We never used it as the company had a driver who would pick you up from LAX and drive the almost three hour trip along the spectacular coast road.

KLM decided that we had to check in at LAX three hours before departure which meant that I had a very early start one morning. I was on my lonesome as some of the other guys had left the night before and others were staying on. So I was first in the check-in queue (with a suitcase filled with all the things that my family wanted from the US) and found myself with over three hours to kill. Duty-free shops can hold my attention span for only so long so I thought about going into a lounge. The card I mentioned above (Privilege Pass) came with a book listing the lounges that accepted the card. The KLM lounges weren't in it but there were a couple in LAX that were. I must admit to being rather nervous as I showed the card at the desk but the lady almost 'bit my hand off' as she took the card and I was in. The one great luxury for me that lounges have is the comfortable seats. I know that you can get free snacks and drinks (of all kinds) but the seats are fantastic. You can shower in some and things are just so relaxing. It wasn't very long after this that my first really important frequent flier card (Silver) arrived from KLM so I never used the other card again.

A Conference on Surveying was scheduled to take place in Teheran and, because we had just sold a system to the Hydrographic Dept. of the National

Oil Company of Iran, it was decided that someone should attend. You've guessed it. I got the short straw. At the time, I was a bit apprehensive but I'm glad I went. It certainly gave me an opportunity that I don't think I'll have again. There was a whole bunch of us from the UK and we all travelled under the auspices of the UK-Iran Trade Partnership (or some such similar title). We had to send our passports away for a couple of weeks (thank goodness for two passports!) so that the visas could be organised and then off we went.

The immigration procedures at Teheran Airport were very similar to those in Saudi so that wasn't so bad and then we were bussed to our hotel. As we were checking in I was approached by a young chap who introduced himself as the local Reson agent. This was news to me as no-one in Reson had informed me of this. It took some time for this to be resolved. It turned out that this company had sold some kit years before but the relationship had never been formalised. This young man and his father hardly left my side all week but the agent/representative agreement was something that they would need to talk to Claus about. They took me out to dinner one night and actually offered me an 'inducement' to get the agreement sorted. I don't take bribes.

The conference took place during the Shi'ite festival of Ashoka when men flay themselves in despair at the death of Imam Ali. As we were driving to dinner, we had to take a detour to miss one of the demonstrations or "the Nutters" as my hosts referred to them!

It was during my time at Reson that Alison started her university life at the Robert Gordon's University (RGU) in Aberdeen training as an engineer. She had completed a careers questionnaire during her last year in Wellington and it seemed that she'd be suited to that path. Why did she choose RGU? Believe it or not, it was because she did some research and discovered that 98.5% of RGU engineering graduates found jobs. That was something that I never thought about when I went to university. It just shows how generations change.

I don't know where she got this from but her Maths' results were always really good. In fact she earned extra money by tutoring school children in mathematics, including Shona, (my PA)'s son.

When I was up in Aberdeen, I would try and take Alison out for a good meal. Her mother was worried in case she wasn't eating properly. One evening we went to a local Indonesian restaurant (Spice Islands). As she was reading the menu Alison asked why some of the items (e.g. Rystafel) were in Dutch. Remember she did have some schooling in Afrikaans. I asked if she hadn't been taught that Indonesia used to be the Dutch East Indies. As she looked back at me blankly, I wondered out loud if I could claim back some of the fees I had paid for her education. I didn't want to know what else she hadn't been taught!

Anyway the food came and I warned her not to try the Beef Rendang as it would be too hot for her. Of course, she did try a morsel (just to see what it was like) and burnt her tongue so much that she's never forgotten that meal!

I was also an unofficial taxi driver so that she could hitch a lift home to Ayr whenever she had some holidays. As we were leaving Aberdeen one Friday evening, she asked me to tell her how her mother and I met. It's such a complicated story that I was still talking about it as we got to Ayr, nearly three hours later. That was one of the reasons that I started writing all of this down.

During her summer holidays she had a number of jobs. She was a waitress in a local hotel, she helped with placing foreign student visitors here for summer courses (from an office in London) and between her last two years she had a summer placement in the Engineering Dept. of the University of Edmonton in Alberta, Canada.

So what were the rest of us going to do for a holiday while she was away? It seemed only fair that we should take Kirsty and Gordon somewhere out of the ordinary. We decided to go to Florida. There was a direct flight from Glasgow to Orlando where we picked up our hire car. As we moved onto the highway, it quickly became obvious that Dorothy was no map reader as she couldn't navigate worth a bent penny. Fortunately Kirsty reached over from the back seat of the SUV, took the map and we had no problem from then on. In fact Dorothy was relegated to the back seat for the rest of the holiday!

Florida is somewhere none of us had ever been so we had many choices of what to see/visit. As we got to our villa a bit late in the evening, we didn't have any breakfast 'things' so we went out to a local diner. The kids liked it so much that we went there nearly every second day. As we sat there eating waffles and 'eggs any style', we discussed where we wanted to visit.

There was a golf course close by and Gordon and I had both brought our clubs. Unlike in Scotland we had two powered caddy carts to help us get round the course. The rules were that Dorothy and Kirsty would drive the carts but unfortunately Kirsty panicked on the way to the first tee and ended up running into the back of Dorothy's and my cart. She wasn't going very fast (luckily) so no damage was done but she drove carefully after that.

Next on the list was Universal Studios. None of us had ever been to an American-style them park and we were blown away by the scale and the variety of it all. One of the details I remember was that the queues were sprayed with a fine mist of water to keep them cool as they waited to get into the attractions. It was so good that we actually spent three days there.

I was really anxious to get to Cape Kennedy and walk around the place where so many space flights started. I mentioned earlier in this tome that, if I had been born American, I would have wanted to be part of the Mercury/Gemini/Apollo programmes. It wasn't to be, of course, but walking round the Space Centre was something special. I was a bit shocked to realise that Cape Kennedy is slap bang in the centre of a Nature Reserve with alligators peeking out of the drainage ditches. One of the exhibits was a chance to touch a piece of 'moon rock' but that was old hat to me as I'd already done that in UCT which was one of the geochemistry departments which analysed the original samples from the moon.

As we drove around, we listened to the local radio (no iPods in these days) and we found that there was to be a gala day at Venice Beach with lots of stalls. As this would be on the Gulf of Mexico shore we decided that it would be worth visiting and, if it was total bust, then there was enough around that area to make the day worthwhile. In the end, it was a good day and there was even a "Palaentology Desk". I went up to speak to the local expert. Florida is a state where you can collect sharks' teeth and I wanted to know if we could possibly go somewhere close by and go fossil hunting. The local expert was a bit dismissive and basically told me that there was nowhere close that I could take my family for the afternoon. I was a bit disappointed – perhaps he didn't think I looked enough like a geologist for him to bother about. In the end we enjoyed the stalls, the planes, and the food and then we decided to head for the beach. The Gulf waters are lovely and warm so we soon were all cavorting about in the sea.

The beach profile had a ridge of sand/shells which meant that the water shallowed about ten to fifteen metres offshore. Once Gordon had discovered this he spent quite a bit of time diving around this ridge (he's a pretty good swimmer). All of a sudden he surfaced with a handful of the ridge material and as he played with it, he shouted, "Look what I've found!" There in the palm of his hand was a shark's tooth. Not a museum specimen but one none the less. Of course, all three kids had collected sharks' teeth in Saudi so he knew what he was looking at. So we spent the next couple of hours searching and finding sharks' teeth. A great afternoon especially when the local beaches had been so disparaged by the local 'expert'! Never listen to experts!!!

We were nearly always exhausted when we got back to the house at night and we always had good nights' sleep. As we were in Florida, we had to visit the Keys and go down to Key West. It's a long drive from near Orlando so we were early to bed and up early to get on the road. Also the 55mph speed limit is a bit frustrating. Thank goodness for cruise control!

The road that connects all the Keys has walls along it to stop vehicles going over into the sea. Fortunately our SUV was high enough off the road to let us see over the wall. Otherwise it would have been a very boring drive. Lovely scenery and obviously the Keys are a rich man's playground. In the end, we were disappointed in Key West, probably because there were road works everywhere and parking was a nightmare. On the way back, we went via Miami and Key Biscayne which is a millionaire's playground! We were pretty tired when we got back and in fact Dorothy had to drive some of the way as I was falling asleep at the wheel.

I'm a fan of baseball and I was determined that the rest of the family should experience what it's like. Dorothy and Kirsty weren't too keen but Gordon was up for it. It turned out that the Cleveland Indians were playing the Tampa Bay Devil Rays in St Petersburg's Tropicana Stadium so off we went. The whole thing took about 5-6 hours. We were there for batting practice and Gordon wanted to catch one of the balls. He didn't have a glove so I told him to not even try. A few minutes later, a young lad came up and gave him a ball he had caught. His father had heard Gordon's and my conversation and told his son to give the ball over. A lovely gesture and Gordon still has that ball today. The whole event was something that is so different to what we have in UK and even Dorothy admitted that she enjoyed it.

While we're talking about holidays, the following year was our last together as a family. If you've got this far, you may have an inkling where we decided to go. Any guesses? I'll give you a few moments.

Alright, we went to South Africa to revisit old haunts. Flying into Johannesburg, we picked up another hired people carrier and went off to the northern suburb of Olivedale to where the Moretons lived. To remind you, Malcolm and Candy were with us in Kimberley and Malcolm and I worked together in Anglo for many years. We stayed with them for a few days and re-lived many nostalgic moments.

We drove round by Oban Ave to our old home, to Alison's primary school in Blairgowrie, to the Sandton Clinic where Kirsty and Gordon were born and by the Wanderers Club.

Then we drove down to Kimberley and stayed for only one night. However that did give us time to show the kids the flats (x2) where we used to live, the maternity hospital where Alison was born, where my old office was and to visit the Kimberley Mine Museum at the 'Big Hole'. Teenagers are loath to be impressed by anything and the three kids were scathing about "how big a hole can it be?" Nevertheless they were impressed when they walked out on the viewing gantry. Walking round the museum and seeing the display of diamonds kept them awestruck.

We also had dinner with Paddy Lawless, an old friend from UCT, who worked as a diamond geologist for De Beers.

We left Kimberley at about lunchtime and headed for Cape Town. It was to take us about ten hours because both Alison and Dorothy were able to do some of the driving. The road across the Karoo is probably the most boring one in South Africa. The scenery doesn't change much from flat and uninteresting. Here I must admit to making a small misjudgment. I miscalculated the distance to Beaufort West and I should have filled up when we had three quarters of a tank. This meant that when Alison was driving she noticed that the fuel gauge was showing 'Empty' and we still had nearly a hundred kilometers to go. Panicking was no use and I told her to keep going, at a steady speed (to conserve fuel), as every turn of the wheels took us closer to the petrol station. What didn't help the situation was that the Sun was setting and I was getting in the neck from Dorothy which probably made her feel better.

Beaufort West lies on the banks of a dry river bed but the road climbs a hill before you can free-wheel down to the town. I must admit that I've never been so glad to see town lights. Filling up meant that we had no more troubles on the way to Cape Town. We showed the children where we had stayed (Lord Milner Hotel) on our first trip to Kimberley and then we arrived in Cape Town about midnight.

When we turned up at Jo's he tossed us the keys to the house as he'd stay with his girlfriend and we'd have the house to ourselves. Not many people would have done that and it was much appreciated.

Dorothy and I have always loved the Cape – just like millions of other people and, although the kids had been there before, they were going to see the region with new eyes. I wanted to take them up to Namaqualand to show them the old field area but Dorothy quickly squashed that idea as she thought they'd be bored for too long.

The most obvious differences were in the new developments and the V&A Waterfront was the *"piece de resistance"*. It has remained that since then. There had also been money spent on the Table Mountain Cableway. New cable cars and new pathways/maps on the top of the mountain made one of the prime tourist spots much more welcoming.

But there is much more to the Cape than that. The scenery is spectacular and the place is made for tourists. Everything from the beaches, the restaurants/cafes and the wine farms are tourist friendly. Not only that but we had a bunch of old friends who knew the children from earlier years and were anxious to see us all again. We spent many afternoons and evenings eating braai food and drinking wine.

There is so much to see and do that we spent most days somewhere different. Cape Point was a fascinating and spectacular place to visit and a couple of days in Hermanus hoping to see some whales (they didn't turn up) were exhilarating. The kids discovered a shop in the Waterfront that sold biltong. Towards the end of the holiday, they pooled their allowances to buy 3kg (that's a lot!) and have it vacuum packed so that they could get it home. It didn't last long when they did!

Gordon and I managed to play a round of golf at Rondebosch while the ladies met up with some friends in the SA National Botanic Gardens at Kirstenbosch.

We all went on a trip to Robben Island where Nelson Mandela had been imprisoned for some considerable time. Rather an eerie place.

We flew up to Jo'burg and then home. It had been a great three weeks.

The end of 1999 meant getting ready for the new Millennium – or at least that was what the powers that be told us. I was/am of the opinion that the new Millennium was and the END of 2000 not at the start. The logic is irrefutable. The centuries start at the number xxx1 as there never was a year '0'. The calendar went from 1BC to 1AD. I've also never heard of the 19.99th Century. How can you call a century the 20th and have the year 2000 in another century? However it was decided that the change in the Millennium was to be at the end of 1999. In the end I thought it was a bit of a damp squib. Even the much-vaunted Millennium Bug failed to materialise. You would have thought at least one aeroplane would have fallen from the sky or one electricity supply would have been interrupted. Another scare story over-hyped by the media.

Being a salesman is not the job I ever wanted for myself. I didn't really enjoy it and, although the travelling may look glamorous to others, it gets pretty tedious after a while. Also there are always the vagaries of the market.

I was trying to convince a company in Jeddah, Saudi Arabia that they needed one of Reson's multibeam echosounders to help them in their coastal survey work. I got as close as actually seeing the purchase order on a desk but I never got to actually handle it.

The final strategy was to fly one of their guys over to Amsterdam so that he could see the unit working on a boat on the canal there. So over he came and I took him round and onto the boat for the demonstration. He seemed impressed but he never did buy. Why didn't he? I really don't know. Perhaps they didn't have the money, which seems unlikely, or didn't think it would help them which was clearly not the case. Then again some people are frightened of 'new' technology and think they're going to be out of a job when actually the units create more work.

The day of the demonstration was also the opening day of the France '98 World Cup and Scotland were playing Brazil in the opening match. I watched that (with the guy from Jeddah) in a bar in downtown Amsterdam. It's alright he was a Greek so there was no Saudi sinning. At one point I thought we had a chance of winning that game but the Brazilians came through in the end.

After that I had to travel to London as there was a big conference/exhibition on where Reson were participating. The hotel was quite a way from the conference/show hall so we hired a 'people carrier' as there were seven or eight Reson people attending. As I was the only Brit, I got the job of driving back and forth. Now, as I'm quite a sensible person, I don't drive in London if I can help it. Unfortunately none of the others knew the city either so imagine the scene with me driving while also navigating with a map on my lap as nobody else could do it. It's just as well that the police weren't watching.

Right across the road from the hotel was a pub that looked reasonable. The hotel bar was the place I wanted to watch Scotland play Norway and then Morocco. The 1-1 draw with Norway left us in with a chance but losing 0-3 to Morocco saw us going home. That result gave me a physical pain in my gut. I didn't know a football result could hurt that much.

Watching the game in the pub was a surreal experience as the sound was muted so that an Elvis impersonator could perform at the other end of the bar!!! Different!!!

Anyway salesmen live and die on their sales figures and I knew mine weren't good. It's also not a good sign when someone from HO comes over to 'help', so it wasn't a great surprise when the axe came. It's always an uncomfortable meeting and things were said on both sides that probably shouldn't have been.

So there I was unemployed again but with some 'redundancy' money to tide me over. I wasn't short of contacts so I started phoning around. One of the calls I made was to my old boss, Glenn Pearson, at Almisehal in Saudi. The call was just to ask him to keep his eyes and ears open for anyone looking for someone like me.

But before I could follow-up anything on that front, I had to get ready to be Torquil's best man. My brother was getting married (eventually!!). He had met a lady from Winchester in Hampshire where the wedding was taking place. I have no idea what the locals thought when all these kilted Scotsman descended on the village of Micheldever (where they were setting up home) for the reception. That was reinforced because Marian had managed to find a piper (in Southampton) so when he started playing they must have thought that the Scots were invading! It was a great day.

When I got back home, I gave Glenn a call just to check up and see if he'd heard anything. He told me of a job that was going in Al Khobar in the Eastern Province but as he explained what it was, something didn't sound right. I asked a couple of questions and he admitted that he wanted me to go into Almisehal's office and clear out some people who were causing disharmony in the organisation. As I knew most of the guys I told Glenn that I didn't want to deprive anyone of a job but he assured me that I didn't do it, the people were still going to go in the near future.

I needed the job so next thing I knew I was off back to Saudi Arabia.

16

Saudi Arabia (Part 2)

Saudi in the year 2000 (1420H) wasn't all that different from what it was like when I left in 1996. As I had been back fleetingly a few times since then, I'd kept up with people that I'd known. However this time there was one big difference. I was on 'single' status whereas before I was there as a married man.

When I'm at home with my family, I'm quite happy not to go out. The family's company is good enough for me. But when you're living alone, getting home from work with only a TV for company can slowly drive you round the bend.

Never mind, that was all in the future. I flew into Riyadh, which I'd never done before, where they X-ray the bags coming into Saudi. Well, you never know what these pesky ex-pats will try to smuggle in, do you? Actually that was a great improvement on the old method which had the customs guys rifling through your open bags. People used to pre-empt that search by putting shoes with the soles upwards (extremely unclean in Islam) or putting a layer of sanitary towels on top. That gave the men (the searchers were all male) the heebie-jeebies! I never tried the towel trick. I think it may have been a bit suspicious!

The next morning I was in the Riyadh HQ of Almisehal – another novelty as we hadn't had an office in Riyadh when I worked in the company before. That's when I learned just how big a problem I was being asked to sort out. I was basically to clear out the whole of the ex-pats in the Dammam office in the Eastern Province. That was going to be an uncomfortable job as I knew them all – some quite well.

It's quite a drive from Riyadh to Dammam; it takes just under 4 hours assuming you don't do some low level flying. The highway has six lanes all the way and you have plenty of time to think. As I drove down I thought about how I was going to handle the whole situation.

Needless to say I was greeted with little enthusiasm although the eastern ex-pats (Filipinos, Indians and Bangladeshis) were pleased to see me. Adnan Almisehal (who was nominally in charge of the office although it would really be me who would be running the show) couldn't stop smiling as he told me how glad he was to see me and to detail what had been going on. The three western ex-pats were less enthusiastic as I think they all realised that their days of having everything all their own way were about to end. In fact within a few days two of them had resigned and so were gone. The last one had his own agenda and it was clear that he was going to leave but on his own terms or so he thought.

Of course I had to get to know or renew contacts with the local customers. Some were easier than others but overall people were glad to see me back. I rejoined the local British Business Association (BBA) where I knew most of the guys.

I was organising an apartment when I was asked if I was interested in getting involved in the local ex-pat football 8-a-side league. Foolishly I told the lad that I had refereed in the past and, before I knew it, the league chairman was on the phone asking me to come along that Thursday afternoon to see if I was any good.

I turned up to find that there were three games of which I would ref the first two. I wanted to make a good impression so I really pushed myself to keep up with the play. The actual refereeing wasn't all that difficult as I believe it's just man management on an open field. By the end of the second game I was drenched in sweat and just about all in. As I came off and looking forward to a rest, Mick Couzens (the guy who ran the league) begged me to do the third game as the other ref was in bed with food poisoning. I couldn't really say no, so I dragged my body around the field again but I slept well that night!!!!

A few weeks later, we were joined by a professional referee, Kevin Bright, who had left Saudi a few years before while suffering from, what was thought to be terminal, cancer. He had fought off the condition and was now back working for British Aerospace. Kevin and I got on very well and he paid me a fine compliment when, after watching me referee a couple of games, he asked me where I had passed my refereeing badge. When I told him that I hadn't actually passed any refereeing tests, he was surprised and said that, from he could see, it was obvious I was a natural! That gave me a lot of confidence and the little hints that he passed on helped me a lot.

Kev and I refereed both this ex-pat league and the internal BAE league. The BAE lads had a clubhouse on their compound which was decorated with framed football shirts which covered all the walls. At the last count, there were over 110 such shirts.

Unfortunately, the cancer recurred in 2004/5 and Kev didn't make it. I was unable to attend his funeral but I will always remember him as a great friend and a fine man.

Work was coming together as I overcame the consequences of so many changes and our technicians were busy getting people, such as the seismic crews, up to speed with using GPS in their work. I also was busy with the Reson SeaBats which were being delivered to Arabian Oil and Aramco.

Another piece of kit that Aramco were considering buying and were asking us to supply was a fairly large ROV (underwater vehicle). Anybody who watches Discovery or National Geographic TV channels has seen one of these. They come in all sizes and shapes but the one that Aramco wanted was a "work" ROV which came in at about $1 million (USD).

As part of the sales process, I had to visit the manufacturer's facility – in Cape Cod, Massachusetts! So I planned to add the sales trip onto my summer break. This meant that I flew from Glasgow to Amsterdam (I always travelled on KLM in these days) and onto Boston. Picking up a hire car I drove south through what was known as the "Big Dig" (I always thought that Boston would be lovely once it was finished) and down to the Cape. It is a beautiful part of the world and, after a couple of days, I was a bit reluctant to leave but I had to. Flying back from Boston to Amsterdam and then onwards to Bahrain where one of my colleagues picked me up left me 'cream-crackered'. Little did I know that I was flying back to a real drama?

You'll remember the colleague who married the girl from Finland under Sharia law? Well, their marriage was falling apart; she was having an affair (with someone she eventually married) and my colleague had assaulted his cuckolder with a ceramic bar ashtray and had to be pulled off him.

Everyone in the ex-pat community was taking sides and I, all of a sudden, was thrown into the middle of it. It took a long time for it all to settle down but eventually it did. The marriage ended (I stood beside him as he petitioned the local court for a divorce), the lovers left for Europe and my colleague also departed for pastures new in the UAE.

Why did he get a divorce? He was a guy who had made a lot of money (on the Stock Exchange) and he wanted his ex-wife to have no rights over any of it. However, he had invested a lot of her money in his name (adding to his profits) and she never saw any of it. That left a bit of a bad taste in my mouth as I didn't think it was very ethical but I suppose he wanted some revenge.

So before I knew it I was the only western ex-pat in the office and life was just bumping along. The seismic companies were ordering gear as was Aramco. Then the office in Riyadh decided to get serious about the burgeoning communications industry. We were involved with Sony Ericsson and heavily involved in pushing out the GSM Mobile network. We actually had a subsidiary company building the GSM towers.

Aramco decided that the company would invest in satellite communications, in particular a system knot as VSAT. All of a sudden, we became the agents for a company from Aberdeen, we had to find a new office and buy a new fleet of large 4x4 vehicles. The VSAT terminals were destined for the deep desert seismic and drilling crews. Some were mobile sites, others more permanent and we even put some on vessels serving the offshore fields. The VSAT on the hydrographic vessel, *Karan 8*, even changed the crew's habits. They used to congregate and chat at the coffee machine but now they met at the VSAT terminal.

There was a serious side as well. There had been occasions when a crew member's family member had been hospitalised or even died and the ship had been out of contact. On the professional side, the ship generated a lot of data when they were surveying. In the past that data had to be physically taken off the boat on tapes or discs. Now the data could be transferred over the VSAT link and processed immediately.

So the quiet office became a hive of activity which actually was a bit of a blessing as days flew by.

Saudi Arabia is peculiar in a lot of ways but one that takes a bit getting used to, is the holiday programme. There are no public holidays such as Christmas, New Year, Bank Holidays, etc. Of course, Saudi doesn't recognise any holidays associated with Christianity.

The Saudi Arabian National Day is Sept 23rd but was NOT an official holiday. Not even the Prophet Mohammed's Birthday was a holiday although most other countries in the region did have it as one.

There were two periods that WERE holidays, both known as Eids. Unlike the National Day, they are scheduled by the Hijra calendar. 'Hijra' translates as 'flight' and dates from the year Mohammed was kicked out of Makkah and fled to Madinah where he could preach Islam in peace. As with everything in Saudi, the holidays are tied to Islam. The first Eid is the few days after the holy month of Ramadan when Muslims fast and study the Koran. The second Eid is tied to the major pilgrimage time of Hajj when about 4 million pilgrims visit Makkah.

The Hijra calendar is a lunar one so the dates advance but about 10 or 11 days a year against the solar Gregorian calendar used by the rest of the world. The Hajj Eid is ALWAYS 70 days after the end of Ramadan.

The company always gave us a week off for both Eids which meant that we actually had 9 days off. Another aspect of these holiday periods is that most of the population is on the move and air fares rocket.

I would keep my annual leave (I was entitled to two return air tickets a year) for the summer and the Xmas/New Year period so I would remain in kingdom for the Eids.

There was downside, though. It was boring!! If I stayed around Khobar, I would go crazy. You can watch only so much TV. So I tried to plan things to do.

For instance there is a set of craters down in the Empty Quarter made when a meteorite broke up as it came down in the early 19th century. Being in the Empty Quarter they periodically filled up with sand and then emptied as the winds blew. The place was known as "Hadidah" which translates as "Place of Iron". I had talked to a few Aramco personnel who had been down near there and had done quite a lot of research so I was pretty well prepared. I didn't keep the trip secret and many people said that they wanted to come along but they had all dropped out by the time to go.

I've travelled a lot off-road and by myself and so I wasn't too concerned. It just reinforced a feeling I have that you can't rely on people. As I planned to be away for about a week, I loaded up 10 days-worth of food and water. I had left my route in the office in case the vehicle broke down or I fell ill or got injured and didn't make it back when I should have. Even though my Nissan Patrol had a double tank, I couldn't take all the fuel I would need so I was depending on the Aramco fuel dumps.

So off I went and all went well until I reached the first dump. There was plenty of diesel but NO petrol. I wasn't out of fuel so I thought I could reach the next dump but I was told that that dump had NO petrol either. Right there and then I knew that I wasn't going to reach the craters and the disappointment was palpable. I did stay out in the deep desert for a couple of nights and the place is really empty. I did see a hawk and some lizards but there were no flies or mosquitoes. At night the stars were awesome. It's a fact of today's world that it's very difficult to be in a place where's there's no sound. The Empty Quarter is such a place. It's rather eerie but after a while remarkably pleasant.

Another trip I took was pretty long – in fact it lasted a week. Again I had to do some research and preparation as I was travelling across the sub-continent. My plans were to visit two sites linked by an ancient civilisation but separated both by distance and political boundaries.

Petra, in Jordan, is a World Heritage site and has huge numbers of visitors every year. Although it has imprints of Roman and Byzantine culture, its major flowering was between 100BC and 100AD when it was the capital of the Nabataean civilisation. It was at the crossroads of so many trading routes and the city grew rich and powerful. Petra is known as the 'Rose City' because the colours of the rocks. It was "lost" for centuries – at least to western eyes – but a German explorer managed to persuade the locals to show him in and the rest, as they say, is history. There is a tradition (myth?) that the wise men bought their gold, frankincense and myrrh there.

However, deep inside Saudi Arabia, about 250 kms northwest of Madinah, lies the place which was the southern 'capital' of the Nabataeans, Mada'in Salah. MS (as I shall refer to it now), known to the Saudis as Al-Hijr, is a protected site in Saudi Arabia, but nowhere near as well-known as Petra. Saudi discourages tourism so the only people who visit MS are bored ex-pats who manage to get away from the cities long enough to make the trip. From anywhere in the kingdom, you need at least two days, perhaps three, to give yourselves enough time to see all there is to see. There are no tour guides, horses, trucks or buggies to take you around so you'd better have a decent 4x4 or you'll get bogged down in the sand as there are no asphalt roads at the site. Nowadays you can get a permit nearby but when I wanted to go there you had to apply for the permit months in advance.

After my last experience, I didn't ask anyone if they wanted to come; I just went. I drove to Riyadh after finishing work on Wednesday afternoon and slept there at a friend's house. It then took me a whole day to drive to Al Ula, the town near MS. Al Ula is mentioned in the Bible as Dadan and has been a settlement for a long time. It is situated round an oasis and you can still see the old mud built buildings.

I spent a good six hours driving around the MS site which includes one of the main stations, now refurbished, of the old Hijaz railway. That's the one that appears in the David Lean epic film "Lawrence of Arabia" starring Peter O'Toole and Omar Sharif. The tombs are spectacular and I wondered about the time taken to excavate them. I must admit that they are an impressive sight.

One of the advantages of being on your own is that you are not held back by your slower companions. You take as little or as much time as you want over something and then you move on. You don't have to wait until the little old lady decides to get back on the bus.

So in the middle of the afternoon, I was off up the road to Tabuk where I had arranged to stay with an old friend in the BAe compound.

I'm going to break off here and write about the Hijaz railway. Originally it ran from Madinah (where Station #1 is) to Amman (Jordan) and onto Damascus in Syria. You can even make an argument for it continuing to Istanbul. It was known locally as the "the Women's Railway" as 'real' pilgrims made the journey by camel caravan. Built by the Ottoman Turks (with a German engineer in charge) as a way of controlling the region, there were a few main stations like Madinah, MS, and Tabuk but additionally there were blockhouses every 10 miles where small squads of soldiers were garrisoned to protect the railway and the passengers. The railway was built in the last throes of the Ottoman Empire and when that fell apart after WW1, and Saudi Arabia emerged as an independent state, the railway fell into disrepair and eventually the track was torn up probably because the new state didn't want any reminders that Turkey used to rule that part of the world.

All that was left were the buildings and the raised ballast of the track. Ex-pats 'discovered' the railway and it became almost a badge of honour to drive along it. The most popular route was south from MS to Madinah although the non-Muslims couldn't get to Station # 1 as it was inside the "*Haram*" or forbidden zone around the Prophet's Mosque. In fact, that route became part of a very popular book about driving tours; so much so that the whole route became picked clean by souvenir hunters. The only things they couldn't take were the buildings, although they tried, and the old rolling stock scattered around the tracks.

There is one junction about 70 or so kilometres northwest of Madinah which was probably used as a shunting point. There is a locomotive and its tender on their side beside the track and it is popularly known as where

Lawrence blew up the Hijaz train as depicted in the famous scene in the movie. Well, it isn't! Lawrence did attack the railway but much further north.

A few words about T. E. Lawrence may be appropriate here. Against all expectations of his senior officers, TEL became an organiser of the warring Arab factions as they rebelled against Turkish rule. The desert was the making of him. All accounts describe him initially as someone who didn't stand out in a crowd but something happened to change him and the history of this part of the world. Cutting away all the innuendoes and legends, he singlehandedly gave the Allies the chance of victory in this theatre of the war. Before he arrived, the Arabs were fighting each other and the Turks were having an easy ride. I suppose his greatest achievements were attacking the port of Aquaba from the landward side when all attacks were anticipated from the sea (shades of Singapore in WW2) and crossing the Sinai Desert alone. He DID attack the railway but I believe that was a gesture to show the locals that the Turks were not all powerful. His story has been written by many authors, all of them much more skilled than me, but his name is still linked with this region and, even 100 years after the events, he is not forgotten. I think of him as the last great Victorian adventurer.

Let's get back to the railway. I'm going to talk a bit about the track going north from MS later on but the remains of the track are evident around Tabuk and north towards Jordan. Once you are in Jordan, it is obvious that the Hijaz railway is not all destroyed. A spur line runs to Aquaba, mainly carrying phosphate to the port, while the main line still runs up to Amman and then onto Damascus. It is possible to ride between the two cities but it gets quite complicated at the border, I believe. I'd still like to do it, though.

Leaving Tabuk, one drives through spectacular scenery to the coast and then north to the Jordanian border. I'd driven through Saudi border posts going into Bahrain, Qatar and Kuwait and they are pretty slick. So was this one but not on the Jordanian side! On the Saudi side the windows are all in order but in Jordan you have to run around from office to office (even waking up the bank clerk so that you can get local currency!) before you've got all the stamps required and you can enter Jordan legally. However it was all done with smiles on both my and their faces. The Jordanians seemed genuinely pleased to have me visit their country.

The road north is excellent and it's all well signposted. The turn-off for Wadi Mousa/Petra is about a third of the way to Amman and by the time I got there it was getting late. As I drove towards Petra, the road started to climb and the temperature started to fall. Don't let anyone tell you that the desert is always warm. It can get pretty cold and, when I had to stop for a comfort break at the side of the road, my teeth were chattering by the time I got back into the cab.

I booked into the Crown Plaza Hotel which is right beside the entrance to Petra and had a very pleasant evening and comfortable sleep.

Up bright and early, off I went into Petra. I'd looked at lots of books and internet pages but the actuality just blew me away. Again, being on my own, I didn't have to wait on anyone else and I didn't have to listen to the standard "patter" of the tour guides. I think the sheer scale was what was breathtaking and the huge tombs put those of MS in the shade. However Petra has problems. The large numbers of visitors could be a problem although I think that they are fairly well controlled. It was actually pretty quiet when I was there this time. The biggest problem is natural. If one compares Petra and MS, one is struck by the greater definition of the sculptures (of all types) in MS. This is due to the rocks being harder and more resistant to erosion. I also believe that MS doesn't get as much rain as Petra so erosion is slower anyway. I'm not sure how that can be countered. Maybe people should visit Petra as soon as they can to see it in its glory.

There are tombs as soon as you enter the site but the real Petra doesn't start until you reach the "*Siq*". This is a 1.5 kilometre long cleft in the rock which doubles as the entrance to Petra. At the top end of it (it drops about a hundred metres along its length) there are the remains of a gateway. If these gates were shut the inhabitants were as safe as anyone in the ancient world. Obviously people walk on the floor of the gully but the walls tower above you. It narrows and broadens along its length but it never gets too narrow – horse carts go up and down it all day. It ends at the tomb known as "The Treasury", the one made famous by the film "Indiana Jones and the Last Crusade". It is possible to imagine the Nabataeans processing down the Siq banging drums and playing pipes during their religious festivals. The area in front of the Treasury can hold many hundreds of people. There is a Siq at MS but it is far shorter although it does have a large cavernous tomb at its mouth much like the one which sits beside the Treasury.

As you walk round, past the amphitheatre, you are struck by the sheer scale and the number of tombs. Of all sizes, it seems every nook and cranny has a tomb. Turning into what is known as the main street, the impressive columns lead onto major courtyards and buildings. MS has no everyday buildings left. There are elephant heads on the tops of columns showing that they once were common hereabouts. These beasts are liable to have been of the same sub-species that Hannibal used when crossing the Alps. The North African elephant is now extinct.

The next climb is to the "Monastery" which was used as a church a few centuries ago. It is a long climb but it is well worth it. Again a wide open area, with an entrance on one side for a procession, sits in front of the rock sculpture. The acoustics would have allowed the assembly to hear every word.

Coming back down into the main part of Petra, I visited the Byzantine mosaics which are under a protective roof but missed the sign for the "High Places". Those would have to wait until my next visit. I spent another night in the hotel and left the next day to drive back to Saudi. I lingered a bit because some of the geology beside the road is spectacular. As I had passed it in the twilight before I hadn't really appreciated its full splendour.

I had arranged to stay another night in the BAe compound in Tabuk but I was so tired after all the driving that I stayed two nights. I knew that the next drive was going to be one of the longest I'd ever done.

Take a look at the map of Saudi Arabia. Tabuk is in the northwest corner. There is a road which runs east and then northeast to Sakakah and then Arar, on the northern border near Iraq. Sakakah has an old hilltop fort/castle (great photo opportunity) and Arar was to become the centre of the new phosphate mining industry in Saudi. That was all in the future though and when I was there the region was a bit of a backwater. The road also brushed the edge of the Nafud desert, which, in my opinion, is far worse than the Empty Quarter, although nowhere near the same size.

Running southeast from Arar is the Tapline Road. It parallels an oil pipeline which, in turn, runs semi-parallel to the Saudi/Iraq border. It is straight as an arrow and is over 500kms long. It is easily the most boring road I have ever driven along and, consequently, the most dangerous. I stopped a couple of times, once for fuel and the other because I felt myself falling asleep. Once I had reached the junction where it joined the road between Khobar and Kuwait, I knew that I was almost home and the feeling was almost euphoric.

I had been away almost a week and had a fund of stories to tell.

About six months later, I was at a function where I fell into a conversation with a guy I knew quite well. Kevin Baynes was from Manchester, a pipeline engineer with Bechtel and an all-round good guy. The contract he was working on with Aramco was either finishing or not being renewed so he was going to be leaving Saudi in less than a year.

He came right to the point. As he was leaving Saudi, he wanted to do the trip I had just done and was I interested in doing it again during the next Eid holiday. Hold me back, as they say! So we planned to retrace my steps but this time at least the driving and the costs would be shared.

We took a bit longer at the sites because there were two of us and Kevin hadn't photographed any of this like I had. I'm only going to mention the differences in our trip. I'm presuming that reading the repetition of what I'd done before would be boring.

When we were in the hotel in Al Ula, we fell into a conversation with a Frenchman who, it turned out, was a local tourist guide. We had already been round MS that day but it was a fascinating chat. He told us that the railway running north from MS was far more interesting than the route south and we could easily make Tabuk, although the track did get a bit rough at the very end. We looked at each other and said, "Why not?"

The next morning found us getting ready to set out when I had a thought. As far as I was aware, there was no documented route (in the public domain) along the northern part of the railway so why shouldn't we produce one? We had a GPS (not a SatNav – this was way before they appeared!) and an odometer, notebook and pen. So setting the route to zero at the hotel car-park, off we went.

To jump ahead, the route, GPS readings and distances were all published in the Eastern Province British Businessmen's Association (BBA) Newsletter. Not perhaps the most prestigious publication but it's there. I'm not sure how many back copies there are but if anyone wants one, I'm sure the BBA could oblige.

As soon as we left the tar road we knew that we had taken good advice. Because there was no easily found published information on this part of the railway, it hadn't been picked clean by souvenir hunters. We took some though and I've still got mine in my garden shed in Scotland. Having driven the southerly half I can say that the scenery is better on the northern route. About halfway to Tabuk there are the remains of one of the major stations serving the railway which was protected by a large Turkish fort. The fort is now surrounded by a fence put up by the Saudis but somehow the locals have managed to use the interior as a scrapyard for old cars!

There is a waterhole nearby (probably the reason why the fort and station were built there) and in the mud at its edge was the paw print of a rather large cat, which I believe belonged to the rare and rarely seen Yemeni leopard. We never saw one but they were around.

Many of the remote blockhouses were protected by low-walled gun emplacements on hills nearby which can still be seen. Another strange site in the desert was low rectangular mounds of black material of about an acre each. At first we had no idea what they were but subsequent research suggested that they were mounds of ballast used to repair the track as needed.

The trip took a bit longer than we thought so we struck out for the tar road before we got to the tunnel and onto Tabuk. The sun was getting lower so discretion took over. On reaching the tar, we headed for Aquaba where Kevin wanted to dive. He was the head of the local dive club and he'd never been down in the Red Sea. So I had a lovely relaxing morning while he went off underwater.

After visiting Petra, we stopped at Wadi Rum, another of T. E. Lawrence's haunts. The locals have named spots "Lawrence's Spring" and "Lawrence's House" – for the tourists – but it is where he did spend a lot of his campaign.

Our route home followed the Tapline as before and again we were away for almost exactly a week. And once again, people were intrigued by our stories.

I suppose that dying is part of living but no matter how and when it happens, it's always a shock to those who are left behind.

As I wrote above, I refereed some of the ex-pat football games. We had many pretty good players around but one of the best was a Welshman, Hugh Lewis. He was in his 30s but still had great ball control and his long range shooting was a joy to behold.

Hugh worked for the courier company DHL and he travelled around the region. On one these trips to Jeddah, on the Red Sea coast of Saudi, he was playing in a friendly football game when he collapsed and died. It turned out that he suffered from an enlarged heart, a condition which had never been diagnosed. He left behind a wife and two small boys.

The whole ex-pat football community was stunned and we held two minute silences for him before each game when the season restarted. That was one of the most emotional things I've ever done on a football field.

One of the other activities I got involved in was the local darts league. In fact I even got to the singles final and won the doubles title. One of my teammates was a guy called Sinclair Ash who had a plummy Home Counties accent. However it turned out that he was born in Edinburgh and moved south as a boy. His wife, Pam, came from Glasgow.

One evening as we were sitting down eating our snack in between the singles and doubles, we fell in a conversation. He told me about his early days in Edinburgh and then asked me where I came from. I told him that the village I grew up in was so small that most Scottish people had never heard of it. He insisted that I tell him and when I said, "Gartmore.", he laughed and said, "You won't believe this but Pam and I were married in Gartmore Church!" I was stunned. It turned out that they knew folk in Aberfoyle and they advised the Ashes to try the minister in Gartmore rather than the one in Aberfoyle.

A couple of months later, Sinclair and Pam were at their house in Spain and were on their way to the airport to return to Saudi when Sinclair complained of feeling unwell.

He died that day in hospital.

If that was not bad enough, now we come to what I think is going to be one of the most difficult bits of this whole treatise to write.

The eleventh of September, 2001 was much like any other day. We had moved to our new office and warehouse space and probably I sent off some of our technicians to the desert with some VSAT equipment.

At about 4.30 in the afternoon, I noticed that my Yahoo internet home page had a small, one line note that a plane had flown into skyscraper in New York. To be honest, I didn't really take much notice; I had things to finish off before I went home. As I was driving home my mobile phone rang. I was expecting this sales rep to turn up the next day. He was flying into Dammam from Qatar and his first words were that he was still coming. I asked why wouldn't he be and he then realised that I was in the dark as to what had happened in New York. He advised me to switch on the TV as soon as I got home.

I did so and watched with increasing horror as the second plane hit. As news bulletins do, the scenes were run over and over again. Like everyone else, I was stunned and just sat there for a couple of hours not really knowing how to react.

There's a primitive urge that people need company in times of hurt or great trouble so I found myself going to the compound club/bar just to talk to someone.

A number of guys had the same idea and I soon realised that I was the only non-American there. We were all rapt at what was unfolding on the TV.

One of the guys was a very experienced engineer and he suddenly said, "Those towers are coming down!" Seemingly the internal structure was such that as soon as the integrity went there was nothing to stop the Twin Towers collapsing. It's a horrible feeling knowing what was going to happen and not being able to do anything other than watch in morbid fascination. That sorts of knocks all those conspiracy theories on the head, doesn't it? Unless of course he was a plant to divert us away from "The Truth"!!

The other quote from that evening was, "They're going to turn Afghanistan into a car park". I can't remember who said it first but no-one disagreed. These guys all knew who was behind it before it became public knowledge.

When I got into my office the following morning, guess what was the main topic of conversation? My Sudanese secretary, a lad called Younis (no female secretaries for us), came into my office with a smile on his face asking if I'd seen what had happened. He left without the smile when I reminded him that the last time someone had done something like this to the US (Japan), they had a couple of atom bombs dropped on them! I think that brought home the gravity of the possible consequences.

As the days went on and it was revealed that 16 out of the 19 hijackers were Saudis, the kingdom started to try and mitigate the damage that would cause. First it was denied that the hijackers were Saudis, then their passports must have been stolen or faked (!), then it was all a Mossad plot and they had switched the blame to the Arabs. The 'Arab Street' quickly latched onto the rumour that all the Jewish workers stayed home that day so none was killed so Israel MUST have been behind it. Unfortunately some people in the Western (American-hating) media also promulgated that story which gave it so much oxygen that even 10 years later it is still extant in the region.

I think the Saudi government realised the implications and eventually enacted laws to suppress home grown terrorists but the man-on-the-street still clings to the belief that the Israelis were behind it all. It doesn't take much thought to find many reasons to deduce why that is ridiculous but the Arabs don't let logic get in way of their prejudices.

The events of that day led to many consequences – the wars in Iraq and Afghanistan to name only a couple – and many more competent and knowledgeable people than myself have written about them. However, the effects were far-reaching but not many have recorded them. We, for instance, saw a lot more security activity. We were stopped at many more checkpoints where our papers were scrutinised and bags, etc. were searched as folks entered shopping malls and the like. All of a sudden the checks on vehicles entering the western compounds were much more rigorous and many social events were postponed indefinitely. Concrete barriers were everywhere and it was almost like we were on lockdown. All of a sudden people just went home and stayed in. Of course, it couldn't go on like that and after a few weeks with no incidents, things started to get back to normal, although it never really returned to the pre-9/11 situation.

It might be a good idea to lighten the mood a little right about now. Believe it or not, one of the many things I did to relieve the boredom after work was to take part in amateur dramatics. For those that know me that may seem a bit improbable but I quite enjoyed it. I was on stage for a couple of productions and even directed a pantomime. It went on stage as the restrictions were lifting and, in fact, was the first big social event for about six months. The two evening performances were dinner theatre and they were both packed. It's the only time that I've been involved in one of these which got a standing ovation. I could be deprecating and say that the audience was just very glad and relieved to be entertained for a change and they would have stood to applaud just about anything, However I'd like to go with that it was a superb performance and production and leave it at that.

I used to go to quiz nights as well and struck up a friendship with three guys Stanley, Graeme and Norman. We made a pretty good team. But I'd like to tell you a couple of stories about Graeme.

He was a world-class skydiver and would go off to the World Championships every year. One year the event was held in the US Mid-West but when Graeme came back he was limping quite badly. He showed us the scars but they didn't seem to be healing. Eventually we persuaded him to go and see a doctor. It turned out that he had broken nearly every bone in his foot which needed pinning and a plaster.

As the foot healed he had to go for physiotherapy in a downtown clinic and, because of the plaster and bandages, he wore shorts. Now shorts are not looked on with favour by conservative Muslims. Next to the clinic in Al Khobar there is a mosque and when Graeme (and Norman who was driving him around) came out of the clinic, one of the mosque's staff (let's call him a mutawah) started giving Graeme some verbal abuse about his shorts. It was all in Arabic so Graeme just shrugged. The mutawah was pointing with his little short stick (which they all carry) at the bandages which covered a barely healed grass scrape/burn. When Graeme attempted to walk off, ignoring this chap, he hit Graeme right across the bandages. The pain must have been intense. Graeme is/was ex-British Forces so he wasn't taking that so he grabbed the mutawah by the throat, pushed him up against the mosque wall and gave him, what is known in polite circles as, a "Glasgow Kiss". The mutawah slumped to the ground and Graeme started to walk off to his car only to see a policeman walk out from under a nearby palm tree. He had seen the whole thing. Graeme had visions of a stretch in a Saudi gaol but the policeman just said (in perfect English), "He's been asking for that for a long time. Off you go."

Mutawahs were not all employed by the Commission (CAVES) or by mosques. Some of them had real jobs some even in Aramco. It happened that one (let's call him Abdullah) was in the same department where Graeme worked as a consultant. Graeme is probably the most irreligious person I've ever met (and I've met a few) so all Abdullah's efforts to convert him to Islam fell on (very) stony ground.

Graeme and a couple of friends went over to Bahrain for a weekend blowout. On the Thursday night they were on a bit of a pub-crawl and stumbled into a dimly lit bar. After a couple of moments as their eyes adjusted, Graeme thought he recognised someone at the other end of the bar. As he went over, he realised that was Abdullah and he was drunk as a skunk! Never one to take a backward step, Graeme went up to him and said, "Hey, Abdullah! You shouldn't be here and you certainly shouldn't be in such a state". Abdullah replied, in a drunken slur, "I am in Bahrain. I am not in Saudi Arabia. Allah cannot see me here!!" So there you have the inspiration for the title of this book.

The year 2002 was the year that finally the Jack family didn't have to worry about school holidays anymore. Alison had already graduated from Robert Gordon's University in Aberdeen with a 2:1 Honours Degree in Mechanical and Offshore Engineering, Kirsty was halfway through her teacher's degree and Gordon went off to Glasgow University to study Chemistry. Kirsty was still living at home as her campus was in Ayr but Gordon moved into Halls of Residence just off Maryhill Road in Glasgow.

Another Ramadan came round with another Eid holiday. What was I going to do? Fortunately I was on a mailing list that showed that the Middle

East branch of the Hydrographic Society was holding a meeting and equipment demonstration in Abu Dhabi halfway through the week. It looked like I was off to the UAE.

I'd been to the UAE many times, mainly to Dubai but I knew a lot of people in Abu Dhabi as there were a few survey companies based there that I dealt with in the past. I drove there just to pass the time. It took about eight hours including crossing the border.

I was booked into the hotel where the meeting was to take place for a couple of nights. After the meeting, there was a reception and, as we were NOT in Saudi Arabia, alcohol was available. I admit I drank more than I should have and went to bed a bit the worse for wear.

My mobile telephone went off somewhere between 2 and 3 in the morning. That wasn't that unusual but this was unexpected as it was during an Eid holiday and people knew I wasn't in Saudi. I answered groggily and heard Kirsty say, "Just to let you know that Gordon's in hospital but he's OK." I must have said something and then she hung up and I fell back on the pillow.

Wakening up in the morning, I thought I'd dreamt it. However I called home to get no reply. I then called Kirsty's mobile. I couldn't get through. It wasn't in range or something. This was getting worrying. Luckily I had numbers for other people except I didn't have Brenda's new number where I thought Dorothy might be. So I called Billy's home (Dorothy's brother) to ask if he knew where she was. He gave me Brenda's number and sounded really concerned but I didn't ask why. I got through to Brenda's house and Dorothy and Kirsty were there.

Now comes the kick in the guts.

The night before Dorothy had been getting ready for a night out with girls from her work when the phone rang. Kirsty answered it and immediately gave it to Dorothy. It was the Western Infirmary in Glasgow telling her that Gordon had been admitted with suspected meningitis. He was stable but she had to come to the hospital. Kirsty drove her up to Glasgow (an hour away) and she went via Brenda's as Brenda was a hospital nurse (at the Royal in Glasgow) and would know something about what was going on.

When they got to the hospital, they were shown into the 'Family Room'. It was only later that Brenda said she had feared the worst as the 'Family Room' is where people are told bad news. However, a couple of folk came by to interrogate Dorothy as to where Gordon had been and who he'd been with. She was in a state and not really in a mood to answer any questions. All she wanted was to see her son.

Eventually she was allowed to see him but she didn't recognise him. He had innumerable tubes coming out of him including a breathing tube, was on oxygen and he was in an induced coma.

We later found out that on the Monday he had complained of not feeling well in an afternoon lab and had gone home early. The next morning his flat-mates had asked him if he was coming to classes. He said he was staying home as he was still ill. When the flat-mates came home in the afternoon, they went into see him. He shut his eyes when they switched the light on and they noticed the rash all over him. One of them recognised the signs of meningitis and called the Residence doctor. He arrived and filled Gordon full of penicillin to stop the infection then rushed him to the Western.

When they got him to the hospital, the staff went to work. Gordon did say that getting the catheter put in was horrible. I believe it took 7 people to hold him while they did it. Basically they shut his organs down and let machines keep him alive.

That was what Dorothy saw and then she had to leave. The doctor told her that the next 12 hours were the critical time. They asked her if they could use a cocktail of drugs that was new to the NHS on Gordon. It had been tested and approved by the FDA in the US but it was still experimental in the UK. Dorothy told them to go ahead. What did she have to lose? There was no way that she was going back to Ayr and so she and Kirsty slept (!) at Brenda's.

So that was the situation when I called. That's a phone call I hope I never have to repeat. Dorothy broke down, I was sobbing and eventually Brenda had to take the phone and tell me that they were going back to the hospital at lunchtime to get an update.

What could I do? Not a lot. I just had to sit around and wait. I told the folk involved in the equipment demonstration what had happened but salespeople are a breed apart. They don't take things like that in and they gaily went off on their sales pitch to someone who didn't give a tinker's toss!

Another point was that in those days mobile phones didn't work everywhere along the roads and I didn't want to be out of reach if I needed to be contacted. Also, as I've said, it was an Eid holiday and planes were full, travel agents were closed and I didn't have enough cash on me to just buy a ticket. I had to get back to Khobar and then organise a flight home. So I decided to stay in Abu Dhabi until I knew what was happening. It was a long time till the next phone call.

A feeling of helplessness is one of the worst feelings in anybody's experience. It's bad enough when you're standing next to whatever or whoever it is you can't help. Try feeling that way 7000 miles away.

When the phone call came, I couldn't believe that it was the same Dorothy on the end of the line. She was almost jaunty. Seemingly Gordon was awake but couldn't talk because of the tubes, etc. He was *compos mentis* and could write questions on a pad. The doctor was astounded and couldn't believe that it was the same guy he'd admitted the night before. It must have been the new drugs cocktail.

He was still covered in sores and his eyes were totally bloodshot so he wasn't out of the woods yet. He was to stay in the Western for a few days and then he was to be transferred to the Beatson Clinic at the Gartnavel Hospital on Great Western Road.

We found out later that he had become quite a celebrity with newspaper articles and spots on the radio. Because he was the first person to have the cocktail administered, he was also a celebrity with the medical students, many of whom came past to photograph and interview him.

So I drove back to Khobar in a lot better frame of mind than I thought I would. Every now and again I would talk to Dorothy on the phone and her mood was getting better every time.

On the Saturday morning I got into the office and immediately told my secretary to get me on the next flight home. When Adnan got in, he asked me if I enjoyed my Eid holiday. I told him I hadn't as Gordon was in hospital and I was leaving that night and I didn't know when I would be back. As it was early December, I knew that I wasn't going to be back before the New Year.

I got home on the Sunday morning and Dorothy and Kirsty took me straight round to the clinic and Gordon in his room. He was so weak that he needed help to go to the bathroom and to shower. It broke my heart to see him like that but I was happy to see him alive. Then Alison walked in with her future husband, Adam. Not the way I had imagined meeting my future son-in-law.

The next few days were a flurry of going to see Gordon and we could see that he was getting better and stronger all the time. Then he got an infection which knocked him back but he even got over that and the day came when we could take him home, just in time for Christmas. It was a family time which meant much, much more than many other Christmases and New Years.

I took Gordon down to our GP's so that he could get his dressings changed and even there he was a celebrity. The nurses all came to see him and ask him how he was.

By the first week in January, it was obvious that he was well and truly on the mend and I could go back to work. He recovered so well that he went back to university in the February so he didn't miss many classes. His was an isolated incident and it was never established where or how he had contracted it. But we all knew how lucky he had been. Thank the Lord for the eagle eyes of his flat mates.

So there I was back in Saudi but I must admit that my heart wasn't in it and my head was elsewhere.

I said above that Saudi in 2000 was much the same as it had been when I had left in 1996. Well, in 2003 it was a very different place. Although September 11th, 2001 had a lot to answer for, that wasn't the only worrying aspect of life inside the kingdom. There had been a number of car bombs and drive-by shootings, in Riyadh especially, targeting western ex-pats. A couple of these had resulted in deaths of BAe personnel such as Robert Dent on the 20th February, 2003 and for a while it was thought they were being sought out. The Saudis couldn't/wouldn't believe that any of the local populace could have been involved in such dreadful acts so they started a rumour that it was a turf war over the illegal supply of alcohol. One of the victims' vehicles had been found with a bottle of home-made wine in it (they were on their way to a barbeque) a fact that the Saudis used to deflect attention away from the fact that a middle-aged married couple had been killed!!

I knew people who were involved in the supply of alcohol and they were not the type to draw attention to themselves. There was no way that they were going to start something like Chicago during Prohibition which the Saudis wanted everyone to think. Unfortunately, many people who should have known better, including Attaches at western Embassies and Consulates and ex-military folk fell for the line. Then came 9/11 and most, if not all, realised that they had been duped.

There WAS an active terrorist community in Saudi Arabia and it was time that the government did something about it.

In the end, the Saudis hummed and hawed not doing much and so, on the evening of May 12th, 2003, the inevitable, which meant that they had to take their collective heads out of the sand, happened.

As most of the city slept, three ex-pat compounds were attacked by home-grown Saudi terrorists – Jadawel, Al Hamra Oasis and the compound of the US company, Vinnell Corp. Vinnell was involved in training the Saudi National Guard (SANG) and I had a lot of business with them as we supplied over 1200 GPS units to SANG. There was a US Military mission who went under the guise of the Office of Procurement Management (OPM) – SANG. Their downtown car park (where I had parked many times) was the site of a car bomb a few months later.

About an hour before midnight, an explosive-packed car tried to get into the Jadawel compound but was stopped by the security guards. The terrorists opened fire killing two and wounding two. The car exploded killing the 5/6 terrorists and a Filipino worker.

At Oasis and Vinnell compounds the terrorists managed to force their way through the gates firing at the guards. Once inside they detonated their bombs devastating both compounds. All of the terrorists died – 12 of them – and good riddance. I hope they enjoyed their plates of white grapes!!!! (There is a school of thought that the Koranic reference to "72 virgins" could actually be "72 white grapes") The irony of that is almost justice. Anyway as far as I'm concerned, all of them are burning in everlasting hell!!

A British ex-pat couple I knew lived on the Oasis Compound. Cliff and Jane Hoban were lovely people. Cliff was always laughing and joking and Jane kept him in order. Thinking about them even now brings a smile to my face. When the compound was attacked they were asleep in their bed. When the car bomb exploded it brought their concrete bedroom ceiling down on them. They literally never knew what hit them. They were so badly crushed that the authorities had to fly their son out from Britain so they could check their DNA.

A total of 35 people died that night and 160 were injured.

The whole country was shocked and the ex-pat community was stunned. Suddenly wives and children were going home because of the situation. Security at compounds became extremely tight and everyone had a worried look on their faces. There was no joking about this!

Then there were more attacks – one at the Holiday Inn in Yanbu (where I'd spent a couple of nights in the past) and a shooting incident near the BAe compound in Tabuk. Another compound near Riyadh was attacked later in the year where 18 people died and 122 wounded. No western ex-pats lived on that compound and the dead residents were all non-Saudi Arabs from Egypt and Lebanon.

The lockdown was claustrophobic and I was feeling very uncomfortable. I spoke to Dorothy on a regular basis and I could tell that she was worried about me. She never nagged and let me decide what I was going to do. I thought long and hard. I was in my early 50s and would I get another job if I left? When the attacks continued, my mind was made up. I was going home.

I had no idea what I was going to do but even stacking shelves in Tesco had its attractions. As a courtesy, I phoned around my contacts and business friends to say goodbye. There was one guy who just seemed to be always out of the office when I called. Rick Gore ran a survey company in Abu Dhabi and I had done business with him before even socialising with him. I was flying out on the Thursday and on the Tuesday I made one last try to catch him.

This time he was in and I told him the news. He asked what I was going to do and I gave him the Tesco line. He then shocked me saying that he needed someone in Baku (Azerbaijan) to cover for the Operations Manager who was on long-term sick leave. Was I interested? I was, so he told me to go home, take a break and to give him a call in a couple of weeks.

It looked like I was heading to the Caspian!!!!

17

Baku, Atyrau and Abu Dhabi

It was only when I got home that I realised how taut my nerve endings were. At last I could relax and not worry about cars that drew up alongside or whether I was being targeted. I must admit that the chance to unwind was a godsend. It was only a few days before all the tension had seeped away. Being back with Dorothy was all it took.

I don't know how much you know (or knew in 2003) about Baku but you're going to learn a lot more. What did I know? Not a great deal, unfortunately. I knew where it was and that it was an oil centre. I knew a couple of guys from the Aberdeen oil industry who had been there, one of whom regarded it as one of the wilderness areas ripe for western business. It had been only a few years since the breakup of the old Soviet Union (hurray!!) and the Azeris were still coming to terms with that fact. However they did recognise that their oil industry was stuck in the past and they needed western expertise.

Believe this or not, my mother knew about Baku! When the Nazis invaded the USSR, they made a beeline for the Baku oilfields (they were always short of fuel) but were stopped at the Battle of Stalingrad a bit further up the Caspian. Mum said that they would listen to radio news bulletins about the battle. I think they knew that if the Germans had reached Baku, they would have been a lot harder to defeat.

As Baku is deep into the old Soviet Union, at the far end of the Caucasus Mountains, western airlines hadn't ever flown there. BA had started services but they were so nervous about what could happen that their first few planes carried extra mechanics and a spare engine!!

I suppose I was going to a relatively civilised Baku but there were fairly recent stories that could have come straight out of the Wild West. It was certainly not a place I would have thought of bringing my family.

This was the first job I ever had where I was a 'contractor' not an employee. The company supplied accommodation in multi-room apartments/flats and when you moved out (going home or offshore) then someone else would move in. Part of what I was in charge of was to organise the sleeping arrangements; the experience would stand me in good stead later on.

The ex-pat Project Managers (based in the office) and survey engineers who were out on the boats both did 'swings' where they worked every day for a number of weeks and would then go home for a break before coming back. One lad, who practiced his bagpipes on board a pipe-laying barge, was offshore for three months and then went so crazy on the night before he was due to fly out that he missed his flight. Unfortunately, as the flights were nearly always full, he had to wait about a week 'on the beach' before he could leave.

Not only did I have to organise beds for the transit guys, I also had to book flights and organise taxis to and from the airport. I knew a couple of the long-term lads from the Gulf and I had had business with the office manager (Paul Froglie) a couple of years ago. He'd moved to Baku just after the SU break-up to start off the whole operation, he'd met a local lass and was now 'in with the bricks'.

We worked long hours and 7 days a week but we did receive a *per diem* allowance which was very welcome. Unfortunately the only evening recreation was drinking in the local bars so that's where the allowance usually went. The food was pretty good and there was a good selection of restaurants.

Our office was in a new tower block which also held the SAS Radisson Hotel and stood on the side of Baku's main square. Believe it or not so was the local McDonald's!

Just over the road were three of the most popular bars called O'Malleys, the Caledonian and the London Wine Lodge. All were owned/run by expats who were married to locals. The LWL had the reputation of having the best kept Guinness in town!

There were a lot of western ex-pats who brought in the much-needed expertise. There were some who had their families with them but they were very much in the minority. All this meant that there were a lot of un-attached men wandering around Baku at night. Needless to say, and because nature abhors a vacuum, there was a flourishing prostitution industry.

There were two classes of girls. There were the bar-girls who were usually not locals and whose purpose everyone knew. However one of the most pleasant ways of spending a balmy evening was to sit outside a bar/restaurant having something to eat and drink watching the parade of pretty Baku girls wandering about.

As well as the bars, restaurants and cafes, there were a lot of stalls selling all sorts of tourist tat. I think the only things that I bought were some Russian dolls.

One aspect of the place was the money. The Azeri currency is the Manat which had an exchange rate of about 5000 to 1USD$. You probably won't believe this but the money exchanges took Scottish notes. Everywhere else you have to have Bank of England notes but not in Baku.

When you immersed in a job, it's a little bit difficult to realise that you are actually taking part in a bit of history. My guys were working on a pipe-laying barge and the pipe was the one which would take the oil from the offshore fields to the trans-Caucasus pipelines. The Soviets had so ruined the on-shore fields that the western firms were more interested in the unexploited fields under the Caspian. They did some rehabilitation work on-shore but it was more of a gesture than anything else.

The pipeline made landfall at a point known as Sangachal and I was particularly gratified a few years later when the terminal there was officially opened.

Baku was the first place that oil was exploited as an industry but had always been in a strategic position. The industry quickly boomed and it could be said that Baku was the catalyst for the present-day worldwide oil industry.

Even before people realised what oil could bring, there were religious sites based on the perpetual gas fires. Folk built fire temples and, although the religion died, the temples are tourist attractions now. However the supply of gas was disrupted during Soviet days and now it has to be piped in to show the tourists the fires.

Talking about religion, Azerbaijan is nominally a Muslim country; the Azeris are ethnic Turks but their idea of Islam is far from that practiced in places like Saudi Arabia. Very few women (if any) are covered, alcohol is everywhere and pork is freely available. I suppose that under the Soviets when religion was discouraged (!!), practices became lax. After the break-up of the Soviet Union, the Iranian mullahs arrived to try and get the Azeris back on the righteous path. After they had railed against the drinking of alcohol, the consumption of pork and the fornication, the mullahs got a two word answer from the locals of which the second word was "off!"

I also saw something which stooped me in my tracks one evening. At an ATM was a Jewish family!!!! The hats, skullcaps and ringlets are unmistakable. It was a sight that I never expected to see in any Muslim country. I was later told that there is quiet a large Jewish community in the Azeri countryside.

Next to one of the temples is the old lab of Dmitri Mendeleev who, as you all know, devised the Periodic Table of the Elements. The other famous 'old boy' of Baku was Albert Nobel (of the Nobel Prizes) who made his fortune here when he invented dynamite to replace the old (more) dangerous explosives.

When you work all day every day it's quite difficult to see anything else other than your office or your accommodation and there is so much to see in the countryside around Baku itself.

South of the city there are three separate interesting sites which are actually close to each other.

The first one is the Gobustan Rock Art where there are many rock carving of people, boats and animals. The people may well be Vikings and one of the boats could well be a Viking longboat. The carvings have been picked out in white against the light brown rocks which makes them easy to see. The animals are standard but the figures can have unusual perspectives which have led some folk to reckon that they represent alien visitors. Then again aliens always fill in the gaps, don't they?

Not very far away is a fenced off rock with a carving in Latin. That would seem remarkable until you notice that the carving signifies that the 12th (X11) Legion had passed by this way. What other language would legionnaires use?

The third locality shows that the Baku area is a tectonically active one. There is rather a large area of mud volcanoes which bubble and pop as gases escape. The area didn't seem very warm but it was still with some trepidation that I put my hand into the bubbling mud. It was pretty cool (temperature wise!) and the mud didn't wash off very easily. There was a slight sulphurous smell but not nearly as bad as I expected. I suppose most of the gas escaping was carbon dioxide.

To go and see these sites I had taken a day off and to round off the trip I went into the hills to the west of Baku. Up there are the gas flares/seeps which have been burning for centuries.

At the start of my second swing through Baku, I spent a month in Abu Dhabi at the regional HQ where I was tasked with overseeing a project where one of our boats was searching for a lost military jet from Bahrain. I suppose you could call it on-the-job training.

Although the search was thorough, the plane was never found. However, the time in Abu Dhabi was pleasant enough. After the month, I headed back to Baku. The flight left from Dubai so I had a chance to meet up with my old friend and colleague from Ferranti ORE days, Dave Hampshire, who was then working there.

My role in Baku changed slightly as Gordon Chudleigh (the guy who had been on sick leave) was back in town. To be honest, I wasn't really doing much and getting a bit bored so when there was a chance remark that someone was needed in Kazakhstan to oversee the end of a project, I volunteered.

I'd never been to Kazakhstan so why not? The only problem for me was that it was the end of November and it was going to be pretty cold. I had some warm clothes as Baku can get cold as well.

I was heading to the town of Atyrau, at the north end of the Caspian Sea where the Ural River enters the sea. Atyrau is the centre of the Kazakh oil industry which is both on-shore and off-shore. Thales had a small project which needed wrapping up and which would take about a month.

To get from Baku to Atyrau, I flew in a Yak 40 aircraft right up the middle of the Caspian. Kazakh Air did not have the greatest safety record so I was a bit nervous but the flight was uneventful. Kazakhstan had the strictest customs declaration sheet I've ever seen. I had to put down everything valuable I was taking into the country including my watch and wedding ring!

Once through into the Arrivals hall, I met my driver and off we went to the office. Atyrau was different to Baku in many ways; it's a different country after all. Two of the major differences are the climate (it's a LOT colder in the winter) and the fact that very few locals speak any English.

Atyrau sits on the Ural River delta which consists mainly of mud. When I was there the temperature hovered around zero. One degree below and the mud froze. One degree above and the mud was, well, mud – horrible, sticky, gooey mud. It was so clinging that you had to have two pairs of footwear, one for outside and one for in the office. Every night I had to wash the mud off my shoes! I used to look forward and welcomed the days when it froze.

Kazakhstan was probably one of the least re-constructed old Soviet republics and still had a lot of 'hangovers' from those days. Not least of these was the bureaucracy and I spent a lot of my time battling with it. Thankfully all of the documents were in Russian so I could hand over the paperwork to my office staff and I just signed things.

So what did I do for recreation? There were bars (!!) and one or two functions that I went to but as they were in Russian I didn't really enjoy them as much as I should have. We had a TV in the company flat but the only channel in English was EuroSport so I had no idea what the world news was. I did watch a lot of winter sports – Biathlon and Cross Country skiing – sports I now know a lot more about than I ever did before.

While I was in Atyrau, the draw was made for the World Cup qualifying sections and, believe it or not, Azerbaijan was drawn in the same group as England. Beckham was coming to Baku!!! I'll say more on that later.

I forget how I found this out but an old friend from Saudi – James Taylor (from Barra) – was also in Atyrau at the same time as me. I knew both him and his family in Khobar. They left there around the same time as I did. Unfortunately we only managed to meet up a few days before I was leaving but we did have a pleasant evening talking about old times.

One aspect of Atyrau which was unusual was the central heating system. In the west central heating is controlled in the individual homes. In Atyrau there was ONE large heating centre and then the hot water was piped throughout the city to the flats/houses. I would have thought that the omni-present aluminium clad pipes were very inefficient but collectivism was still the local mindset.

The Italian Oil Company ENI was the principal partner in the region and right next to their newly built HO was an Irish Pub! Maybe the locals thought that it would make the ex-pats feel at home. These new builds contrasted sharply with the 'old' Soviet buildings. There was never any doubt which was which.

I didn't have a lot of time to spend in "O'Neill's" but I had a couple of lunches there. However, when I was in Atyrau, the 2003 Rugby World Cup was being held in Australia. Believe it or not I watched the final (which England won) live in that bar – the middle of the old USSR. A bit different from watching 3 day old film of the Sweden vs. Brazil 1958 World Cup Final! That brought home to me how far we've come in communications during my lifetime.

Then it was time to leave. I'd done what I had to do and I was heading home for Christmas. First I had to get back to Baku. So it was off to the airport which stood a little way outside the town and well away from the mud of the delta.

269

I haven't mentioned this before but this area of Kazakhstan is flat. In fact it's so flat you can almost see the curvature of the Earth. The mountainous views of Kazakhstan are from the eastern part of the country. The flat terrain is probably the reason that the Baikonur Cosmodrome is sited in central Kazakhstan.

Because it's flat, there is nothing to stop the wind from hurtling in from Siberia. The buildings in the town shelter you somewhat but out at the airport there's very little protection.

After clearing check-in, passport and customs, the departure lounge was a joke. I stood there for what seemed like an age and could see the Yak 40 (destination Baku) only about 100 yards away. When the transit bus pulled up to take us to the plane, I thought that it was a little too over-protective. I would have been quite happy to have walked across the tarmac.

Little did I know!! The bus pulled up about 10 yards from the rear of the aircraft. The Yak 40 is boarded by steps underneath the tail plane. By the time I got to those steps, I was doubled up with the pain caused by the wind out of Siberia. I have never been that cold and I was well wrapped up.

I wasn't sorry to say goodbye to Atyrau. It was an experience, no doubt, and I did pick up a couple of nice souvenirs. I would have liked to have bought a fur hat but couldn't find a shop that sold them.

A couple of hours later I was back in Baku. I was in town for one night and then I'd catch the BA flight to Heathrow and onto Glasgow.

As I had the afternoon free I went off to explore the old centre of Baku. I climbed the Maiden's Tower which was probably the central keep during medieval times and sat at a pavement café just relaxing.

Thales was in the midst of a takeover battle with Fugro (a Dutch based survey company) so nearly everyone was a bit concerned about their future employment. As I was a 'contractor', my future was pretty unclear and Rick Gore was open enough to tell me that he couldn't guarantee any further work after the end of the year.

So I didn't know if I was going to be back. That evening I had some farewell drinks when a thought crystallised in my head. Remember the World Cup draw and the fact that England (and Beckham) were going to be playing Azerbaijan?

Gordon was still in Glasgow University and I thought that he'd get unbelievable street-cred if he walked into the student bar wearing an Azeri football top when that game was on. But where was I going to get one?

No-one seemed to know but one of the bar-staff phoned a contact and told me that the Azeri FC may have sold them. Where was the Azeri FC? Outside the bar was a 'tame' taxi driver who would take drunks back to their accommodation if they couldn't walk. He would take me to the FC's offices.

At the Azeri FC, we walked in and my driver started asking if they sold them. One of the office staff shook his head but then went back to the telephone. Another official began talking to me in quite good English and told me the guy on the phone was calling some sports shops to see if they had any strips. It turned out the guy that I was talking to was the FIFA authorised Azeri referee and he had refereed all round Europe.

I assume that most people have either seen or heard of the 1966 World Cup Final when England's 3rd goal was given by the 'Russian' linesman as being over the goal line. That 'Russian' linesman was actually an Azeri and was/is a national figure.

The guy on the phone eventually found a store and told my driver where it was so off we went. The rain was pelting down, I was with a driver who couldn't speak English, going to who knew where in a city I didn't know and we seemed to be driving forever. We even passed another McDonald's in some far out part of town. Did I mention that Baku was the 4th largest city in the old Soviet Union?

We drove and drove and then I could see a strip mall of shops with one still lit up. This was the sports store and they did have Azeri football kits. At USD$8.00 each I bought one for Gordon and one for myself!

We got back to the bar and I showed the clientele what I'd bought. Someone asked where I'd got them but I told him I had no clue. He'd have to ask the taxi driver!!

The next morning I was onto the BA flight to Heathrow. As we left Baku, out of the port side I could see Mt. Ararat sticking up above the clouds. It was a beautiful sight.

Landing at Heathrow, it turned out that the December fog was in and disrupting the schedules. Although we were on time, our parking stand was still occupied, so we sat for about an hour. All this meant that I almost missed my connection to Glasgow and the inevitable happened. My luggage didn't make it.

It took over two days for the bags to turn up in Ayr!

18

Singapore

Christmas and New Year came and went and we all had a good time. Then it was time to think about what I was going to do. I hadn't checked my emails for a while so my inbox was rather full when I got round to it.

After sifting through the spam, I came across an email that Gordon Chudleigh had forwarded from my office account in Baku. It had been forwarded a couple of times but had originated in Aberdeen and basically asked me to call an old friend, Dave Curry, when I got the email.

So I called him.

After the courtesies, he came straight to the point. He needed someone to run his company branch office in Singapore and was I interested?

Of course I was!! He dampened my enthusiasm somewhat by asking me to go to Aberdeen for an interview and he intimated that he did have someone else in mind for the job, someone who was already in Singapore.

The thought ran through my mind, "So why did you want me to call?" Then I realised that he didn't want to seem too keen to have me!

So up I went for the interview after which he said that he had to give the other guy a chance to respond. After waiting about two weeks and hearing nothing I thought I wasn't going to lose anything by calling him up. So I did to find that he was travelling but that he would be back in a few days.

So that you don't get bored, I got the job and I was off to Singapore.

Although I'd been to India and China, I'd never made it to SE Asia or anywhere near Singapore. When my mother heard that was where I was off to, all the stories of WWII came out again.

Singapore is unique. From Changi Airport, which is without doubt one of the finest in the world, to its Metro system, its health system, etc. – everything works!!

The offshore companies are concentrated on the east end of the island around the Loyang Offshore Base and Seatronics had their offices there. Loyang and Changi run into one another. Most of the accommodation in Singapore is in flats/apartments. It really the only way that the population can be housed and not overflow the land. I had one in Loyang Gardens for those folk who know the area.

Because of the restricted land area, Singapore has a really clever way of regulating its car population. The authorities have decided that the island can support only so many cars. So to get a car, one has to wait for one to be scrapped, exported or otherwise leave the register. Thus getting a car is not just a case of turning up at the showroom and ordering it. It's quite a process but eventually one arrives. The one I had for the duration of my stay was a Hyundai Sonata.

Given all that, Singapore has a brilliant public transport system. The Metro (or MTS) moves millions of people a year and stretches throughout the island. It is continually being upgraded and expanded. The buses are regular and clean and the taxis are everywhere and pretty cheap.

You may be able to remember that I was diagnosed as a diabetic about a dozen years before. I'm not going into all the ins and outs of diabetes but it does affect the small capillaries which carry blood to the extremities. However the smallest capillaries are in the back of the eye, in the retina and diabetics routinely suffer from Diabetic Retinopathy (DR) where the capillaries start to leak. It was explained to me that the high sugar in the blood acts like an acid and eats away at the vessel walls.

I've always had good, even excellent, eyesight so imagine my disappointment when I realised that I needed reading glasses. I went off to my optician but she referred me to the Eye Clinic in the Ayr Hospital. That's when DR was diagnosed but I had a problem. I was flying to Singapore two days later!

I didn't know it at the time but Singapore has some of the best eye doctors in the world. It's said that over 95% of the population wear spectacles so my condition was almost normal. I got first class treatment which impressed the folk back home. However they did catch up.

Seatronics supplied rental equipment to (mainly) the offshore industry. This comprised anything from small cameras and lights to large underwater survey vehicles. I must admit I'd never rented any equipment before so it was all a new experience to me.

Soon after I arrived I also realised that I'd been pitched into a very difficult situation which was not of my doing. The previous occupant of my position had been 'naughty' and was basically fired. As part of his dismissal he had signed a document in which he agreed not to compete with Seatronics' business for 2 years. He didn't stick to it and so was caught up in a court case with the company.

Unfortunately for me he had a lot of friends in the local industry. Although British, he had lived and worked in Singapore for about twenty years and had married a local girl. The problem I had was that I was looked on as the 'baddy', having taken over his office and so it was very difficult to do business with his friends for some time. In fact I was pointedly ignored at some of the popular 'watering holes'.

But the 'watering holes' were of some benefit. I met a father and son (the Robbs) from Aberdeen who worked together in the industry. They were mad keen golfers so they asked me along to make up the numbers. Now Singapore has many fine golf courses but to play at the weekend is prohibitively expensive.

But there is an alternative. Over the Straits of Malacca, lie some islands belonging to Indonesia where the golf is much more affordable. So we would head over there on a Saturday morning for a relaxing round. The fast ferries were usually packed but the first time I went, I was concerned that we wouldn't be able to get on the first tee. I shouldn't have worried. As we got off and turned right to go to the course, the vast majority turned left onto another ferry. They were all ethnic Chinese and what do the Chinese love to do? Gamble!! At the time the only gambling in Singapore was on the horses but there was a floating casino where they were all headed!

As Indonesia is a separate country, passports and visas were required but that was all in the price and the paperwork was minimal. You checked in your bag of clubs and they magically appeared on the 1st tee! Unfortunately an Indonesian visa took up a page in your passport.

I spent many happy mornings on the golf courses there.

One of the drawbacks of the trip was that the ferry terminal in Singapore used to be packed as multiple ferries would arrive at around the same time. This led to long frustrating queues at Passport Control. I was standing there one afternoon when I noticed that there was a queue with hardly anybody in it marked "Access Control" and those who did use it were speeding through. What was the story there?

After I got through Passport Control, I had a wait for my clubs to appear so I wandered over to the desk next to the "Access Control" line.

It turned out that if you were Singaporean or had a resident's Green Card (I did), you could get an Access Control Card which carried your fingerprints. You slotted the card into the gate, put your thumb on a reader and, hey presto, you were through. I wanted one!

I needed to go to Changi Airport with my passport, Green Card, two passport photos, SNG$30 and apply. Needless to say I was there on the Monday and forty minutes later I had the card. Once again Singapore efficiency showed itself.

I had to travel to Bangkok for the day on business later that week and was leaving on the 0600hrs flight. When I got to the passport desks, the place was packed but the Access Control line was empty. Over I went, slotted my card in, pressed my thumb on the little window and I was through. The little trouble I went through to get the card was fully justified by this first use!!

Singapore is well known for its ban on chewing gum. If the ban was not in place, the island would quickly become a tip. However some other activities are also banned and the most important is spitting. If you go anywhere else in SE Asia the locals spit habitually and constantly. Try flying on a Chinese airline with everyone spitting throughout the flight. As most of Singapore's population is ethnic Chinese, this has been a re-education and total change in behavior. The health benefits are obvious.

Although you can take almost anything Duty Free into Singapore when you arrive, you cannot bring any tobacco products such as cigarettes. Singapore has one of the strictest laws against promoting smoking anywhere. Packs are covered in images of cancerous mouths, throats and tongues whereas the Duty Free ones don't. There have been many instances of people being detained when taking a cigarette out of a plain pack!

One weekend, the Robbs asked me to a birthday barbeque where I made some more social contacts.

Probably the most important had nothing to do with work. This guy ran the social cricket side for the Australian and New Zealand Association (ANZA). He asked if I could play and before I knew it I was in the side. I would play for the next two years but it also gave me the opportunity to learn a new skill.

As the games were social rather than in a serious league, there were no official umpires. The 'umpires' on the day were taken from those guys in the side batting who weren't 'in'. You stood for a few overs then someone else would take over. I always enjoyed doing it so I asked if there were Umpire Training Courses run by the local Cricket Union. No one knew for sure so I called the Union up on the Monday morning to learn that a course was starting that evening.

So I became a qualified cricket umpire and took that skill back to Scotland where I still umpire today.

The first game I ever umpired officially was between Singapore Cricket Club II versus Singapore Cricket Club III on the Pedang in the middle of the city. Talk about rivalry!! However it was a good introduction and I loved every minute.

The clubhouse of the Singapore Cricket Club is extremely imposing. As I walked in for the first time, I looked around and thought, "Yup, the Brits have been here!"

For a time I contemplated joining one of the sporting clubs. I looked into it and actually was taken round the grounds and amenities of the British Club which I thought would probably be the most appropriate. I was impressed until I was taken into the main bar. There was nothing wrong with the décor or ambience. However in the corner sat a caricature of the colonial Brit, tweed jacket, military tie and, at 10 o'clock on a Saturday morning, becoming severely inebriated. There was no danger that I was even going to give myself a chance of turning into something like that so I never did join. The easy relaxed atmosphere of the ANZA group was just right for me.

I'm not a great concert goer but I did go to see Elton John in a concert (just him, a piano and a microphone) in Dubai. However I've always loved the Eagles and they were to give a series of concerts around SE Asia including Singapore. They played for three and a half hours, performed thirty-three songs and didn't hit a bum note. It was a great night.

The office in Singapore had responsibility for the whole of SE Asia and Australasia. I've always believed that to find out what your customer wants, it's always better to have met with them. That's why, even today, trade shows and exhibitions are so important.

I always like to visit my customers and did so regularly in Singapore. Sometimes it was just for a chat which I hope broke up their routine.

As I wrote above, I visited Bangkok in Thailand but I also visited Jakarta in Indonesia on a semi-regular basis.

I also made a couple of trips to Perth where I managed to meet Deidre and Rob Dunne who had been our next door neighbours in Johannesburg. I visited New Zealand as well, flying into Auckland, then onto New Plymouth and Wellington.

The first time I was in Perth, the Dunnes took me on a sightseeing tour which ended up in Freemantle. We were ordering some food and discussing some AFL game that was on the TVs in the restaurant (I knew very little about AFL then) and referrals to third umpires when this guy at the next door table turned around and asked if we were cricket umpires. I explained that I was but Rob wasn't. He asked if I lived in Perth and I explained that I was visiting from Singapore. Right there and then he said that the local cricket scene was in dire need of umpires so if I DID move to Perth I was to contact him. He gave me both his telephone number (he was the chairman of a local club) and the number of the WA Umpires' Association.

Dorothy made a couple of trips out to Singapore which she loved. She enjoyed the walks and the shopping as well as the nightlife and social scene.

However because I could get home only a couple of times a year, I missed some important events. The major one was Kirsty's graduation from Paisley University as a B. Ed. Then she was off to be a primary school teacher. We re-did the graduation photos about six months later when I was home.

Singapore is a treasure trove of history. When Raffles founded the city it was not a foregone conclusion. Settlements further north in Penang and in Indonesia (e.g. Jakarta) had greater claims. However the Dutch weren't going to give up Jakarta and it has to be said that only a visionary would have chosen the overgrown island of Singapore. Probably the one major aid in that decision was the fact that the island had probably the best natural harbour in the region – even if it was overgrown with mangroves. That facility has, of course, changed over the years and has contributed to Singapore's growth. As it stands on the Straits of Malacca, it is at one of the great crossroads (and bottlenecks) of marine trade in the world. Take a look at any map showing goods travel by sea in SE Asia and note how all the routes converge at Singapore. It's almost an unfair advantage!

Of course as well as being in an advantageous position regarding trade routes, Singapore is also in a strategic military position for much the same reasons.

Hence the importance it held in many conflicts culminating in WWII. As I mentioned early on my father was on his way to Singapore with his RAF squadron when the island fell to the Japanese Imperial Army. I've never been in the forces and am not a military historian by any means but there is no doubt that the campaign the Japanese conducted coming down the Malay Peninsula was a brilliant one.

Of course, there is the shorthand version that 'all the guns were pointing the wrong way' and that is what it is – a shorthand version (and misleading). There was one battery guarding the entrance to the harbour (on the south side of the island) which did have its guns pointing seaward but that was where you would expect them to bear!!

The swiftness of the advance southwards and the fact that Singapore IS an island which got nearly all its fresh water from the Malay mainland meant that once the Japanese captured the causeway, the end was inevitable. That didn't stop heroics and last ditch/gap attempts at resistance. However it soon became clear that surrender was the only option. There certainly was no chance of the garrison being relieved.

Someone once said, "War is Hell", a sentiment that most war veterans would agree with. As the "Hell" word has been used, I have no idea what word should be used for what happened to the captured soldiers and civilians after that surrender on 15th February, 1942. Dante may have had a term but "Seven Shades of Purgatory" may come close.

It's very difficult for someone like me who has never had to go through anything like that to fully appreciate the horrors that were perpetrated. Museums, black and white photos and grainy, jerky film footage tell only part of the story.

One of the most sobering mornings I ever spent anywhere was at the Kranji War Memorial. Row upon row of gravestones all meticulously kept, towering granite blocks inscribed with names of those whose remains were never found and, in one corner, a heart-breaking section where the children, nurses and other civilians are buried. Thousands upon thousands of casualties lie there and, in the corner of the park, a little hut where a man sits with the records. If you want to find the grave of a relative, he will look him/her up and direct you to the exact spot.

Even although Singapore has developed enormously since 1942, it has never forgotten. The Changi POW camp where unspeakable things happened is long gone but is remembered by a little memorial on the exact spot. People rush by it but it's there.

But let's get back to more pleasant things.

A great delight of Singapore is the sheer number and choice of restaurants and food stalls. Prices range enormously but for a couple of Singapore dollars you can eat like a king. Although Chinese food predominates, other Asian cuisines are common. There is an area called 'Little India' and western tastes are also catered for.

However there is one aspect of the Singaporean diet which is bizarre. There is a fruit called a Durian. It looks like a melon with rather large pimples. It supposedly has an exquisite taste but it smells disgusting. The smell is so disgusting that durians are banned from all public buildings (especially hotels) and the MTS system and stations. The great mystery in my mind is – who was the brave soul that ignored the smell and actually ate the fruit?

As well as the restaurants, there are a whole lot of bars. Sidewalk hostelries with relatively cheap drinks as well as glitzy rooftop hotel bars where a beer costs the Earth sit opposite each other on the same street.

There is of course one bar that everyone has to visit and one drink that everyone has to try, at least once. The Raffles Hotel in downtown Singapore has been fully renovated from a ruined shell making it now one of the leading hotels in the city. It is famous for its Long Bar where fans with blades shaped like dried coconut leaves keep you cool and the floor is covered with peanut shells (the ONLY place in Singapore where you MUST throw your discarded shells on the floor) and where, somewhere before 1915, a barman called Niang Tong Boon developed the Singapore Sling, a pink coloured cocktail. Not my cup-of-tea but Dorothy and I tried it and even bought a couple of the glasses that it is served in.

A random thought is that most modern cocktails were developed during the US Prohibition era to make the bathtub booze palatable. (I exclude the gin and tonic which was developed so that taking quinine to combat malaria was enjoyable rather than a chore.) So does that make the Singapore Sling one of the oldest surviving cocktails?

I must admit that when I left Saudi Arabia in 2003, I did have doubts about whether I was doing the right thing. It was a bit of "going into the unknown". But events that unfolded on the 29th of May, 2004 proved that I had made the correct decision.

Terrorists of the Saudi-based branch of Al-Qaeda attacked several locations in Al Khobar killing 22 people of 10 different nationalities in the process. During the attacks 14 of the attackers were killed or captured but 3 escaped.

The lone American (Frank Floyd) was killed as he sat in his office in the Al Khobar Petroleum Center, where I used to have an office (!). When asked if he was Christian or Muslim, he answered Christian and promptly had his throat cut. Two of his fellow workers (both Filipino) suffered the same fate. Frank and I used to have a coffee and a chat together every now and again. We weren't friends but we knew each other.

Michael Hamilton was someone that I had had a passing acquaintance with. We were both members of the BBG but we had very little direct dealings. He was high up in Apicorp (Arab Petroleum Investments Corporation) and happened to be leaving the Apicorp compound when it was attacked. Two guards and a young Egyptian boy (in the school bus) were killed before Michael was pulled (still alive) from his shot-riddled vehicle. He was then tied to the back of their 4x4 vehicle and dragged through the streets for about 500 metres. He was totally unrecognisable when his body was found dumped under an overpass.

Then the terrorists tried to attack the Al Bustan complex (where I used to live) but were beaten off by the guards. So they moved along the road to the large Oasis 3 complex. There they went on the rampage. They killed two security guards and two children on the school bus, injuring another four, two critically. Another security guard managed to get the rest of the children off the bus and away to a safe area. The terrorists then burst into the residential part of the compound slitting the throats of any non-Muslims they could find. Starting with beheading two chefs (one Italian and the other Swedish) in the Italian restaurant, they moved onto the Indian (Hindu) workers where they killed eight.

They took 54 people hostage and held them on the sixth floor and booby-trapped the exits. Believe it or not three of the terrorists managed to climb down the walls and stole a car enabling their escape all while the compound was surrounded by soldiers because by this time the security forces had woken up.

During the night there were a couple of rescue attempts but the booby traps kept the rescuers back. Early the next morning Saudi forces were dropped from two helicopters. They freed the hostages, killed two of the terrorists and captured another; most of the perpetrators had escaped however. Rumours of them having help from the Saudi Security Forces abounded.

All this unfolded in front of my eyes on my TV in Singapore. I could see roads, buildings and compounds that I knew well being blown up and shot at and I must admit I worried about my friends who were still living there but my overwhelming emotion was relief that I wasn't there.

I was travelling through Changi Airport one day and I had some spare time before my flight. I decided to log onto one of the internet terminals which had just been installed. Imagine my surprise to find an email from Sue (from Steve and Sue) Goodlad our old friend from Cape Town days. They now lived in Thailand but Sue was going to be in Singapore as their son was going to be in a rugby tournament there.

A few emails later, we arranged for me to pick Sue up at a downtown hotel – one I didn't recognise. As she came out to the car, she exclaimed, "That's nothing but a brothel! Just you wait till I get ahold of that ******* that booked this hotel!" I could hardly drive for laughing. However, we did spend a great few hours catching up sitting outside on Boat Quay.

By the end of 2005, it was obvious to me (and probably others) that the sales figures weren't so good and it was no surprise that my contract wasn't to be renewed. I did have some time left in Singapore to see if I could find another job but I couldn't. Actually one did come up after I was back in Scotland but it disappeared when they realised they would have to fly me out for an interview and then relocate me

So I was unemployed again. I must admit that I thought that I would have no trouble finding another one as the oil business was in a bit of a boom and I had found jobs during downturns. So Xmas and New Year 2006 wasn't a fun time.

It doesn't really matter how much money you get as you're laid off/made redundant/fired it seldom lasts till the next pay cheque whenever that is. But it does ease some of the problems for a while.

Fortunately, I had an insurance policy which paid the mortgage. That is a HUGE relief. There's a drive to pursue mis-selling of such policies but I have no complaints. It paid for itself many times over.

Dorothy was still working but had been told that she'd reached her salary 'ceiling' unless she re-trained as a para-legal. That she wasn't going to do so we weren't laughing and joking a lot. She didn't earn a huge amount but it kept us ticking over. I was reading the local paper one day and a job advert jumped out at me. It was for someone like Dorothy and the money was considerably better. After much persuasion she applied for it and got it. The only downside was that it was in Troon, not in Ayr, so she'd have to drive there every day rather than just walk. It was a wise decision to change as the firm she worked for before ended up laying people off and she would have been one to go.

But we had one happy occasion to look forward to. Alison was to be married in March. I had met Adam briefly when Gordon was ill but we'd had time to get acquainted since. Dorothy had been travelling quite regularly up to Aberdeen so she knew him a bit better. They had met when Alison started her first job, after graduating from Robert Gordon's University, at Amec, an engineering firm in Aberdeen.

Men have a different perspective on most things from women but it culminates in preparations for a wedding. Men, once they've hired or sorted out their suit or kilt, are either worrying over the speech they're required to make or celebrating that they're not making a speech! Women, on the other hand, worry over THE dress, the cake, the table decorations, the music (church and reception), the invitations, the bridesmaids, the church flowers, their attire, the photographer and the guest list amongst others. It's a wonder they have time to get stressed but get stressed they do.

Alison and Adam had decided that all the males in the bridal party would wear the same tartan in their kilts. That made a total of seven – groom, best man, the two dads and three ushers. As Adam and I were the only ones ever to have put on a kilt before, it was a hilarious morning spent in the kilt hire shop. Adam is from Durham and his Dad, brother (best man) and his three best friends (the ushers) are all from there as well and were a bit leery of wearing kilts.

The weather was cold and snow was on the ground (March in Aberdeen – not really surprising!) but that didn't take anything away from the occasion. I must admit that giving my daughter away was rather emotional but the reception in Elphinstone Hall of Aberdeen University was a great time. Alison demanded a picture of her with all the 'kilts'. It looked a bit like the Highlanders' charge at Culloden!!

So a few weeks later they were off to Calgary, Alberta in Canada. They now live in St John in New Brunswick. How they got there is another story – perhaps one for them to tell.

Then Gordon graduated B. Sc. (Hons) in Chemistry from Glasgow University (like his dad). He was off to industry to work.

I had to 'sign on' at the Job Centre. This was a condition of the insurance company so that my mortgage would be paid. After my first 'interview' I was told that I wasn't getting any benefits (I hadn't paid National Insurance for years and my wife was working so there was money coming into the house) and the Job Centre had no hope of helping me find a job so I was basically on my own. Perhaps I should have claimed to be a political refugee!!!!

I like to observe people and the Job Centre gave me a couple of stories that those that have never had to 'sign on' may be interested in.

One of the conditions of the process is that you have to turn up every fortnight to actually sign on the dotted line. At the same time one of the staff asks you what you've done to find a job. My staff member had to go and get somewhere and I started to look around the open-plan office. At the next desk another man was doing the same as me and after had finished he jumped up and left the office. I wasn't far behind him so imagine my surprise when I saw him running a flower stall on a corner of Ayr High Street!! I was 99% sure it was the same guy so should have I reported it?

Yes, I should have but I didn't.

Sometimes I had to wait to get the right person to sign the insurance form. Then the procedure changed and I had to wait in a room with folk who had complaints about the system. It was really illuminating listening to their gripes.

Their language, although crude at times, showed what they thought of the system. They referred to their 'pay' never 'benefits' and one was outraged because she hadn't been 'paid' when she had been abroad on holiday!!!! Every one of them knew their 'rights' but not one talked about getting a job.

I perhaps should have been outraged but mainly I was sad and disappointed. It was just a snapshot of the benefits culture but one that may be more mainstream than commonly thought.

Money was getting tight. Dorothy's money wasn't going very far and we got to the stage where we HAD to use a credit card to pay for the groceries. We then paid back the minimum amount so the total kept rising. It was not ideal but at least we had the option. My job hunting wasn't working and it wasn't for the lack of trying. I did get interviews but nothing came of them. One did call back about a year later but I was elsewhere (see below) so they were a bit late.

Before we knew it, Christmas and New Year were here. It wasn't the most lavish but having Kirsty and Gordon around made up for a lot.

19

Saudi Arabia (Part 3)

One afternoon early in January 2007, just after the festivities had finished and it was all a bit flat, the telephone rang.

The voice (in a broad Australian accent) at the other end asked for me. After the pleasantries were over, he asked if I would be interested in a job as an Operations Manager in a small junior mining company operating in Saudi Arabia. I would have been happy with a job anywhere at this point so I said yes. He then rang off saying that his CEO would call me the next day.

I was a bit bewildered as he hadn't told me the company, the CEO's name or where they had got my name. I told Dorothy about the call and she, in her no nonsense way, said that I shouldn't hold my breath.

At that time telemarketers were the bane of my life. If we got a dozen calls a day, 90% were from folk trying to sell us something. One of the common ones was for mobile phones and, believe it or not, it was usually young Australian girls on the other end of the phone selling the darn things.

So the phone rings and this female Australian voice asks to speak to "Jack Allan Mackenzie". I've been down this road before so I say that there's no-one here of that name. The normal response from one of these telemarketers is "OK, then who are you? You'll do". The response I got this time was "Oh, I'm sorry. I must have the wrong number".

I then realised that this lassie wasn't selling mobile phones so, before she could hang up, I said, "But I'm Allan Mackenzie Jack, if that helps". After she stopped laughing, she explained that she was the CEO of Vertex, the junior mining company that her colleague, Ralf Stagg, had referred to the previous day.

Twenty minutes later, at the end of a fairly rigorous telephone interview, Ines Scotland decided that I'd do and I could start applying for a visa to get to Jeddah in Saudi Arabia as that was where the company's Saudi office was.

What was it that someone once said? "Never say never!" After saying that it would be a cold day in hell before they got me back in Saudi Arabia, I was on my way back. Oh, well, it's not just for the 'Eagles' that Hell Freezes Over!!!!

Flying into Jeddah on the BMI flight, I must admit I wondered what I was getting myself into. Of course I knew that Saudi had gold mines (all government run) but this was the first time that I'd heard of a junior mining company getting involved in the sector.

Saudi Arabia had realised that the way that they looked at mining had to change. They'd down the 'bigger the better' way and it hadn't worked. The big companies such as Rio Tinto, Petrohunt and BHP Billiton had been around but nothing had happened. They had spent a lot of money with no rewards. Part of the problem was that they HAD to have a Saudi partner, with 51% of the business, who basically was a financial drain and with no technical expertise. So they decided to change and the new Mining Code came out in 2005 with some very interesting provisions. The FOREIGN company could do business in mining without a Saudi partner, prospecting licences could be no bigger than 100 sq. kms, and all profits could be re-patriated. The company still had to jump through the Saudi regulatory hoops but the mood had improved.

Vertex was registered in Bahrain because it was easier and the finance business there is much more in tune with western banking than Saudi was/is.

So this is what I was heading to. After getting through passport control and customs at Jeddah (much easier to write than it actually is) I was met by both Ines and the company driver, Abdul Rahman. He is an interesting character. Although born and bred in Jeddah (which he knows like the back of his hand), he is a Yemeni and he walks with a pronounced limp caused by a stiff knee. He came off a motorbike and suffered a fair few injuries. He is an excellent driver and it was only after he had driven me round Jeddah for a few weeks that I felt comfortable doing it on my own.

Abdul Rahman was a taxi driver sitting outside the hotel that Ines and Ralph Stagg had been staying at when they used him to drive them around Jeddah. He did such a good job, they offered him a permanent one with the company (Employee # 001).

I was dropped off at the company villa and would be collected in the morning to go into the downtown office.

The office was open-plan although part was being closed off to be a meeting room. I realised that we'd only just moved in as we didn't have any partitions. I was introduced to Brett Butlin (Employee #2) who was the company geologist and with whom I would work closely for the next few years. Rob Holland was a friend of Brett's who was over to have a look-see to decide whether he wanted to come and work for us. He and Brett had worked together before on other projects.

My role was to support these guys, run the office and supply all the necessary back-up to keep the venture going. There was a secretary, Syed, who was useless. In fact, I didn't believe that he could be as useless as he was but he kept proving it so he had to go.

Vertex had an office in Bahrain and two guys were based there. Sam Arul (Employee #3) was the general do everything guy, but was/is brilliant in IT. Abdullah Al Masri (Employee #5) was the company accountant who would eventually transfer to Jeddah. That wasn't really a hardship for him as he was a Jeddah lad anyway.

So guess who was Employee #4? That's correct – me!

It might have been a small team but one that did it right.

However, if I was to support these guys, I had a problem. Although I knew a bit about Saudi, I knew nothing about Jeddah. I'd been in the city a few times but only overnight at the most. I knew nobody so I certainly didn't have the circle of contacts I might have had in Dammam/Khobar.

What's a man to do?

Go back to first principles.

When I was in Khobar I was on the committee of the British Business Association (BBA) whose name is self-explanatory. As I never throw a business card away, I had the phone number of the chairman of said BBA. There had to be an equivalent in Jeddah, surely?

I called up Geoff Fennah and asked him if he knew of anybody I could contact over this side. He gave me the number of a John White who was on the committee of the British Business Group (BBG).

So I called John up and introduced myself. After a chat he promised to email me an enrollment form for the BBG and we hung up. About thirty seconds later my phone rang and it was John White. 'Believe it or not," he said, "I've got someone in my office that knows you!!"

Now you could have knocked me down with a feather! Paul Raven (who it was) had been on my darts team in Khobar and had lived on the Al Bustan compound where I had lived. Thanks to those two I met a lot of British (and other) ex-pats over the next few weeks and so I was off and running. The BBG directory gave me a lot of contact information and I was able to find lease vehicles, apartments on compounds and companies for health insurance, plumbing and electrical contractors.

However, I was a bit of an anomaly as nearly every other expat was in Teaching, Health or Finance. The most common remark was "Oh, I didn't know that Saudi had a mining industry!"

The company had ten prospecting licences but the one we were concentrating on was one called Jabal Sayid. We had to concentrate on one as we had such a small team. As we grew, we looked at the others.

Jabal Sayid (JS) was a 'success story' from the 1960's, 70's and 80's when the Saudi Government realised that they had a large part of the kingdom which they knew very little about as an economic resource.

The western part of Saudi is a part of the Arabian-Nubian shield, a complex of basement (Precambrian) rocks which was known to contain metal deposits. The shield had been torn apart by the opening of the Red Sea but both sides had gold mines.

The 'ancients' had worked copper and gold deposits for thousands of years in western Saudi Arabia in the region known as the Hijaz. Copper is really easy to find as it tends to stain the country rocks green. The difficult part is finding payable deposits as a little bit of malachite goes a long way.

Gold doesn't stain the rocks but once you've seen gold, you never forget it. The mine at Mahd adh Dhahab (translates as Cradle of Gold) has been worked, on and off, for about three thousand, five hundred years. It may well have been one of King Solomon's Mines.

However, the 'ancients' had a couple of problems. They didn't have the mining techniques to go very deep although some of their workings have given me some worries. They must have used small children to get to some of the depths. Also they had to rely on their eyes. Once the grains of gold got too small to see, they walked away.

So buried ore-bodies were never found and they didn't understand the clues like gossans that modern geological prospectors do.

Sometime in the late 50's, the Saudis decided that they had to find out what they had. They invited the French BRGM and the US Geological Survey to come and map the entire region. It was a great success and these maps are still used today.

That actually shows up another characteristic of the Saudi nature. These maps were produced 40-50 years ago and have never been updated. They have had no input from the age of satellites, GPS or anything modern. There is an attitude that it's been done and doesn't need improving or updating.

As part of the mapping exercise, JS was just part of an area to be mapped. Then someone realised that the top of one of the hills was gossanous. This prompted a programme of geochemical analyses and drilling that outlined copper and zinc rich bodies. At the time, you couldn't give copper and zinc away and, although they put down a 2 km. decline (large enough for trucks), it was never going to be profitable and they walked away.

Before we came along, a couple of companies had re-looked at the site but they too had deemed it too small and not rich enough.

To many people that could have been discouraging but geologists are by nature optimistic and there are many, many stories of companies walking away from a prospect and another taking it up and making a mine out of it. It's usually due to not drilling enough holes, not drilling deep enough or over a wide enough area. It also wouldn't be the first time that the second company analysed for something that the first company hadn't.

The whole thing was a gamble and we had to make it pay off. We did have a lot of historical data but it was significant that nearly every one of our drillholes intersected something richer, wider or deeper than anyone else had found. We never took a backward step and that kept the money flowing and us getting toward the point where we knew that JS was going to be a mine.

I was working an eight and two week rotation which I really enjoyed. At the beginning, I was travelling on a business visit visa which meant that I had to leave the country on a 'visa run' every 30 days. Actually we made it 28 days to allow us some slack time if planes got delayed or vehicles broke down. It also meant that folk knew which day of the week was their day to travel.

So I visited Bahrain and Dubai, where I met up with Keith and Judy Martin (from UCT days). Keith worked for Repsol, the Spanish oil company, and had been seconded from Madrid to the UAE on some acquisition project.

One of my 'visa runs' was due in mid-September which happened to be also right in the middle of Ramadan. There was no way that I was going to go to another Muslim country at that time of year so where could I go? Israel was out (for obvious reasons) and Saudi is surrounded by Muslim countries. However there is a country that fitted and was only a two hour flight away.

Cyprus was ideal and the best thing was that the weekend included the Saudi National Day so I got a four day break out of it.

As we progressed we got more personnel on board (I even got my Saudi Residence Permit or Iqama) and we were doing OK. We even got a better drilling company as contractors (Fugro from Dammam – one of my old contacts) and we were doing really well. I was running around Jeddah (to the Saudi Geological Survey – SGS – and the DMMR – the Deputy Ministry for Mineral Resources) as well as to and from JS (and other prospects).

As we got more people I could hand some of my workload over which allowed me to take Fridays off and even leave the office early on Thursdays.

I did have a problem, though. There's not much to do in Jeddah. Nearly every ex-pat goes diving (but it has never really appealed to me) and the others go camping in the desert which I did in my work!

So I was dying of boredom.

The compound has a small shop which stocked essentials like milk, bread etc. I was stocking up one Friday morning when I struck up a conversation with a woman I knew (Wendy Barsby). We were chatting about things like the weather when she asked me if I'd ever done any acting. I admitted that I had so she invited me along to rehearsals that afternoon. So I joined the Red Sea Players and never looked back. I'm not sure I became a star but I enjoyed it.

2007 went by in a flash. We were so busy that we had no idea that the months were just flying by.

I've always tried to be home for Christmas and New Year. I did work over that period once back in 1993/4 and realised that I was being stupid.

Since Alison, Kirsty and Gordon have grown up and have been doing their own 'things' at Hogmanay (New Year), Dorothy and I have been going to a hotel for the festivities. This has a number of advantages. No planning is involved and someone else clears up the mess. By 2007 we'd been doing it for about 5 years along with Dorothy's brother and sisters (plus spouses). Adam and Alison joined us one year and assorted nieces and nephews have tagged along as well.

This Christmas and New Year we had my mother staying with us so she came along to the hotel. Believe it or not she was turning 90 in the February but she was still up dancing at 0330hrs on New Year's morning!! I was worried that she'd be overdoing things but one of the party remarked that it wouldn't matter. She'd had a great time and she'd remember this New Year for however long she had left.

So it was back to Saudi and the excitement of getting our 'ducks in a row' so that we could apply for a Mining Licence. It would take over a year to get all the data together and put the Definitive Feasibility Study (DFS) in a form that we could submit to the government (and the market). It actually took the Saudis over a year to approve the Mining Licence (taking about 6 months even to open the application) but that's a story for another day.

Keith and Judy had been in touch. They wanted to visit Petra and they knew that I'd been there a couple of times. We arranged a tour and Dorothy would come along as well. It is a good idea to time your visits to places like Petra at the right time of year so that it is not too hot and you're not surrounded by hordes of other tourists.

We decided that we would go in September but a few weeks before, I got the news that my mother was ill and in a hospice in Stornoway. Torquil and Marian had been alerted by her neighbours and had travelled up from Hampshire.

As I was due home for my two week break very soon, I decided to go and see for myself how my mother was. I flew up from Glasgow and was collected by one of my mother's friends. She took me straight round to the hospice where it was obvious that my mother was gravely ill. She had lost a lot of weight, she couldn't digest certain foods and she looked really gaunt.

I was in no doubt that she was dying but no-one seemed to know how long she had left. The hospice nurses' job was to keep her alive and comfortable and I don't think doctors ever want to give you a definite time limit. The consensus was that she had months rather than weeks left.

I spent a few days with her and took her on a last trip to Calbost in Lochs where her mother grew up and where she had spent many happy childhood summer holidays. Her body might have been giving up but her mind was as sharp as ever. All through that car journey she told me stories of those holidays. I only wish that I'd had a tape recorder with me.

But I had to leave. The hospice had all of my and Torquil's contact details so they would let us know of any change.

Dorothy and I were off to Petra to meet up with Keith and Judy. We booked into a hotel in Amman and then we went off to Wadi Mousa, the present day town on the outskirts of Petra. We strolled around the site for two days, visiting even the 'High Places' a part that I hadn't been to before. There is a theory that the High Places are the spot where Moses looked over into the 'Promised Land', the land that he was never to enter.

Leaving Petra we went to Wadi Rum to find that it had become much more commercialised since I'd been there a few years before. Then you could drive around in your own vehicle with a guide. Now you had to hire a 4x4 with a guide. At least there was a café/restaurant on the site which didn't exist before.

We then visited Aqabah looking across the gulf to Eliat (in Israel) and the Sinai Peninsula driving back to the hotel in Wadi Mousa to spend the night

The next morning we drove down the mountains into the Jordan Valley. Judy had picked up a stomach bug and was feeling pretty low so we had to make a few 'pit stops'.

Everyone has heard of the Dead Sea, the lowest point on the continents, and its very peculiar, extremely salty water. There are a number of resorts along its banks and we spent most of the afternoon in one of them. We floated in the Sea and even plastered some so-called therapeutic mud on ourselves. The oiliness of the water is very strange and the many shower points where you can get clean are welcome.

As the Sun began to set we drove back to Amman and our hotel as we were all leaving the next day. I was the designated taxi driver to first take Keith and Judy to the airport for their flight to Dubai and then to take Dorothy to get her flight back to London and Glasgow.

My flight to Jeddah was near midnight. Amman airport is pretty small and there's not a lot to do there. In fact it's pretty boring, which is a great disappointment, when you've spent a few days being inspired by the local attractions.

Anyway back to Jeddah I went and back into the routine.

Again the weeks flew by but all too soon I got the news that my mother had deteriorated and she had only a few days left.

Jumping on a plane (sounds impressive, doesn't it?) I rushed home and then up to Stornoway again. This time it was Torquil who met me and took me straight round to the hospice.

Mum had deteriorated considerably. If not comatose, she was close to it. I'm not sure that she recognized me (or Torquil) and it was obvious that I'd only just made it in time.

Early the next morning (16th November) at just after 2 o'clock, she passed away. She was the last of her generation in our family so, in truth, it was the end of an era.

It doesn't matter how organised a person is (and my mother was), once they have died there's still a mess to clear up. It's inevitable that you get mired in closing bank accounts, visiting lawyers, organising services and a burial and getting rid of the detritus of a life. Someday someone will do it for each one of us.

The Free Church has its own 'rituals' although I doubt if anyone from the Free Church would use that term. One of the things they do is have a service in memory of a member who has died. They call it a 'Wake' but it is nothing like the conventional idea of one. As my mother had stipulated in her will that she was to be buried with my Dad in Gartmore, the 'Wake' would be the only chance for our extended family to say goodbye. My goodness, there were cousins there that I hadn't seen in years/decades.

Getting the coffin to Gartmore was going to be awkward, we thought, but a young lad from Stornoway had been killed near Edinburgh in a vehicle accident and his body was being shipped to Lewis for burial. The hearses swapped coffins at Ullapool neatly solving the problem.

We trooped to Gartmore for the funeral service but, because of the bureaucracy of the local Council, had to come back the next day for the internment. It was a consolation that Torquil and I had grown up with the local undertaker which smoothed a lot of paths.

I then went back to Jeddah.

20

You've Got to Stop Somewhere

December 29th 2008 dawned as a normal winter's day in Ayr. Perhaps it was a bit squally and a bit cold. There was nothing remarkable about it except when the telephone rang and it was Alison letting me hear the first magical cries of our first grandchild, Iona Maclean Brown. Dorothy was at work and I was just about to go and pick her up. I left Kirsty talking to her sister and then we called back when Dorothy got home.

I said before that I always wanted to be a Dad. I must admit that I thought I'd used up all the parental emotions with the three kids so I was totally unprepared for what I feel for that little one.

It's a pity that my mother didn't live long enough to become a great grandmother but she almost did. Maybe it's the circle of life. One life ends and another begins. But that's too philosophical for me!

If I look back over the period of time covered in this book, I realise that I've been very lucky.

I grew up in the 50's when life was much simpler and more carefree (at least for a young boy).

I grew up in the country with fresh air and healthy living.

I never had to go to war (Thanks USA)

I attended a great school (McLaren High) before the blight of comprehensive education hit it.

I studied at two fantastic universities (Glasgow and Cape Town).

I met and married a wonderful girl. Probably the best thing I ever did.

I managed to father three unbelievably fantastic children.

I've travelled the world and realised that home is a great place to be.

I'm a proud Scot and a proud Briton.

So that's the end of this book but not the end of the story.

In David Niven's autobiography "The Moon's a Balloon", he passes on the advice to stop writing when you get to the end so this is where I shall.

Acknowledgements

An autobiography spans such a long period that it is difficult to isolate only a few people to thank. I could list my school teachers, school friends, university lecturers and classmates, my work colleagues through the years and all the unsung people that have helped in innumerable ways to make my journey all that easier. However, that would fill many pages. So here I must be ruthless and select only a few.

Dorothy, my wife, has always been supportive in all that I've done. She read and critiqued early drafts of this manuscript and I took on board her criticism.

My children, Alison, Kirsty and Gordon, were the primary reason that I wrote all this down. Alison prompted it all by asking a simple question that took three hours to answer. Hopefully they'll have a better understanding of both their father and where they come from after reading this.

I hope that the stories that I tell which involve people other than myself don't embarrass anyone. That is not the intention. These stories are mine. Other people may have different recollections. If memories differ, neither is right or wrong. We all look at things through different lenses.

My thanks go to all that have helped in getting the book published, especially Brian Birch who helped with the layout and made helpful comments on the manuscript, and Wayne Boughen for the cover art.

Although this story is mine and mine alone, it would not have been nearly so interesting to write, and hopefully to read, if I hadn't met so many great characters along the way.

All omissions and errors are the author's alone.